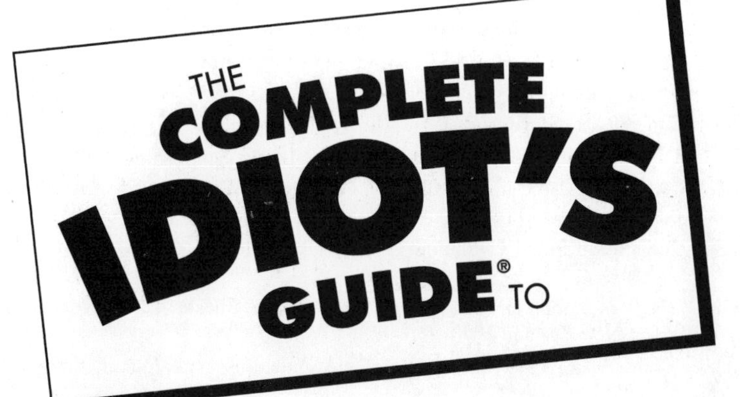

Great Quotes for All Occasions

by Elaine Bernstein Partnow

ALPHA
A member of Penguin Group (USA) Inc.

ALPHA BOOKS

Published by the Penguin Group

Penguin Group (USA) Inc., 375 Hudson Street, New York, New York 10014, USA

Penguin Group (Canada), 90 Eglinton Avenue East, Suite 700, Toronto, Ontario M4P 2Y3, Canada (a division of Pearson Penguin Canada Inc.)

Penguin Books Ltd., 80 Strand, London WC2R 0RL, England

Penguin Ireland, 25 St. Stephen's Green, Dublin 2, Ireland (a division of Penguin Books Ltd.)

Penguin Group (Australia), 250 Camberwell Road, Camberwell, Victoria 3124, Australia (a division of Pearson Australia Group Pty. Ltd.)

Penguin Books India Pvt. Ltd., 11 Community Centre, Panchsheel Park, New Delhi—110 017, India

Penguin Group (NZ), 67 Apollo Drive, Rosedale, North Shore, Auckland 1311, New Zealand (a division of Pearson New Zealand Ltd.)

Penguin Books (South Africa) (Pty.) Ltd., 24 Sturdee Avenue, Rosebank, Johannesburg 2196, South Africa

Penguin Books Ltd., Registered Offices: 80 Strand, London WC2R 0RL, England

International Standard Book Number: 978-1-59257-741-5
Library of Congress Catalog Card Number: 2007939746

10 09 08 8 7 6 5 4 3 2 1

Interpretation of the printing code: The rightmost number of the first series of numbers is the year of the book's printing; the rightmost number of the second series of numbers is the number of the book's printing. For example, a printing code of 08-1 shows that the first printing occurred in 2008.

Printed in the United States of America

Publisher: *Marie Butler-Knight*
Editorial Director: *Mike Sanders*
Senior Managing Editor: *Billy Fields*
Acquisitions Editor: *Michele Wells*
Development Editor: *Nancy D. Lewis*
Production Editor: *Kayla Dugger*
Copy Editor: *Jeff Rose*
Cover Designer: *Bill Thomas*
Book Designer: *Kurt Owens*
Indexer: *Johnna Vanhoose Dinse*
Layout: *Brian Massey*
Proofreader: *Mary Hunt*

To my sisters, each of whom is a special inspiration to me in different ways:
Judith Partnow Hyman (big sister)—the joy of family and how to love
Susan Partnow (little sister)—the importance of service and the greater good
Susan Witkovsky (soul sister)—the ways of the inner journey.

Contents at a Glance

Appendixes

Introduction

There are many ways to organize a book of quotations. Some go by contributor; most go by individual subject; others, like this one, go by general subject. Twenty-three chapters divide this collection into such categories as marriage, graduation, parenthood, home, children, loss and death, illness, adventure, and more.

Often a quote you'll find in one chapter could just as easily fit into another. As you glance through the quotes, searching for just the right one, you will sometimes see a single slash (/) and sometimes a double (//). A single slash designates a line break and occurs most frequently with poems and song lyrics. A double slash signifies either a verse break, if a poem; a paragraph break in prose; or, in plays, a different character speaking.

A word about "Attributions": I made every attempt to find original or at least secondary sources for each quote. But sometimes, I just couldn't track it down, even though I was 95 percent sure that the quote was properly attributed. If I've erred with any of them, the fault is entirely my own and I stand corrected—in fact, I'd love to be corrected! If you know where it came from, please write and let me know.

Two appendixes have been included as well. Appendix A is a Selected Bibliography. *Selected* because, while most of the titles that appear throughout the text are complete, with authors or editors and year of publication right there on the page, some titles are too darn long. I was more interested in your being able to keep your eye bouncing along the pages than your taking in a bunch of authorial credits. So I abbreviated some titles and created the bibliography where you could find them *in toto*, should you wish to. So when you see a title after a quote *without a year of publication*, that is your cue to look it up in the selected bibliography (as in *Jokes*, Getlen; the complete title: Getlen, Larry, *The Complete Idiot's Guide to Jokes*, 2006).

Appendix B is an alphabetical who's who. It provides a thumbnail sketch that shows when the person was born and, if he or she is no longer with us, when they died. Also it provides information about what nation they were born in and reside, what their occupations are, whether or not they've won any major awards, and *major*, major achievements. It is by no means comprehensive, but is meant to give you a taste of and a context for each of the persons whose words adorn these pages. To make it more convenient for you to find a quote from a specific person, the page numbers are included for your reference.

To make this book as useful as possible for you, an index by keyword is included. Here you can look up topics as diverse as knowledge and danger (or do they not go together, as in, "A little knowledge is a dangerous thing"?). By the way, a variation of that axiom was first used in 1709 by Alexander Pope, who is *not* one of our contributors.

On almost every page you'll find one quote that's been set aside from the others: the best of the best. This is my favorite quote on that page. It was very hard to do. Sometimes I cheated by putting a series of quotes together in one "best of the best." It'd be fun to know which ones you'd have picked. Write and tell me, or send me your favorite quotes, at QuotableGal@aol.com, and I'll consider including them in the next collection.

Acknowledgments

Dozens of wonderful resources on the Internet enabled me to gather the information needed to complete this book. I thought I'd share just a few that were particularly helpful; perhaps they will be to you, too.

en.wikiquote.org (quotes)

en.wikipedia.org (biography)

www.thepeaches.com/music/composers (lyrics)

www.gutenberg.org/browse/authors (Project Gutenberg: books)

catalog.loc.gov (Library of Congress: years of publication)

www.imdb.com (Internet Movie Database; biography)

www.poets.org (The Academy of American Poets: quotes & biography)

digital.library.upenn.edu/women (A Celebration of Women Writers: biography, links)

Several print publications were helpful to me as well. Those I used the most are listed here:

Andrews, Robert, ed., *The Columbia Dictionary of Quotations*, 1993 (Columbia University Press)

Frank, Leonard Roy, ed., *Quotationary*, 2001 (Random House)

Getlen, Larry, ed., *The Complete Idiot's Guide to Jokes*, 2006 (Alpha Books)

Miner, Margaret, and Hugh Rawson, *The New International Dictionary of Quotations*, 3rd edition, 2000 (Signet)

And, of course, *The New York Times Review of Books.*

My agent Janet Rosen of Sheree Bykofsky & Associates went well beyond the usual duties of an agent by providing me with some wonderful quotations. My friend Arthur A. Seidelman scoured the vast resources of his mind for some superb quotes from his favorite playwrights. My sister Susan Partnow sent me a wonderful list of quotes related to her passion, peace activism. My family and friends were most forgiving at my neglect of them. Leonard Frank, my technical editor, offered up a pile of excellent new quotations. In fact, the entire team at Alpha Books was so superb, they made the project a joyful undertaking, despite some harrowing timelines: Michele Welles and Nancy Lewis, in particular, were a delight to work with. My heartfelt gratitude to all these dedicated, wonderful people.

But most of all, I have to thank my husband, Turner Browne. We were in the final stages of rebuilding our home (lost to Hurricane Dennis in 2005) when I was contracted for this book. We moved in as I was finishing it. Many of the burdensome tasks that had been my responsibility were shifted to his capable but already weary shoulders. He truly exhausted himself in order to give me the time to write and, as usual, saw to it that I was well-fed and watered. What would I do without him!

Special Thanks to the Technical Reviewer

The Complete Idiot's Guide to Great Quotes for All Occasions was reviewed by an expert who double-checked the accuracy and appropriateness of what you'll find here. Special thanks are extended to Leonard Roy Frank.

Brooklyn native Leonard Roy Frank graduated from the Wharton School of the University of Pennsylvania in 1954. He is the editor of *Influencing Minds: A Reader in Quotations* (Los Angeles, Feral House, 1995); *Random House Webster's Quotationary* (New York, Random House, 1998); and, since 2000, seven other collections of quotations for Random House. He has lived in San Francisco since 1959.

Trademarks

All terms mentioned in this book that are known to be or are suspected of being trademarks or service marks have been appropriately capitalized. Alpha Books and Penguin Group (USA) Inc. cannot attest to the accuracy of this information. Use of a term in this book should not be regarded as affecting the validity of any trademark or service mark.

I Do, I Do

Daughter just got engaged? Friend getting married? Celebrating your anniversary? Your divorce? Marriage—or the dissolution of it—is one of the preeminent experiences of our lives. Here are some sallies to greet the occasion.

• • •

"Marriage, n. The state or condition of a community consisting of a master, a mistress and two slaves, making in all, two.
—Ambrose Bierce, *The Devil's Dictionary*, 1906"

When my fiancé proposed it was very romantic. He turned off the TV. Well, he muted it. During the commercial. —Wendy Liebman, glee mail, wendyliebman.com, 2002

Men who have a pierced ear are better prepared for marriage. They've experienced pain and bought jewelry. —Rita Rudner, *Tickled Pink*, 2001

I realized on our first wedding anniversary that our marriage was in trouble. Fang gave me luggage. It was packed. My mother damn near suffocated in there. —Phyllis Diller, *Women in Comedy*, Martin and Segrave

There was altogether too much candor in married life; it was an indelicate modern idea, and frequently led to upsets in a household, if not divorce. —Muriel Spark, *Memento Mori*, 1959

I did have a talent—and I was married to her for 38 years. —George Burns, oft-repeated line about his wife, Gracie Allen

Marry an outdoors woman. Then if you throw her out into the yard for the night, she can still survive. —W. C. Fields, *W. C. Fields & Me*, Carlotta Monti with Cy Rice, 1971

That's what a man wants in a wife, mostly; he wants to make sure o' one fool as 'ull tell him he's wise. —George Eliot, *Adam Bede*, 1859

I am his awful wedded wife. —Goodman Ace, *Easy Aces* radio show, 1930s–1940s

What could be more absurd than to assemble a crowd to witness a man and a woman promising to love each other for the rest of their lives, when we know what human creatures are—men so thoroughly selfish and unprincipled, women so vain and frivolous? —Emily Eden, *The Semi-Attached Couple*, 1830

Marriage has many pains, but celibacy has no pleasures. —Samuel Johnson, *The History of Rasselas, Prince of Abissinia*, 1759

Men often marry their mothers .... —Edna Ferber, *Saratoga Trunk*, 1941

> If you live to be a hundred, I want to live to be a hundred minus one day, so I never have to live without you.
>
> —A. A. Milne, *Winnie the Pooh*, 1926

Every time a woman makes herself laugh at her husband's often-told jokes she betrays him. The man who looks at his woman and says "What would I do without you?" is already destroyed. —Germaine Greer, *The Female Eunuch*, 1971

Marriage is nature's way of keeping people from fighting with strangers. —Alan King, *Jokes*, Getlen

Why, Benjamin Franklin says a man without a woman is like a half a pair of scissors. —Anita Loos, *Happy Birthday*, 1947

It's having the same man around the house all the time that ruins matrimony. —Texas Guinan, nightclub act

To keep your marriage brimming, / With love in the loving cup, / Whenever you're wrong, admit it; / Whenever you're right, shut up. —Ogden Nash, "A Word to Husbands," *Marriage Lines*, 1964

To marry is to halve your rights and double your duties. —Arthur Schopenhauer, *The World as Will and Representation*, 1819

Any intelligent woman who reads the marriage contract, and then goes into it, deserves all the consequences. —Isadora Duncan, *My Life*, 1927

Husbands are chiefly good as lovers when they are betraying their wives. —Marilyn Monroe, *Marilyn Monroe In Her Own Words*, 1990

Marriage is the operation by which a woman's vanity and a man's egotism are extracted without an anaesthetic. —Helen Rowland, *A Guide to Men*, 1922

Books and marriage go ill together. —Molière, *Les Femmes Savantes*, 1672

Marriage is a bribe to make a housekeeper think she's a householder.

—Thornton Wilder, *The Matchmaker*, 1954

If variety is the spice of life, marriage is the big can of leftover Spam. —Johnny Carson, *Jokes*, Getlen

We would have broken up except for the children. Who were the children? Well, she and I were. —Mort Sahl, stand-up routine

There is a rhythm to the ending of a marriage just like the rhythm of a courtship—only backward. You try to start again but get into blaming over and over. Finally you are both worn out, exhausted, hopeless. Then lawyers are called in to pick clean the corpses. —Erica Jong, *How to Save your Own Life*, 1977

I think a bad husband is far worse than no husband .... —Margaret Cavendish, *Sociable Letters*, 1664

> My wife Mary and I have been married for forty-seven years and not once have we had an argument serious enough to consider divorce; murder, yes, but divorce, never.
>
> —Jack Benny, stand-up routine

Love, the quest; marriage, the conquest; divorce, the inquest. —Helen Rowland, *Reflections of a Bachelor Girl*, 1903

I never hated a man enough to give him his diamonds back. —Zsa Zsa Gabor, quoted in *The Observer* (London), 1957

It's bad enough when married people bore one another, but it's much worse when only one of them bores the other. —Marie von Ebner Eschenbach, *Aphorisms*, 1905

When the rabbi said, "Do you take this woman?" sixteen guys said, "We have." —Joan Rivers, *The Haunted Smile*, Epstein

"I don't hate him," Athenaise answered … "It's jus' being married that I detes' an' despise." —Kate Chopin, "Athenaise," 1895

One man's folly is another man's wife. —Helen Rowland, *Reflections of a Bachelor Girl*, 1903

You know marriage is making a big comeback. I know personally that in Hollywood people are marrying people they never married before. —Bob Hope, www.BobHope.com, 2007

The only good thing about marriage is becoming a widow. —Isabel Allende, *Daughter of Fortune*, 1999

A widow is a fascinating being with the flavor of maturity, the spice of experience, the piquancy of novelty, the tang of practiced coquetry, and the halo of one man's approval. —Helen Rowland, *A Guide to Men*, 1922

The problem with marriage is that it ends every night after making love, and it must be rebuilt every morning before breakfast. —Gabriel Gárcia Márquez, *Love in the Time of Cholera*, 1985

> “When you see what some girls marry, you realize they must hate to work for a living.
> —Helen Rowland, *Reflections of a Bachelor Girl*, 1903”

The keeping of an idle woman is a badge of superior social status. —Dorothy L. Sayers, essay

A man in love is incomplete until he has married—then he's finished. —Zsa Zsa Gabor, quoted in *Newsweek* (New York), 1960

… this marrying I do not like: 'tis like going on a long voyage to sea, where after a while even the calms are distasteful, and the storms dangerous: one seldom sees a new object, 'tis still a deal of sea, sea; husband, husband, every day—till one's quite cloyed with it. —Aphra Behn, *The Dutch Lover*, 1673

Marriage is a wonderful institution, but who wants to live in an institution? —Groucho Marx, *Jokes*, Getlen

Marriage is lonelier than solitude. —Adrienne Rich, "Paula Becker to Clare Westhoff," *Dream of a Common Language*, 1978

Marriage. The beginning and the end are wonderful. But the middle part is hell.
—Enid Bagnold, *The Chinese Prime Minister,* 1964

Love is moral without legal marriage, but marriage is immoral without love. —Ellen Key, *The Morality of Women and Other Essays*, 1911

So I am beginning to wonder if maybe girls wouldn't be happier if we stopped demanding so much respeckt [sic] for ourselves and developped [sic] a little more respeckt for husbands. —Anita Loos, *A Mouse Is Born*, 1951

... most of us carry into marriage not only our childlike illusions, but we bring to it as well the demand that it *has* to be wonderful, because it's *supposed* to be. —Eda J. Le Shan, *How to Survive Parenthood*, 1965

All married couples should learn the art of battle as they should learn the art of making love. —Ann Landers, *Ann Landers Says Truth Is Stranger ...*, 1968

... Lady Janet ... never has any opinion but mine: this is what I call the only solid foundation to build matrimonial happiness upon; and so I have made up my mind to marry. —Marguerite Blessington, *The Two Friends*, 1835

two by two in the ark of / the ache of it. —Denise Levertov, "The Ache of Marriage," *O Taste and See*, 1963

And I've learned a long time ago that the only people who count in a marriage are the people who are in it. —Hillary Rodham Clinton, interview with Matt Lauer, *The Today Show*, 1999

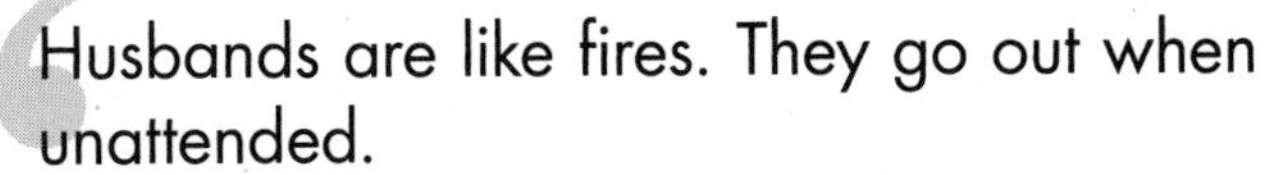

> Husbands are like fires. They go out when unattended.
>
> —Zsa Zsa Gabor, quoted in *Newsweek* (New York), 1960

Always remember, Peggy, it's matrimonial suicide to be jealous when you have a really good reason. —Clare Boothe Luce, *The Women*, 1936

Marriage involves big compromises all the time. International-level compromises. You're the U.S.A., he's the U.S.S.R., and you're talking nuclear warheads. —Bette Midler, quoted by Tom Seligson, *Parade* (New York), 1989

Never go to bed mad. Stay up and fight. —Phyllis Diller, *Housekeeping Hints*, 1966

A lady's imagination is very rapid; it jumps from admiration to love, from love to matrimony in a moment. —Jane Austen, *Pride and Prejudice*, 1813

Marriage is a business of taking care of a man and rearing his children … It ain't meant to be no perpetual honeymoon. —Clare Boothe Luce, *The Women*, 1936

Instead of marrying "at once," it sometimes happens that we marry "at last." —Colette, *Gigi*, 1944

If a woman *doubts* as to whether she should accept a man or not, she certainly ought to refuse him. If she can hesitate as to "Yes," she ought to say "No," directly. —Jane Austen, *Emma*, 1815

I'm getting married on April 12th. My fiancé and I still haven't decided on the year …. —Wendy Liebman, glee mail, wendyliebman.com, 2003 engagement

At every party there are two kinds of people—those who want to go home and those who don't. The trouble is, they are usually married to each other. —Ann Landers, *International Herald Tribune* (Paris), 1991

Marry rich. Buy him a pacemaker, then stand behind him and say "boo." —Joan Rivers, *Funny Women*, Unterbrink

My husband walks in the door one night, he says to me, "Roseanne, don't you think it's time we sat down and had a serious talk about our sex life?" I say to him, "You want me to turn off *Wheel of Fortune* for that?" —Roseanne Barr, *The Haunted Smile*, Epstein

I have yet to hear a man ask for advice on how to combine marriage and a career. —Gloria Steinem, www.haruth.com/WomenToWomen.htm

> Together wing to wing and oar to oar.
> —Robert Frost, "The Master Speed" (inscribed on the gravestone of Frost and his wife)

No woman with an ounce of sense gets married to be entertained, she marries to be maintained. —Isabel Allende, *Daughter of Fortune*, 1999

I quite thought he was honest when he said he didn't believe in marriage—and then it turned out that it was a test, to see whether my devotion was abject enough. —Dorothy L. Sayers, *Strong Poison*, 1930

Wasn't marriage, like life, unstimulating and unprofitable and somewhat empty when too well ordered and protected and guarded. Wasn't it finer, more splendid, more nourishing, when it was, like life itself, a mixture of the sordid and the magnificent; of mud and stars; of earth and flowers; of love and hate and laughter and tears and ugliness and beauty and hurt? —Edna Ferber, *Show Boat*, 1926

There is no subject on which more dangerous nonsense is talked and thought than marriage. —George Bernard Shaw, *Getting Married*, 1908

Welcome to the World 2

Babies, toddlers, children—you love 'em, or you can't stand 'em. But where would the world be without 'em? Whether you consider them rug rats or cherubs, if you're looking to congratulate a new addition to the world, here are some hilarious as well as dear ways to do it.

• • •

Babies are such a nice way to start people. —Don Herold, quoted by Lawrence J. Peter, *The Peter Prescription*, 1972

"When a new baby laughs for the first time a new fairy is born, and as there are always new babies there are always new fairies."
—J. M. Barrie, *Peter & Wendy*, 1911

"The joy, the reason to believe," my mother said, "the hope for the world, the baby, holy with possibility, that is all of us at birth." —Tillie Olsen, *Mother to Daughter, Daughter to Mother*, 1984

The crimson rose / plucked yesterday, / the fire and cinnamon / of the carnation, // the bread I baked / with anise seed and honey, / and the goldfish / flaming in its bowl. // All these are yours, baby born of woman, / if you'll only go to sleep. —Gabriela Mistral, "If You'll Only Go to Sleep," *Tenderness*, 1924

As he saw it, childbirth was long hours for short wages. —Alice Fulton, "Happy Dust," *The Missouri Review* (Columbia), 1997

If men were equally at risk from this condition—if they knew their bellies might swell as if they were suffering from end-stage cirrhosis, that they would have to go nearly a year without a stiff drink, a cigarette, or even an aspirin, that they would be subject to fainting spells and unable to fight their way onto commuter trains—then I am sure that pregnancy would be classified as a sexually transmitted disease and abortions would be no more controversial than emergency appendectomies. —Barbara Ehreinreich, "Their Dilemma and Mine," *The Worst Years of Our Lives*, 1991

> May all your genes be recessive!
> —Johnny Carson, *The Johnny Carson Show*

... lifestyles and sex roles are passed from parents to children as inexorably as blue eyes or small feet. —Letty Cottin Pogrebin, "Down with Sexist Upbringing," *The First Ms. Reader*, Klagsbrun

My mom says I'm a super-special wonderful terrific little guy. / My mom just had another baby. / Why? —Judith Viorst, *If I Were in Charge of the World and Other Worries ...*, 1981

There was a little girl, / Who had a little curl, / Right in the middle of her forehead. / When she was good, / She was very, very good, / But when she was bad she was horrid. —Henry Wadsworth Longfellow, "There Was a Little Girl"

A toddling little girl is a centre of common feeling which makes the most dissimilar people understand each other. —George Eliot, *Scenes of Clerical Life*, 1857

... what is the use of being a little boy if you are going to grow up to be a man. —Gertrude Stein, *Everybody's Autobiography*, 1937

Children are all foreigners. —Ralph Waldo Emerson, journal entry, 1839

Only children know what they are looking for. —Antoine de Saint-Exupéry, *The Little Prince*

Between the dark and the daylight, / When the night is beginning to lower, / Comes a pause in the day's occupation, / That is known as the Children's Hour. —Henry Wadsworth Longfellow, "The Children's Hour," 1860

A child's a plaything for an hour. —Mary Ann Lamb, "Parental Recollections," *Poetry for Children*, 1809

Nothing you do for children is ever wasted. They seem not to notice us, hovering, averting our eyes, and they seldom offer thanks, but what we do for them is never wasted. —Garrison Keillor, "Easter," *Leaving Home*, 1987

Every child is in a way a genius; and every genius is in a way a child. —Arthur Schopenhauer, "On the Vanity and Suffering of Life," *The World as Will and Representation*, 1819

> A baby is God's opinion that the world should go on.
>
> —Carl Sandburg, *Remembrance Rock*, 1948

For little boys are rancorous / When robbed of any myth, / And spiteful and cantankerous / To all their kin and kith. —Phyllis McGinley, "What Every Woman Knows," *Times Three*, 1960

… that wild, unknown being, the child, who is both bottomless pit and impregnable fortress …. —Colette, "Look!", 1929

Children are not our creations but our guests. —John Updike, quoted by Anatole Broyard, *Aroused by Books*, 1974

We in the West do not refrain from childbirth because we are concerned about the population explosion or because we feel we cannot afford children, but because we do not like children. —Germaine Greer, *Sex and Destiny*, 1984

Thou straggler into loving arms, / Young climber up of knees, / When I forget thy thousand ways, / Then life and all shall cease. —Mary Ann Lamb, "A Child," *Poetry for Children*, 1809

All God's children are not beautiful. Most of God's children are, in fact, barely presentable. —Fran Lebowitz, *Metropolitan Life*, 1978

It is destroying, dissolving him utterly, this helpless warmth against him, this feel of a child. —Tillie Olsen, "Hey Sailor, What Ship?," *Tell Me a Riddle*, 1960

The child endures all things. —Maria Montessori, *The Absorbent Mind*, 1949

So long as little children are allowed to suffer, there is no true love in this world. —Isadora Duncan, *This Quarter* (Paris), Autumn 1929

Children's liberation is the next item on our civil rights shopping list. —Letty Cottin Pogrebin, "Down with Sexist Upbringing," *The First Ms. Reader*, Klagsbrun

Children are the only form of immortality that we can be sure of. —Peter Ustinov, attributed

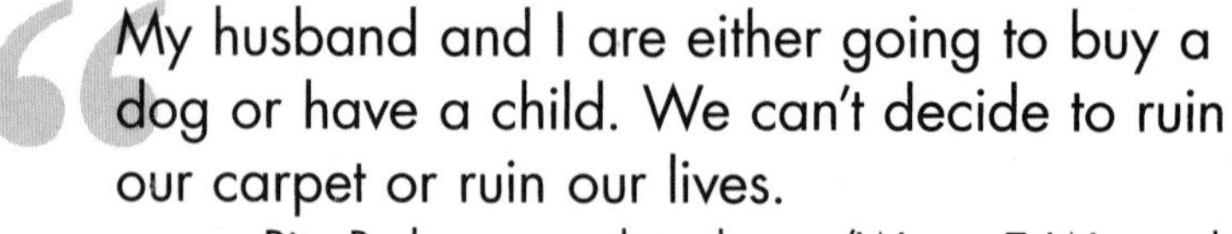

> My husband and I are either going to buy a dog or have a child. We can't decide to ruin our carpet or ruin our lives.
>
> —Rita Rudner, www.haruth.com/WomenToWomen.htm

Posterity is the world to come; the world for whom we hold our ideals, from whom we have borrowed our planet, and to whom we bear sacred responsibility. —Bill Clinton, *First Inaugural Address* (Washington, D.C.), 1993

A child is fed with milk and praise. —Mary Ann Lamb, "The First Tooth," Brother, *Poetry for Children*, 1809

Child, with many a childish wile, / Timid look, and blushing smile, / Downy wings to steal thy way, / Gilded bow, and quiver gay, / Who in thy simple mien would trace / The tyrant of the human race? —Joanna Baillie, *Basil*, 1798

Children's talent to endure stems from their ignorance of alternatives. —Maya Angelou, *I Know Why the Caged Bird Sings*, 1969

At the core of every child is an intact human. —Riane Eisler, *Tomorrow's Children*, 2000

Well, you have children so you know: little children little troubles, big children big troubles—it's a saying in Yiddish. Maybe the Chinese said it too. —Grace Paley, "Zagrowsky Tells," *Later the Same Day*, 1985

> "A baby is an inestimable blessing and bother.
> —Mark Twain, letter to Annie Webster, 1 September 1876"

Father asked us what was God's noblest work. Anna said men, but I said babies. Men are often bad; babies never are. —Louisa May Alcott, diary entry (1843), *Her Life, Letters, and Journals*, Edna D. Cheney, ed., 1889

A child's spirit is like a child, you cannot catch it by running after it; you must stand still, and, for love, it will soon itself come back. —Arthur Miller, *The Crucible*, 1953

I'll tell you about babies. Whenever I see one, I want to give it a cigar and discuss the Common Market. —Muriel Resnik, *Any Wednesday*, 1963

In the name of motherhood and fatherhood and education and good manners, we threaten and suffocate and bind and ensnare and bribe and trick children into wholesale emulation of our ways. —June Jordan, "Old Stories: New Lives," *Moving Towards Home: Political Essays*, 1989

I can't get over my disappointment in not being a boy. —Louisa May Alcott, *Little Women*, 1868

... I think children are a little like plants. If they grow too close together they become thin and sickly and never obtain maximum growth. We need room to grow. —Peace Pilgrim, *Her Life and Work*

Women's Liberation is just a lot of foolishness. It's the men who are discriminated against. They can't bear children. And no one's likely to do anything about that. —Golda Meir, quoted in *Newsweek* (New York), 1972

I want to have children, but my friends scare me. One of my friends told me she was in labor for 36 hours. I don't even want to do anything that feels GOOD for 36 hours. —Rita Rudner, www.haruth.com/WomenToWomen.htm

Death and taxes and childbirth! There's never any convenient time for any of them! —Margaret Mitchell, *Gone with the Wind*, 1936

Obviously there is pain in childbirth. But giving birth is also a moment of awe and wonder, a moment when the true miracle of aliveness, and of a woman's amazing part in that miracle, is suddenly experienced in every cell of one's body. It is in that sense truly an altered state of consciousness. —Riane Eisler, *Sacred Pleasure*, 1996

Suddenly it seemed my little shut-in had been cooped up long enough. Suddenly it wanted liberty. It was coming like a locomotive headlight. It was coming quick as scat. God Almighty! Now this baby was helping. Now this baby wanted to be born. —Alice Fulton, "Happy Dust," *The Missouri Review*, 1997

We begin life with loss. We are cast from the womb without an apartment, a charge plate, a job or a car. —Judith Viorst, *Necessary Losses*, 1986

I'm not sure if my husband is going to be there when I actually have the baby. He said the only way he's going to be in the room when there's a delivery is if there's a pizza involved. —Rita Rudner, *Tickled Pink*, 2001

But what's more important. Building a bridge or taking care of a baby? —June Jordan, *New Life, New Room*, 1975

Infancy conforms to nobody: all conform to it, so that one babe commonly makes four or five out of the adults who prattle and play to it. —Ralph Waldo Emerson, "Self-Reliance," *Essays: First Series*, 1841

> "At last, there came the joyful whisper, "a fine boy," perhaps the only moment of a fine boy's existence in which his presence is more agreeable than his absence."
>
> —Emily Eden, *The Semi-Detached House*, c. 1860s

A soiled baby, with a neglected nose, cannot be conscientiously regarded as a thing of beauty. —Mark Twain, *Answers to Correspondents*, 1865

Diaper backward spells repaid. Think about it. —Marshall McLuhan, quoted in *Vancouver Sun* (British Columbia), 1969

In a world that is cutting down its trees to build highways, losing its earth to concrete ... babies are almost the only remaining link with nature, with the natural world of living things from which we spring. —Eda Le Shan, *The Conspiracy Against Childhood*, 1967

Of all the animals, the boy is the most unmanageable. —Plato, *Theaetetus*

Although she still had three months to go, Mindy already felt the hefty, protective tug of maternal obligation. Indeed, the bond was so strong she was considering not having the umbilical cord cut right away, but leaving it intact so she could keep track of her child's whereabouts until he or she was at least twenty-one. —Rita Rudner, *Tickled Pink*, 2001

Why is it that we rejoice at a birth and grieve at a funeral? It is because we are not the person involved. —Mark Twain, *Pudd'n'head Wilson*, 1894

Madam, there's no such thing as a tough child—if you parboil them first for seven hours, they always come out tender. —W. C. Fields, radio show

... there is one order of beauty which seems made to turn the heads not only of men, but of all intelligent mammals, even of women. It is a beauty like that of kittens, or very small downy ducks making gentle rippling noises with their soft bills, or babies just beginning to toddle and to engage in conscious mischief—a beauty with which you can never be angry, but that you feel ready to crush for inability to comprehend the state of mind into which it throws you. —George Eliot, *Adam Bede*, 1859

> Plastic surgery must be like childbirth without the child ... After a while, if you're satisfied with the results, you forget the pain and want to do it again.
>
> —Rita Rudner, *Tickled Pink*, 2001

3

Hello Muddah, Hello Faddah

When a child is born, so are a mother and a father … and from that triple birth a wellspring of joys, woes, and conundrums spews forth for the new mom and dad. One that goes on for years and years … and years. Forewarned is forearmed.

• • •

Having a child is surely the most beautifully irrational act that two people in love can commit. —Bill Cosby, *Fatherhood*, 1986

It is a national shame that many Americans are more thoughtful about planning their weekend entertainment than about planning their families. —Hillary Rodham Clinton, *It Takes a Village and Other Lessons Children Teach Us*, 1996

> "What Business had you to get Children, without you had Cabbage enough to maintain 'em?"
>
> —Susanna Centlivre, *The Gamester*, 1705

Familiarity breeds contempt—and children. —Mark Twain, *Mark Twain's Notebook*, Albert Bigelow Paine, ed., 1935

May you fight all the day like a dog and a cat, / And yet ev'ry year produce a new brat. —Mary Wortley Montagu, "Epithalamium," *Letters*

If you have never been hated by your child, you have never been a parent. —Bette Davis, *The Lonely Life*, 1962

... sometimes the very faults of parents produce a tendency to opposite virtues in their children. —Maria Edgeworth, *Maneuvering*, 1809

I've also discovered the world is full of mothers who've done their best and still hurt their daughters: that we have daughters everywhere. —Alice Walker, "Sunniness and Shade," *Anything We Love Can Be Saved*, 1997

Oh, high is the price of parenthood, / And daughters may cost you double. / You dare not forget, as you thought you could, / That youth is a plague and a trouble. —Phyllis McGinley, "Homework for Anabelle," *Times Three*, 1960

No one is more susceptible to an expert's fearmongering than a parent. —Stephen D. Levitt and Stephen J. Dubner, *Freakonomics*, 2005

Two parents can't raise a child any more than one. You need a whole community—everybody—to raise a child. —Toni Morrison, quoted by Bonnie Angelo, *Time* (New York), 1989

I look after my young, I can't look after the world .... —Gregory Maguire, "Uprisings," *Wicked*, 1995

Children aren't happy with nothing to ignore, / And that's what parents were created for. —Ogden Nash, "The Parent," *Happy Days*, 1933

Her [mother's] constant care blurs into the maternal mists while his [father's] few alcohol rubs are as memorable as if they were anointments by a prophet. —Letty Cottin Pogrebin, *Deborah, Golda, and Me*

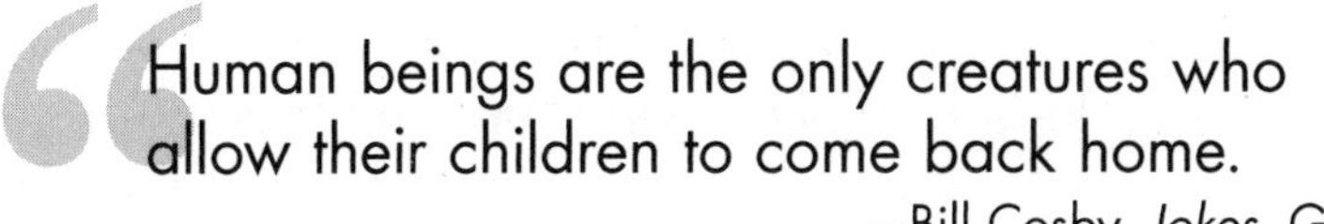

Human beings are the only creatures who allow their children to come back home.

—Bill Cosby, *Jokes,* Getlen

With him for a sire and her for a dam, / What should I be but just what I am? —Edna St. Vincent Millay, "The Singing-Woman from the Wood's Edge," *A Few Figs from Thistles*, 1920

I have no sympathy with the old idea that children owe such immense gratitude to their parents that they can never fulfill their obligations to them. I think the obligation is all on the other side. —Elizabeth Cady Stanton, diary entry (1880), *Elizabeth Cady Stanton*

For success in training children the first condition is to become as a child oneself ... to be as entirely and simply taken up with the child as the child himself is absorbed by his life. —Ellen Key, *The Century of the Child*, 1909

I love my parents and they're wonderful people, but they were strict, and I still look for ways to get even. When I got my own apartment for the very first time and they came to stay with me for the weekend, I made them stay in separate bedrooms. —Elayne Boosler, *Funny Women*, Unterbrink

Parents of young children should realize that few people, and maybe no one, will find their children as enchanting as they do. —Barbara Walters, *How to Talk with Practically Anybody About Practically Anything*, 1970

Oh, what a tangled web do parents weave / When they think that their children are naïve. —Ogden Nash, "Baby, What Makes the Sky Blue?"

I figure when my husband comes home from work, if the kids are still alive, then I've done my job.

—Roseanne Barr, *The Haunted Smile,* Epstein

Nobody who has not been in the interior of a family can say what the difficulties of any individual of that family may be. —Jane Austen, *Emma*, 1815

When a child enters the world through you, it alters everything on a psychic, psychological and purely practical level. You're just not free anymore to do what you want to do. And it's not the same again. Ever. —Jane Fonda, quoted by Danae Brook, *Los Angeles Weekly* (Los Angeles), 1980

A mother's life, you see, is one long succession of dramas, now soft and tender, now terrible. Not an hour but has its joys and fears. —Honoré de Balzac, "Letters of Two Brides," *La Press*, 1841–1842

Of course, everybody knows that the greatest thing about Motherhood is the "Sacrifices," but it is quite a shock to find out that they begin so far ahead of time. —Anita Loos, *A Mouse Is Born*, 1951

Being a mother is a noble status, right? Right. So why does it change when you put "unwed" or "welfare" in front of it? —Florynce Kennedy, quoted by Gloria Steinem, *Ms.*, 1973

My breasts have fed three children, nurtured and sustained their bodies and built them up in twelve ways. If they wanna lay down after that, by god they deserve the rest. —Roseanne Barr, *My Life as a Woman*, 1989

It takes a woman twenty years to make a man of her son, and another woman twenty minutes to make a fool of him. —Helen Rowland, *Reflections of a Bachelor Girl*, 1903

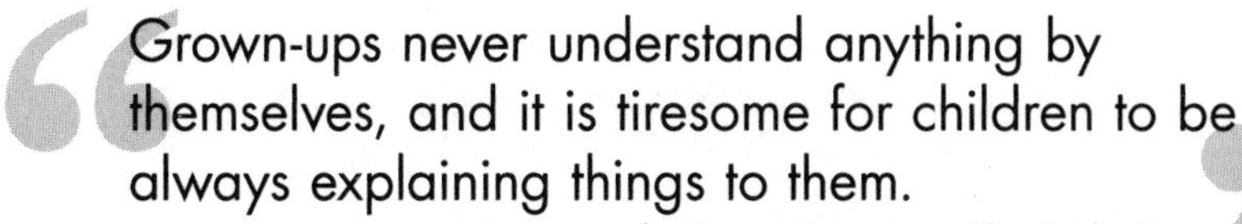

—Antoine de Saint-Exupéry, *The Little Prince*

She discovered with great delight that one does not love one's children just because they are one's children but because of the friendship formed while raising them. —Gabriel Garcia Marquez, *Love in the Time of Cholera*, 1985

A mother, who is really a mother, is never free. —Honoré de Balzac, "Letters of Two Brides," *La Press*, 1841–1842

I supposed I could have stayed home and baked cookies and had teas, but what I decided to do is fulfill my profession. —Hillary Rodham Clinton (with Claire G. Osborne), *The Unique Voice of Hillary Rodham Clinton*, 1997

To depend upon a profession is a less odious form of slavery than to depend upon a father. —Virginia Woolf, *Three Guineas*, 1938

Always obey your parents, when they are present. —Mark Twain, "Advice to Youth," speech (Boston), 15 April 1882

> It is funny the two things most men are proudest of is the thing that any man can do and doing does in the same way, that is being drunk and being the father of their son.
>
> —Gertrude Stein, *Everybody's Autobiography*, 1937

A father is always making his baby into a little woman. And when she is a woman he turns her back again. —Enid Bagnold, *Autobiography*, 1969

Blessed indeed is the man who hears many gentle voices call him father! —Lydia Maria Child, *Philothea: A Romance*, 1836

The thing to remember about fathers is, they're men. / A girl has to keep it in mind. —Phyllis McGinley, "Girl's-Eye View of Relatives: First Lesson," *Times Three*, 1960

If men started taking care of children, the job will become more valuable. —Gloria Steinem, quoted by Claudia Wallis, *Time* (New York), 1989

[Why is it] there are never any evil stepfathers. —Margaret Atwood, "Unpopular Gals," *Good Bones and Simple Murders*, 1994

I cannot think of any need in childhood as strong as the need for a father's protection. —Sigmund Freud, *Civilization and Its Discontents*, 1931

It is a wise father that knows his own child. —William Shakespeare, *The Merchant of Venice*, 1596

That is natural enough when nobody has had fathers they begin to long for them and then when everybody has had fathers they begin to long to do without them. —Gertrude Stein, *Everybody's Autobiography*, 1937

Parents, you have caused my misfortune, and you have caused your own. —Arthur Rimbaud, "Nuit de l'Enfer" (1874), *Collected Poems*, Oliver Bernard, ed., 1962

Children are being given a false picture of what it means to be human. We tell them to be good and kind, nonviolent and giving. But on all sides they see media images and hear and read stories that portray us as bad, cruel, violent, and selfish. —Riane Eisler, *Tomorrow's Children*, 2000

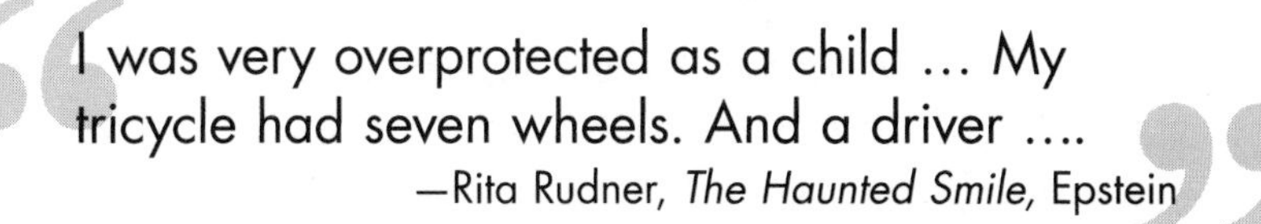

"What are you thinking about, Bel-Gazou?" // "Nothing, Mother." // An excellent answer. The same that I invariably gave when I was her age. —Colette, "The Priest on the Wall," *My Mother's House*, 1922

We find a delight in the beauty and happiness of children that makes the heart too big for the body. —Ralph Waldo Emerson, "Illusions," *The Conduct of Life*, 1860

Kids even have play dates. Playing is now done by appointment. Whatever happened to, "You show me your wee-wee, and I'll show you mine?" —George Carlin, *Jokes*, Getlen

So does the name you give your child affect his life? Or is it your life reflected in his name? —Stephen D. Levitt and Stephen J. Dubner, *Freakonomics*, 2005

> Warmth is the vital element for the growing plant and for the soul of the child.
> —Carl Jung, "The Gifted Child," (1942) *The Development of Personality,* R. F. C. Hull, tr., 1954

Where parents do too much for their children, the children will not do much for themselves. —Elbert Hubbard, *Notebook*

Children aren't coloring books. You don't get to fill them with your favorite colors. —Khaled Hosseini, *The Kite Runner*, 2003

It is not a bad thing that children should occasionally, and politely, put parents in their place. —Colette, "The Priest on the Wall," *My Mother's House*, 1922

We have kept our children so busy with "useful" and "improving" activities that we are in danger of raising a generation of young people who are terrified of silence, of being alone with their own thoughts .... —Eda La Shan, *The Conspiracy Against Childhood*, 1967

When your children are teenagers, it's important to have a dog so that someone in the house is happy to see you. —Nora Ephron, *I Feel Bad About My Neck*, 2006

At every step the child should be allowed to meet the real experiences of life; the thorns should never be plucked from his roses. —Ellen Key, *The Century of the Child*, 1909

Those who have lived in a house with spoiled children must have a lively recollection of the degree of torment they can inflict upon all who are within sight or hearing. —Maria Edgeworth, *The Manufacturers*, 1803

In the final analysis it is not what you do for your children but what you have taught them to do for themselves that will make them successful human beings. —Ann Landers, *Ann Landers Says Truth Is Stranger ...*, 1968

The best way to keep children home is to make it pleasant—and let the air out of the tires. —Dorothy Parker, quoted in *Utne Reader* (Minneapolis), 1991

How sharper than a serpent's tooth it is / To have a thankless child! —William Shakespeare, *King Lear*, 1608

"I like children—properly cooked."

—W. C. Fields, *By Himself*, Fields

Children begin by loving their parents; after a time they judge them; rarely, if ever, do they forgive them. —Oscar Wilde, *A Woman of No Importance*, 1893

Home for the Holidays 4

New Year, Thanksgiving, Passover, anniversaries, and that annual celebration some of us relish and some of us abhor—birthdays. These quotes will give you something to munch on other than Christmas cookies.

• • •

Call a truce, then, to our labors—let us feast with friends and neighbors. —Rudyard Kipling, "Christmas in India," 1890

Christmas won't be Christmas without any presents. —Louisa May Alcott, *Little Women*, 1868

A lovely thing about Christmas is that it's compulsory, like a thunderstorm, and we all go through it together. —Garrison Keillor, "Exiles," *Leaving Home*, 1987

Christmas to a child is the first terrible proof that to travel hopefully is better than to arrive. —Stephen Fry, attributed

Christmas at my house is always at least six or seven times more pleasant than anywhere else. We start drinking early. And while everyone else is seeing only one Santa Claus, we'll be seeing six or seven. —W. C. Fields, quoted in *Newsweek* (New York), 1947

"If all the year were playing holidays, / To sport would be as tedious as to work.

—William Shakespeare, *Henry IV, Pt. 1*, 1597"

"Maybe Christmas," he thought, "doesn't come from a store." / "Maybe Christmas … perhaps … means a little bit more!" —Dr. Seuss, *How the Grinch Stole Christmas!*, 1957

… I watched the tall plain trees that ring three sides of it being pruned in what seemed a crazily brutal way …. Then, magically, for Christmas Eve and the formal opening with its speeches and music, the tall trees turned into arbres de Noel, twinkling with thousands of little lights the color of champagne.—M. F. K. Fisher, *A Considerable Town*, 1948

I celebrated Thanksgiving in an old-fashioned way. I invited everyone in my neighborhood to my house, we had an enormous feast, and then I killed them and took their land. —Jon Stewart, "Holidays," *Jokes*, Getlen

For Thanksgiving last year I made a seventeen-pound turkey … pot pie. —Wendy Liebman, *The Haunted Smile*, Epstein

Embarrassing moment for President Bush today. He called the pope to wish him a happy Passover. —Jay Leno, *Jokes*, Getlen

Re: Jewish holidays: My mother, my aunts, my own grandmothers float back to me, young and vibrant once more, making days holy in the sanctuaries of their kitchens, feeding me, cradling me, connecting me to the intricately plaited braid of their past …. —Faye Moskowitz, *And the Bridge Is Love*, 1991

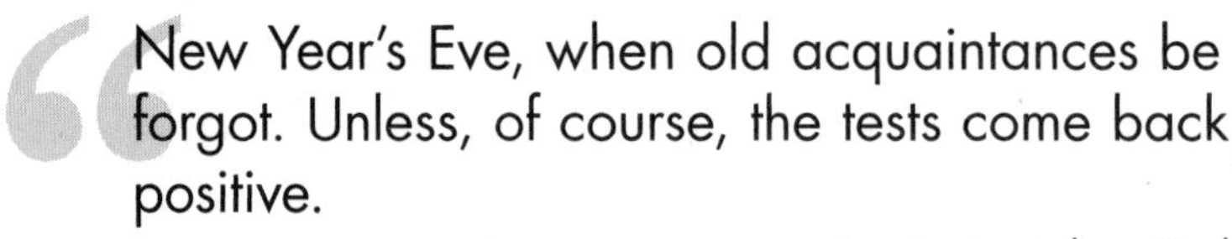

New Year's Eve, when old acquaintances be forgot. Unless, of course, the tests come back positive.

—Jay Leno, *Jokes*, Getlen

The only way to spend New Year's Eve is either quietly with friends or in a brothel. —W. H. Auden, *Table Talk*

May I join you in the doghouse, Rover? / I wish to retire till the party's over. —Ogden Nash, "Children's Party," *Many Years Ago*, 1945

... the little festive atmosphere of strangeness, of excitement, that only a holiday bedroom brings. This is ours for the moment, but no more. While we are in it, we bring it life. When we have gone, it no longer exists, it fades into anonymity. —Daphne du Maurier, *Don't Look Now*, 1970

A two-year-old is kind of like having a blender, but you don't have a top for it. —Jerry Seinfeld, stand-up routine

When I was One, / I had just begun. / When I was Two, / I was nearly new. / When I was Three / I was hardly me. / When I was Four, / I was not much more. / When I was Five, I was just alive. / But now I am Six, I'm as clever as clever, / So I think I'll be six now for ever and ever. —A. A. Milne, "The End," *Now We are Six*, 1927

Children were pretty things at three years old; but began to be great plagues at six, and were quite intolerable at ten. —Maria Edgeworth, *The Manufacturers*, 1803

Perhaps a modern society can remain stable only by eliminating adolescence .... —Eric Hoffer, *Reflections on the Human Condition*, 1973

O Adolescence, O Adolescence / I wince before thine incandescence .... —Ogden Nash, "Tarkington, Thou Should'st Be Living in This Hour," *Versus*, 1949

When you are seventeen you aren't really serious. —Jean-Paul Sartre, "Roman," *Collected Poems*, Oliver Bernard, ed., 1962

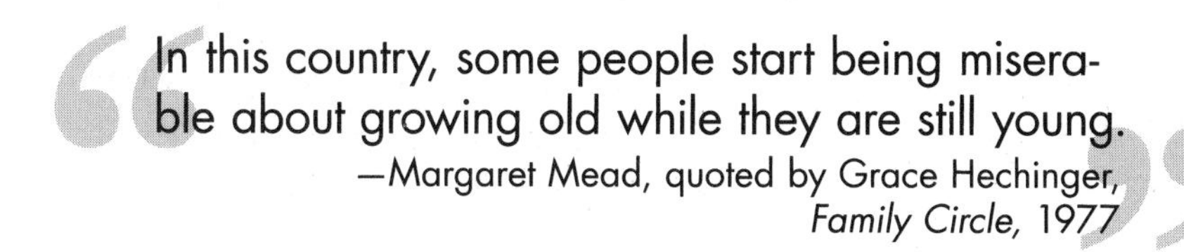
In this country, some people start being miserable about growing old while they are still young.
—Margaret Mead, quoted by Grace Hechinger, *Family Circle*, 1977

Youth smiles without any reason. It is one of its chiefest charms. —Oscar Wilde, *The Picture of Dorian Gray*, 1891

Oh, my God. I've just told you how old I am. Nobody knows how old I am. I'm going to have to kill you now. —Rita Rudner, *Tickled Pink*, 2001

Towering is the confidence of twenty-one. —Samuel Johnson, letter (1758), quoted by James Boswell, *The Life of Samuel Johnson*

But it's hard to be hip over thirty / When everyone else is nineteen. —Judith Viorst, *It's Hard to Be Hip Over Thirty and Other Tragedies of Married Life*, 1968

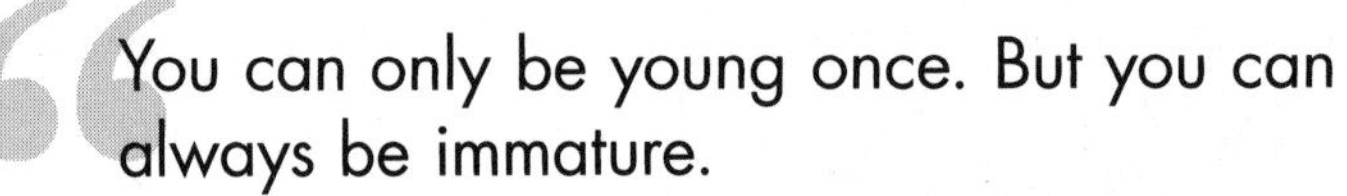

Thirty-five is a very attractive age. London society is full of women of the highest birth who have, of their own free choice, remained thirty-five for years. —Oscar Wilde, *The Importance of Being Ernest*, 1895

A woman, till five-and-thirty, is only looked upon as a raw girl, and can possibly make no noise in the world till about forty. —Mary Wortley Montagu, *Letters*

I was thirty-seven years old and still discovering who I was. —Julia Child (with Alex Prud'Homme), *My Life in France*, 2006

I don't plan to grow old gracefully. I plan to have face-lifts until my ears meet. —Rita Rudner, attributed

At twenty, a man feels awfully aged and blasé; at thirty, almost senile; at forty, "not so old"; and at fifty, positively skittish.—Helen Rowland, quoted by F. P. Adams et al., *The Book of Diversion*, Adams

"Except ye become as little children," except you can wake on your fiftieth birthday with the same forward-looking excitement and interest in life that you enjoyed when you were five, "ye cannot enter the kingdom of God." One must not only die daily, but every day we must be born again. —Dorothy L. Sayers, *Creed or Chaos? and Other Essays in Popular Mythology*, 1947

I am not young enough to know everything. —J. M. Barrie, *The Admirable Crichton*, 1903

The world's anguish is caused by people between twenty and forty. —William Faulkner, interview, *Writers at Work*, Cowley

I've never understood why people consider youth a time of freedom and joy. It's probably because they have forgotten their own. —Margaret Atwood, "Hair Jewelry," *Dancing Girls*, 1982

Youth is something very new: twenty years ago no one mentioned it. —Coco Chanel, quoted by Marcel Haedrich, *Coco Chanel, Her Life, Her Secrets*, 1971

No hanky, no panky. At my age, foreplay is brushing my teeth … when I can remember where I put 'em. —Rita Rudner, *Tickled Pink*, 2001

> You know you're getting old, when your back starts going out more than you do.
>
> —Phyllis Diller, *Housekeeping Hints*, 1966

"Maturity," Bokonon tells us, "is a bitter disappointment for which no remedy exists, unless laughter can be said to remedy anything." —Kurt Vonnegut, *Cat's Cradle, or Ice-Nine*, 1963

You are young, and then you are middle-aged, but it is hard to tell the moment of passage from one state to the next. —Doris Lessing, *The Summer Before the Dark*, 1973

You know you're getting old when you get that one candle on the cake. It's like, "See if you can blow this out." —Jerry Seinfeld, stand-up routine

> Perhaps middle-age is, or should be, a period of shedding shells; the shell of ambition, the shell of material accumulations and possessions, the shell of the ego.
>
> —Anne Morrow Lindbergh, *Gift from the Sea,* 1955

Who would return to the youth he is forever pretending to regret? —Agnes Repplier, "Some Aspects of Pessimism," *Books and Men*, 1888

The youth gets together his materials to build a bridge to the moon, or perchance a palace or temple on the earth, and at length the middle-aged man concludes to build a woodshed of them. —Henry David Thoreau, journal entry, 14 July 1852

Was it for this I uttered prayers, / And sobbed and cursed and kicked the stairs, / That now, domestic as a plate, / I should retire at half-past eight? —Edna St. Vincent Millay, "Grown-Up," *A Few Figs from Thistles*, 1920

Old is always 15 years from now. —Bill Cosby, *Jokes*, Getlen

> First you forget names, then you forget faces. Next you forget to pull your zipper up, and finally you forget to pull it down.
>
> —George Burns, *Jokes,* Getlen

The muddle of old age is not that one is old, but that one is young. —Oscar Wilde, attributed

Nothing so dates a man as to decry the younger generation. —Adlai Stevenson, speech, University of Wisconsin (Madison), 1952

Old age isn't a battle. Old age is a massacre. —Philip Roth, *Everyman*, 2006

I don't need you to remind me of my age, I have a bladder to do that for me. —Stephen Fry, "Trefusis Returns!," *Paperweight*, 1993

A man knows when he is growing old because he begins to look like his father. —Gabriel Gárcia Márquez, *Love in the Time of Cholera*, 1988

I'll soon be sixty. And at a certain point, the definition of young is anyone who is a year younger than you are. —Bill Clinton, quoted by David Remnick, "The Wanderer," *New Yorker* (New York), 18 September 2006

Being over seventy is like being engaged in a war. All our friends are going or gone and survive amongst the dead and the dying as on a battlefield. —Muriel Spark, *Memento Mori*, 1959

To be seventy years young is sometimes far more cheerful and hopeful than to be forty years old. —Oliver Wendell Holmes Sr., letter to Julia Ward Howe on her 70th birthday, 1889

It feels great to be 95. I mean, for those parts of me that still have feeling. —Bob Hope, *Jokes*, Getlen

... old age is like a plane flying through a storm. Once you're aboard, there's nothing you can do. You can't stop the plane, you can't stop the storm, you can't stop time. So one might as well accept it calmly, wisely. —Golda Meir, quoted by Oriana Fallaci, *L'Eurepeo*, 1973

Every man desires to live long, but no man would be old. —Jonathan Swift, "Thoughts on Various Subjects," *Miscellanies in Prose and Verse*, 1727

The greatest problem about old age is the fear that it might go on too long. —A. J. P. Taylor, interview, *The Observer* (London), 1981

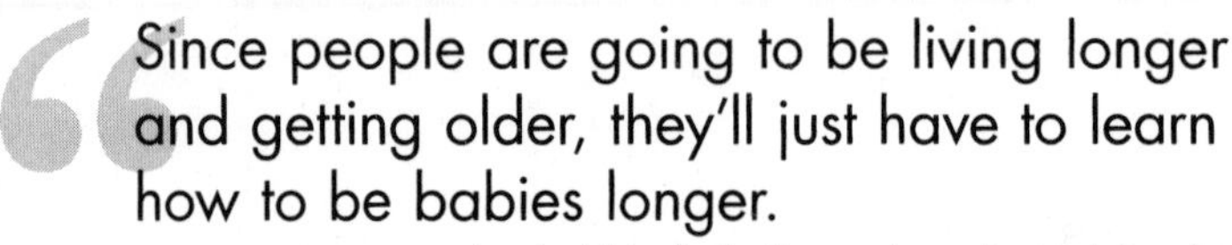

> Since people are going to be living longer and getting older, they'll just have to learn how to be babies longer.
>
> —Andy Warhol, *From A to B and Back Again*

I don't believe in aging. I believe in forever altering one's aspect to the sun. Hence my optimism. —Virginia Woolf, Diary entry (1932), *The Diary of Virginia Woolf*, Anne O. Bell, ed., 1982

In youth we learn; in age we understand. —Maria von Ebner Eschenbach, *Aphorisms*, 1905

A man's years should not be counted until he has nothing else to count. —Ralph Waldo Emerson, attributed

Women are as old as they feel, and men are old when they lose their feelings. —Mae West, *Wit and Wisdom*, Weintraub

Wrinkles should merely indicate where the smiles have been. —Mark Twain, *Following the Equator*, 1897

Few envy the consideration enjoyed by the oldest inhabitant. —Ralph Waldo Emerson, "Old Age," *Society and Solitude*, 1870

Time and trouble will tame an advanced young woman, but an advanced old woman is uncontrollable by any earthly force. —Dorothy L. Sayers, *Clouds of Witness*, 1956

I'm very pleased to be here. Let's face it, at my age I'm very pleased to be anywhere. —George Burns, attributed

School Daze

5

Is it your daughter's graduation day? Did your son just get accepted to the college of his choice? Was your hubby promoted from assistant to associate professor? Did your mom get tenure? Trying to make a point with the school board or at a PTA meeting? You're bound to find just the right line among these sometimes witty, sometimes inspirational quotes.

• • •

A good education is not so much one which prepares a man to succeed in the world, as one which enables him to sustain a failure. —Dr. Bernard Iddings Bell, www.bard.edu

> In the first place God made idiots. This was for practice. Then He made School Boards.
>
> —Mark Twain, *Following the Equator,* 1897

Focusing your life solely on making a buck shows a certain poverty of ambition. It asks too little of yourself … because it's only when you hitch your wagon to something larger than yourself that you realize your true potential. —Barack Obama, commencement address, Knox College (Galesburg, Illinois), 2005

Genius at first is little more than a great capacity for receiving discipline. —George Eliot, *Daniel Deronda*, 1874–1876

Constant effort and frequent mistakes are the stepping stones of genius. —Elbert Hubbard, *The Philosophy of Elbert Hubbard*, Elbert Hubbard II, comp., 1930

If my brothers saw me writing poems, they'd call me a queer and then it'd be all over school and I'd have to fight my way home every day. You know, most guys think you're a sissy if you like this stuff. —Gloria Naylor, *Linden Hills*, 1985

Curiosity is not a sin …. But we should exercise caution with our curiosity … yes, indeed. —J. K. Rowling, *Harry Potter and the Goblet of Fire*, 2000

It is often easier to fight for principles than to live up to them. —Adlai Stevenson, speech, "The Nature of Patriotism" (New York), 27 Aug 1952

He says a learned woman is the greatest of all calamities. —Maria von Ebner Eschenbach, *The Two Countesses*, 1893

> It is nothing short of a miracle that the modern methods of instruction have not yet entirely strangled the holy curiosity of inquiry ….
>
> —Albert Einstein, *Albert Einstein: Philosopher-Scientist*, Paul Schilpp, ed., 1951

Certainly the prolonged education indispensable to the progress of Society is not natural to mankind. —Winston Churchill, *Roving Commission: My Early Life*, 1930

Education is in danger of becoming a religion based on fear; its doctrine is to compete. —Eda J. Le Shan, *The Conspiracy Against Childhood*, 1967

A Bachelor of Arts is one who makes love to a lot of women, and yet has the art to remain a bachelor. —Helen Rowland, *A Guide to Men*, 1922

Education is our passport to the future, for tomorrow belongs to the people who prepare for it today. —Malcolm X, attributed

You can use a hammer to build with or you can use a hammer to destroy. —Molly Ivins, column, *Fort Worth Star-Telegram*, 1992

Service means you get as well as you give, your life is changed as you change the lives of others … it is the way we find meaning in our lives, both individually and collectively. —Hillary Rodham Clinton, speech, Youth Service Day, The White House (Washington, D.C.), 1993

Say not, "When I have free time I shall study"; for you may perhaps never have any free time. —Hillel, quoted in *Sayings of the Fathers*

No study, pursued under compulsion, remains rooted in the memory. —Plato, *The Republic*

You will find that the truth is often unpopular and the contest between agreeable fancy and disagreeable fact is unequal. For, in the vernacular, we Americans are suckers for good news. —Adlai Stevenson, commencement address, Michigan State University (East Lansing), 1958

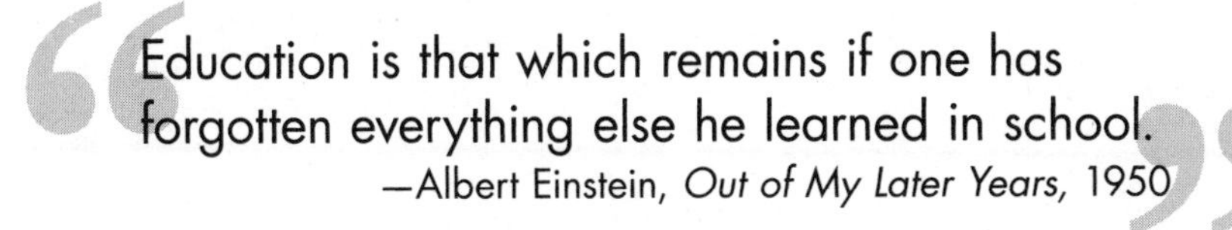

When I was in high school, I was in the French club. We didn't really do anything. Once in a while, we'd surrender to the German club. —Brian Kiley, *Jokes*, Getlen

Anyone who would attempt the task of felling a virgin forest with a penknife would probably feel the same paralysis of despair that the reformer feels when confronted with existing school systems. —Ellen Key, *The Century of the Child*, 1909

A teacher affects eternity; he can never tell where his influence stops. —Henry Adams, *The Education of Henry Adams*, 1907

To me education is a leading out of what is already there in the pupil's soul. To Miss Mackay it is a putting in of something that is not there, and that is not what I call education, I call it intrusion .... —Muriel Spark, *The Prime of Miss Jean Brodie*, 1961

Such ignorance. All the boys were in military schools and all the girls were in the convent, and that's all you need to say about it. —Katherine Anne Porter, quoted by Henry Allen, *Los Angeles Times* (Los Angeles), 1974

You must train the children to their studies in a playful manner, and without any air of constraint, with the further object of discerning more readily the natural bent of their respective characters. —Plato, *The Republic*

But were you to give up that impossible idea [of security] and focus on freedom, on connection, on compassion—I tell you, it's a glorious life! —Eve Ensler, quoted by Marianne Schnall, www.feminist.com, 2006

Sure he's too much a gentleman to be a scholar. —Aphra Behn, *Sir Patient Fancy*, 1678

A certain light was beginning to dawn dimly within her—the light which, showing the way, forbids it ... but the beginning of things, of a world especially, is necessarily vague, tangled, chaotic, and exceedingly disturbing. —Kate Chopin, *The Awakening*, 1889

> They are called finishing-schools and the name tells accurately what they are. They finish everything ....
>
> —Olive Schreiner, *The Story of an African Farm*, 1883

The people I'm furious with are the Women's Liberationists. They keep getting up on soapboxes and proclaiming women are brighter than men. That's true, but it should be kept quiet or it ruins the whole racket. —Anita Loos, quoted in *The Observer* (London), 1973

Man's knowledge of things will begin to be matched by man's knowledge of self. The significance of a smaller world will be measured not in terms of military advantage, but in terms of advantage for the human community. It will be the triumph of the heartbeat over the drumbeat. —Adlai Stevenson, speech (Springfield, Illinois), 1952

They know enough who know how to learn. —Henry Adams, *The Education of Henry Adams*, 1907

Begin with that most terrifying of all things, a clean slate. And then look, every day, at the choices you are making and when you ask yourself why you are making them, find this answer: for me, for me. —Anna Quindlen, commencement address, Mount Holyoke College (South Hadley, Massachusetts), 1999

The things we have to learn before we can do, we learn by doing. —Aristotle, *Nicomachean Ethics*, c. 325 B.C.E.

Training is everything. The peach was once a bitter almond; cauliflower is nothing but cabbage with a college education. —Mark Twain, *Pudd'n'head Wilson*, 1894

Willie had left school after the ninth grade. He said there was really nothing more they could teach him. He knew how to read and write and reason. And from here on in, it was all propaganda. —Gloria Naylor, *Linden Hills*, 1985

> You can't learn everything you need to know legally.
>
> —John Irving, *Trying to Save Piggy Sneed,* 1996

One looks back with appreciation to the brilliant teachers, but with gratitude to those who touched our human feelings. —Carl Gustav Jung, "The Gifted Child," (1942) *The Development of Personality*, R. F. C. Hull, tr., 1954

What is the use of transmitting knowledge if the individual's total development lags behind? —Maria Montessori, *The Absorbent Mind*, 1967

My brain: it's my second favorite organ. —Woody Allen, *Sleeper*, 1973

I've got more brains in my little finger than I have in my entire head! —Goodman Ace, *Easy Aces* radio show, 1930s–1940s

Never trust anything that can think for itself if you can't see where it keeps its brain. —J. K. Rowling, *Harry Potter and the Chamber of Secrets*, 1999

> "What the brain does by itself is infinitely more fascinating and complex than any response it can make to chemical stimulation."
>
> —Ursula K. Le Guin, *The Lathe of Heaven*, 1971

My nephew is in high school. He's a member of the abstinence society, where a group of students have pledged to maintain their virginity. We had something similar at my high school—it was called the math club. —Brian Kiley, *Jokes*, Getlen

Nothing would more effectively further the development of education than for all flogging pedagogues to learn to educate with the head instead of with the hand. —Ellen Key, *The Century of the Child*, 1909

You don't appreciate a lot of stuff in school until you get older. Little things, like being spanked every day by a middle-aged woman—stuff you pay good money for later in life. —Emo Philips, *Jokes*, Getlen

I must have a prodigious quantity of mind; it takes me as much as a week sometimes to make it up. —Mark Twain, *The Innocents Abroad*, 1869

Grant that I may be successful in molding one of my pupils into a perfect poem, and let me leave within her deepest-felt melody that she may sing for you when my lips shall sing no more. —Gabriela Mistral, "The Teacher's Prayer," *Desolacion*, 1922

True knowledge consists in knowing things, not words. —Mary Wortley Montagu, letter (1753), *Letters*

You've got to get obsessed and stay obsessed. —John Irving, *The Hotel New Hampshire*, 1981

We should be careful to get out of an experience only the wisdom that is in it—and stop there; lest we be like the cat that sits down on a hot stove-lid. She will never sit down on a hot stove-lid again—and that is well; but also she will never sit down on a cold one any more. —Mark Twain, *Following the Equator*, 1897

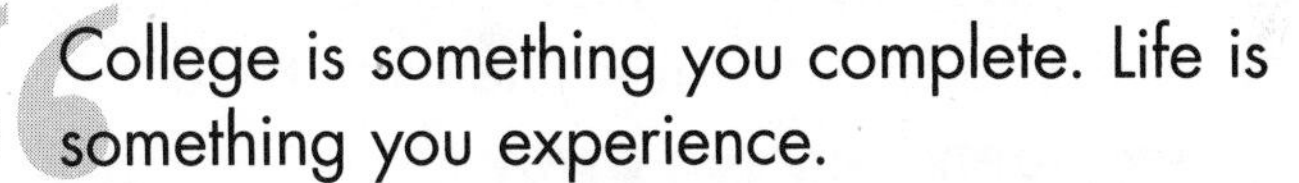

College is something you complete. Life is something you experience.

—Jon Stewart, commencement address, College of William and Mary (Williamsburg, Virginia), 20 May 2004

I won't say ours was a tough school, but we had our own coroner. We used to write essays like "What I'm Going to Be *If* I Grow Up." —Lenny Bruce, *Jokes*, Getlen

Don't you believe 'em when they say that what you don't know won't hurt you. Biggest lie ever was. See it all and go your own way and nothing'll hurt you. If what you see ain't pretty, what's the odds! See it anyway. Then next time you don't have to look. —Edna Ferber, *Show Boat*, 1926

There can be no education without leisure, and without leisure education is useless. —Sarah Josepha Hale, *Godey's Lady's Book* (*passim*), 1837–1877

… the lovely satisfying unity of things—the wedding of the thing learnt and the thing done—the great intellectual fulfillment. —Dorothy L. Sayers, quoted by Barbara Reynolds, *Dorothy L. Sayers: Her Life and Soul*, 1993

Is an intelligent human being likely to be much more than a large-scale manufacturer of misunderstanding? —Philip Roth, *The Counterlife*, 1969

No facts taught here are worth anything until students have assimilated them, correlated them, interpreted them. It is the student, not the bit of knowledge, that we are teaching. —Dr. Bernard Iddings Bell, motto, www.bard.edu

I'm not a fan of facts. You see, the facts can change, but my opinion will never change, no matter what the facts are. —Stephen Colbert, *The Colbert Report*

> She always says, my lord, that facts are like cows. If you look them in the face hard enough they generally run away.
> —Dorothy L. Sayers, *Clouds of Witness,* 1956

If we value the pursuit of knowledge, we must be free to follow wherever that search may lead us. The free mind is not a barking dog, to be tethered on a ten-foot chain. —Adlai Stevenson, speech, University of Wisconsin (Madison), 1952

Upon the subject of education, not presuming to dictate any plan or system respecting it, I can only say that I view it as the most important subject which we as a people can be engaged in. —Abraham Lincoln, address to the people of Sangamo County, 1832

So this gentlemen said, "A girl with brains ought to do something else with them besides think." —Anita Loos, *Gentlemen Prefer Blondes*, 1925

Keep the Faith

It's hard enough to know what gift to buy for a bar mitzvah or first communion, but it's even harder to find just the right words to write to someone special for a sacred occasion. Among these bons mots, you're sure to find some help.

• • •

Religion, n. A daughter of Hope and Fear, explaining to Ignorance the nature of the Unknowable. —Ambrose Bierce, *The Devil's Dictionary*, 1906

> The supreme reality of our time is our indivisibility as children of God and the common vulnerability of this planet.
>
> —John F. Kennedy, speech, joint session of the Dail and the Seanad (Dublin, Ireland), 1963

We're a people of rainbow hues and multiple faiths. If that heritage has taught us nothing else by now, it should have taught us this: It's ignorant to think you can judge a man's soul by looking at his face. —Leonard Pitts, column, *The Miami Herald* (Miami), 2001

Money is not required to buy one necessary of the soul. —Henry David Thoreau, *Walden*, 1854

Religion without humanity is a poor human stuff. —Sojourner Truth, interview, Battle Creek, Michigan, c. 1877

Art and religion first; then philosophy; lastly science. That is the order of the great subjects of life …. —Muriel Spark, *The Prime of Miss Jean Brodie*, 1961

Religions are different roads converging on the same point. —Mohandas Gandhi, *Hind Swaraj or Indian Home Rule*, 1938

Religion, like water, may be free, but when they pipe it to you, you've got to help pay for the piping. And the piper! —Abigail Van Buren, "Dear Abby," newspaper column, 1974

Not everybody feels religion the same way. Some it's in their mouth, but some it's like a hope in their blood, their bones. —Tillie Olsen, "O Yes," *Tell Me a Riddle*, 1960

It was the schoolboy who said, "Faith is believing what you know ain't so." —Mark Twain, *Following the Equator*, 1897

Now I ask you what is the impulse that comes from the possession of even the kindest heart compared to real faith in God and a hereafter. Without it one just plods on. —Alice B. Toklas, *Staying On Alone*, Edward Burns, ed., 1973

I have come to think that up and down the double helix of our DNA the molecules of faith and reason chatter away …. It is in our interest, as well as the interest of the world, that they remain on good speaking terms. —Bill Moyers, quoted in the *Tallahassee Democrat* (Tallahassee, Florida), 2006

He wears his faith but as the fashion of his hat; it ever changes with the next block. —William Shakespeare, *Much Ado About Nothing*, 1600

The religion that is afraid of science dishonors God and commits suicide. —Ralph Waldo Emerson, journal entry, 1831

> Sure there's different roads from this to Dungarvan—some thinks one road pleasanter, and some think another; wouldn't it be mighty foolish to quarrel for this?—and sure isn't it twice worse to try to interfere with people for choosing the road they like best to heaven?
>
> —Marguerite Blessington, *The Repealers,* 1833

Anyhow, I say, the God I been praying and writing to is a man. And act just like all the other mens I know. Trifling, forgetful [sic], and low-down. —Alice Walker, *The Color Purple*, 1982

Do not judge the gods, young man, they have painful secrets. —Jean-Paul Sartre, *The Flies*, 1943

And again: No more gods! no more gods! Man is King, Man is God!—But the great Faith is Love! —Arthur Rimbaud, "Soleil et Chair," *Collected Poems*, Oliver Bernard, ed., 1962

I have a warm personal relationship with God; I often picture her smiling wryly and saying, in the words of Shakespeare's Puck, "Lord, what fools these mortals be!" —Anna Quindlin, quoted in *Newsweek* (New York), 2001

Watch out for people who call themselves religious; make sure you know what they mean—make sure *they* know what they mean! —John Irving, *A Prayer for Owen Meany*, 1989

> The effect of the consolations of religion may be compared to that of a narcotic.
>
> —Sigmund Freud, *The Future of an Illusion,* 1927

We have just enough religion to make us hate, but not enough to make us love one another. —Jonathan Swift, "Thoughts on Various Subjects," *Miscellanies in Prose and Verse*, 1727

There is no waste with God. He cancels nothing but redeems all. —Dorothy L. Sayers, quoted by Barbara Reynolds, *Dorothy L. Sayers: Her Life and Soul*, 1993

> "The kind of people claiming to be in communication with God today … they are enough to drive a *real* Christian crazy!"
> —John Irving, *A Prayer for Owen Meany*, 1989

They always throw around this term "liberal elite." And I kept thinking to myself about the Christian right: what's more elite than believing that only you will go to heaven? —Jon Stewart, *Jokes*, Getlen

Jewishness cropped up and has never successfully been put down since. —P. J. O'Rourke, *Republican Party Reptile*, 1987

I am a Jew … If you prick us, do we not bleed? if you tickle us, do we not laugh? if you poison us, do we not die? and if you wrong us, shall we not revenge? —William Shakespeare, *The Merchant of Venice*, 1596

If the statistics are right, the Jews constitute but one percent of the human race. It suggests a nebulous dim puff of star dust lost in the blaze of the Milky Way …. Yet he has made a marvelous fight in the world, in all the ages; and has done it with his hands tied behind him. —Mark Twain, "Concerning the Jews," *Harper's Magazine* (New York), 1899

It is possible that the next Buddha will not take the form of an individual. The next Buddha may take the form of a community, a community practicing understanding and loving kindness, a community practicing mindful living. And the practice can be carried out as a group, as a city, as a nation. —Thich Nhat Hanh, article in *Inquiring Mind* (Berkeley, California), 1994

The face of terror is not the true faith of Islam; that's not what Islam is all about. Islam is peace. —George W. Bush, address, Islamic Center of Washington, 2001

The true Islam has shown me that a blanket indictment of all white people is as wrong as when whites make blanket indictments against blacks. —Malcolm X, quoted by Magnus Bassey, *Malcolm X: The Seeker of Justice*, 2003

The United States is not a Christian nation any more than it is a Jewish or a Mohammedan nation. —John Adams, Treaty of Tripoli, 1797

> What is faith worth if it is not translated into action?
>
> —Mohandas Gandhi, quoted by D. G. Tendulkar, *Mahatma*, 1961

Scriptures, n. The sacred books of our holy religion, as distinguished from the false and profane writings on which all other faiths are based. —Ambrose Bierce, *The Devil's Dictionary*, 1906

Re: the Bible: It is full of interest. It has noble poetry in it; and some clever fables; and some blood-drenched history; and some good morals; and a wealth of obscenity; and upwards of a thousand lies. —Mark Twain, Letter (1909), *Letters From the Earth*, Bernard Augustine De Voto, ed., 1962

Prayer is a concentration of positive thought. —Peace Pilgrim, *Her Life and Work*

Prayer is translation. A man translates himself into a child asking for all there is in a language he has barely mastered. —Leonard Cohen, "F.," *Beautiful Losers*, 1970

Asked if she worshiped regularly: Honey, at my age, I don't do anything regularly. —Selma Diamond, *Funny Women*, Unterbrink

When I was a kid, I used to pray every night for a new bicycle. Then I realized that the Lord, in his wisdom, doesn't work that way. So I just stole one and asked him to forgive me! —Emo Philips, stand-up routine, 1985

Pray, v. To ask that the laws of the universe be annulled in behalf of a single petitioner confessedly unworthy.
—Ambrose Bierce, *The Devil's Dictionary,* 1906

The Soul unto itself / Is an imperial friend— / Or the most agonizing Spy— / An Enemy—could send —Emily Dickinson, No. 683, *Poems*, Johnson

What soul is without flaws? —Arthur Rimbaud, *A Season in Hell*, 1873

Go out and be born among gypsies or thieves or among happy workaday people who live with the sun and do not think about their souls. —Pearl S. Buck, "Advice to Unborn Novelists," 1949

Spirituality can be—indeed, must be—deeply rational. —Sam Harris, *The End of Faith*, 2005

He said that knowledge was of little use without wisdom, and that there was no wisdom without spirituality, and that true spirituality always included service to others. —Isabel Allende, *Daughter of Fortune*, 1999

I have seen some souls so compressed that they would have fitted into a small thimble, and found room to move there—wide room. —Olive Schreiner, *The Story of an African Farm*, 1883

A single Screw of Flesh / Is all that pins the Soul —Emily Dickinson, No. 262, *Poems*, Johnson

Of the enemies of the soul— / the world, the devil, the flesh— / the *world* is the most serious and most dangerous. —Gabriela Mistral, "We Were All to Be Queens," *Felling*, 1938

His soul is about the size of a toenail. —Ursula K. Le Guin, *The Eye of the Heron*, 1978

We will try to be holy, / We will try to repair the world given to us to hand on. / Precious is this treasure of words and knowledge and deeds / that moves inside us. —Marge Piercy, *The Art of Blessing the Day*, 1999

In essence, the search of so many people today for the mystical wisdom of an earlier time is the search for the kind of spirituality characteristic of a partnership rather than a dominator society. —Riane Eisler, *The Chalice and the Blade*, 1994

> The secret of seeing is to sail on solar wind. Hone and spread your spirit till you yourself are a sail, whetted, translucent, broadside to the merest puff.
>
> —Annie Dillard, *Pilgrim at Tinker Creek,* 1974

Pure Spirit, one hundred degrees proof—that's a drink that only the most hardened contemplation-guzzlers indulge in. —Aldous Huxley, *Island*, 1962

The further the spiritual evolution of mankind advances, the more certain it seems to me that the path to genuine religiosity does not lie through the fear of life, and the fear of death, and blind faith, but through striving after rational knowledge. —Albert Einstein, *Out of My Later Years*, 1950

The difference between science and religion is the difference between a willingness to dispassionately consider new evidence and new arguments, and a passionate unwillingness to do so. —Sam Harris, Article in *The Huffington Post*, 2006

The soul can split the sky in two, / And let the face of God shine through. —Edna St. Vincent Millay, "Renascence," 1917

Everyone's conscience in religion is between God and themselves, and it belongs to none other. —Margaret Cavendish, *Sociable Letters*, 1664

Of Consciousness, her awful Mate / The Soul cannot be rid —Emily Dickinson, No. 894, *Poems*, Johnson

> To you I'm an atheist; to God, I'm the Loyal Opposition.
>
> —Woody Allen, *Stardust Memories,* 1980

If God existed, and if He cared for humankind, He would never have given us religion. —Martin Amis, article in *The Guardian* (London), 2002

Religion has become so pallid recently, it is hardly worthwhile being an atheist. —Paddy Chayefsky, *The Tenth Man*, 1959

Anybody can observe the Sabbath, but making it holy surely takes the rest of the week. —Alice Walker, letter to the editor, *Ms.* (1974), *In Search of Our Mothers' Gardens*, 1983

A belief is a lever that, once pulled, moves almost everything else in a person's life. —Sam Harris, *The End of Faith*, 2005

Why is it more ridiculous to arraign ecclesiastics for their false teaching and acts of injustice to women, than members of Congress and the House of Commons? —Elizabeth Cady Stanton, *The Woman's Bible*, 1895

Do not, as some ungracious pastors do, / Show me the steep and thorny way to heaven, / Whiles, like a puff'd and reckless libertine, / Himself the primrose path of dalliance treads. —William Shakespeare, *Hamlet*, 1600

Spiritual leadership should remain spiritual leadership and the temporal power should not become too important in any Church. —Eleanor Roosevelt, letter to Cardinal Francis Spellman (1949), quoted by Joseph P. Lash, *Eleanor: The Years Alone*, 1972

There's No Place Like Home

First apartment? First time homeowner? Newly moved into the neighborhood? Whether the new place is a tiny studio apartment or a stately mansion, moving and making a new home can be distressing, exciting, and scary. Whatever the emotion, help is on the way. If you can't be there to lend a hand, mark the occasion with one of these quotes.

• • •

"Home" is any four walls that enclose the right person. —Helen Rowland, *Reflections of a Bachelor Girl*, 1903

Nothing succeeds like address. —Fran Lebowitz, *Metropolitan Life*, 1978

Home wasn't built in a day. —Goodman Ace, *Easy Aces* radio show, 1930s–1940s

> I'm not going to vacuum 'til Sears makes one you can ride on.
>
> —Roseanne Barr, www.haruth.com/WomenToWomen.htm

Maybe it will take a woman to clean up the House. —Nancy Pelosi, referring to the House of Representatives, interview with Barbara Walters, 2006

The labor of keeping house is labor in its most naked state, for labor is toil that never finishes, toil that has to be begun again the moment it is completed, toil that is destroyed and consumed by the life process. —Mary McCarthy, "The *Vita Activa*," *The New Yorker*, (New York), 1958

... the whole process of home-making, housekeeping and cooking, which ever has been woman's special province, should be looked on as an art and a profession. —Sarah Josepha Hale, *Godey's Lady's Book*, c. 1859

> I'm a wonderful housekeeper. Every time I get a divorce I keep the house.
>
> —Zsa Zsa Gabor, interview

Cleaning your house while your kids are still growing / Is like shoveling the walk before it stops snowing. —Phyllis Diller, *Housekeeping Hints*, 1966

"Housewives" is a term I employ that means anybody who has ever had to clean up somebody else's shit and not been paid for it .... —Roseanne Barr, *My Life as a Woman*, 1989

... one of the best gifts of the gods ... a good, faithful housekeeper ... But for this noble, self-sacrificing woman, much of my public work would have been quite impossible. —Elizabeth Cady Stanton, *Stanton*, Stanton

Re: the family maid: She used to come over and make tuna salad and we'd watch *Let's Make a Deal* while my mom cleaned the house. —Sandra Bernhard, *Funny Women*, Unterbrink

Viciousness in the kitchen! The potatoes hiss. —Sylvia Plath, "Lesbos," *Ariel*, 1965

Perhaps all artists were, in a sense, housewives: tenders of the earth household. —Erica Jong, "The Artist as Housewife: The Housewife as Artist," *Ms. Reader*, Klagsbrun

... there is something dangerous about being a housewife. —Betty Friedan, *The Feminine Mystique*, 1963

I have too many fantasies to be a housewife ... I guess I *am* a fantasy. —Marilyn Monroe, quoted by Gloria Steinem, *Ms. Reader*, Klagsbrun

It is certainly true that housekeeping cares bring with them a thousand endearing compensations. They are a woman's peculiar joy, and women are apt to be light-hearted.—Marceline Desbordes-Valmore, letter to her son and daughter (1840), *Memoirs*, Sainte-Beuve

But I think women dwell quite a bit on the duress under which they work, on how hard it is just to do it at all. We are traditionally rather proud of ourselves for having slipped creative work in there between the domestic chores and obligations. I'm not sure we deserve such big A-pluses for all that. —Toni Morrison, quoted by Jean Strouse, *Newsweek* (New York), 1981

> I hate housework! You make the beds, you do the dishes—and six months later you have to start all over again.
>
> —Joan Rivers, quoted in *Woman Talk,* Michèle Brown and Ann O'Connor eds., 1984

Housekeeping ain't no joke. —Louisa May Alcott, *Little Women*, 1868

It is a proud moment in a woman's life to reign supreme within four walls, to be the one to whom all questions of domestic pleasure and economy are referred. —Elizabeth Cady Stanton, *Eighty Years and More*, 1898

I'm nine years behind in my ironing. I bury a lot in the backyard. —Phyllis Diller, *Women in Comedy*, Martin

"Woman's work! Housework's the hardest work in the world. That's why men won't do it." —Edna Ferber, *So Big*, 1924

The problem lay buried, unspoken for many years in the minds of American women …. Each suburban housewife struggled with it alone. As she made the beds, shopped for groceries, matched slipcover material, ate peanut butter sandwiches with her children, chauffeured Cub Scouts and Brownies, lay beside her husband at night, she was afraid to ask even of herself the silent question: "Is this all?" —Betty Friedan, *The Feminine Mystique*, 1963

Men such as him do not have to clean up the messes they make, but we have to clean up our own messes, and theirs into the bargain. In that way, they are like children, they do not have to think ahead, or worry about the consequences of what they do. —Margaret Atwood, *Alias Grace*, 1996

> "While civilization has been improving our houses, it has not equally improved the men who are to inhabit them."
>
> —Henry David Thoreau, *Walden*, 1854

A man in the house is worth two in the street. —Mae West, *Wit and Wisdom*, Weintraub

A man builds a fine house; and now he has a master, and a task for life: he is to furnish, watch, show it, and keep it in repair, the rest of his days. —Ralph Waldo Emerson, "Work and Days," *Society and Solitude*, 1870

There was no loneliness in the living room. So it was a good part, and maybe the best part of the house. —June Jordan, *New Life, New Room*, 1975

Ah! happy is the man whose early lot / Hath made him master of a furnish'd cot —Joanna Baillie, "A Reverie," *Fugitive Verses*, 1790

It is the time you have wasted for your rose that makes your rose so important. —Antoine de Saint-Exupéry, *The Little Prince*

Should not every apartment in which man dwells be lofty enough to create some obscurity overhead, where flickering shadows may play at evening about the rafters? —Henry David Thoreau, *Walden*, 1854

The more women become rational companions, partners in business and in thought, as well as in affection and amusement, the more highly will men appreciate *home*—that blessed work, which opens to the human heart the most perfect glimpse of Heaven, and helps to carry it thither, as on an angel's wings. —Lydia Maria Child, No. 34, *Letters from New York*, 1852

The home was a closed sphere touched only at its edge by the world's evolution. —Ellen Key, *The Renaissance of Motherhood*, 1914

We need not power or splendor; / Wide hall or lordly dome; / The good, the true, the tender, / These form the wealth of home. —Sarah Josepha Hale, "Home," *Poems for Our Children*, 1830

I had three chairs in my house; one for solitude, two for friendship, three for society. —Henry David Thoreau, *Walden*, 1854

Those comfortably padded lunatic asylums which are known, euphemistically, as the stately homes of England. —Virginia Woolf, "Lady Dorothy Nevill," *The Common Reader*, 1925

> "We said there warn't no home like a raft, after all. Other places do seem so cramped up and smothery, but a raft don't. You feel mighty free and easy and comfortable on a raft."
>
> —Mark Twain, *The Adventures of Huckleberry Finn*, 1885

Ah, I like the look of packing crates! A household in preparation for a journey! … Something full of the flow of life … Movement, progress …. —Lorraine Hansberry, *A Raisin in the Sun*, 1958

I'll dig in / into my days, having come here to live, not to visit. / Grey is the price / of neighboring with eagles, of knowing / a mountain's vast presence, seen or unseen. —Denise Levertov, "Settling"

I can tell by your eye shadow, you're from Brooklyn, right? … Me too. My mother has plastic covers on all the furniture. Even the poodle. Looked like a barking hassock walking down the street. —Elayne Boosler, *Funny Women*, Unterbrink

What is the use of a house if you haven't got a tolerable planet to put it on? —Henry David Thoreau, *Familiar Letters*, 1865

The Indian … stands free and unconstrained in Nature, is her inhabitant and not her guest, and wears her easily and gracefully. But the civilized man has the habits of the house. His house is a prison. —Henry David Thoreau, journal entry, 26 April 1841

"No matter how dreary and gray our homes are, we people of flesh and blood would rather live there than in any other country, be it ever so beautiful. There is no place like home."
—L. Frank Baum, *The Wonderful Wizard of Oz,* 1900

The ornament of a house is the friends who frequent it. —Ralph Waldo Emerson, "Domestic Life," *Society and Solitude*, 1870

Work a lifetime to pay off a house—You finally own it and there's nobody to live in it. —Arthur Miller, *Death of a Salesman*, 1949

A house in which there are no people—but with all the signs of tenancy—can be a most tranquil good place. —Muriel Spark, "The Portobello Road," *Collected Stories: I*, 1968

Moolah

Paying bills, learning to budget, understanding the stock market, investing wisely—these are important lessons to learn, and to teach. Sometimes your kid—or even your spouse—may resist. So may your boss. Find a quote to make it fun, inspiring, or at least palatable.

• • •

There are two times in a man's life when he should not speculate: when he can't afford it, and when he can. —Mark Twain, *Following the Equator*, 1897

> A fool and her money are soon courted.
> —Helen Rowland, *A Guide to Men*, 1922

Money doesn't bring courage, I learned. It's the other way around. —Suze Orman, *The Courage to Be Rich*, 1999

Put not your trust in money, but put your money in trust. —Oliver Wendell Holmes, *The Autocrat of the Breakfast Table*, 1858

Sometimes your best investments are the ones you don't make. —Donald Trump (with Tony Schwartz), *Trump: The Art of the Deal*, 1987

Prosperity is the best protector of principle. —Mark Twain, *Following the Equator*, 1897

Success in investing doesn't correlate with I.Q. once you're above the level of 25. Once you have ordinary intelligence, what you need is the temperament to control the urges that get other people into trouble in investing. —Warren Buffett, interview, *Business Week* (New York), 1999

The way to become rich is to make money, my dear Edna, not to save it .... —Kate Chopin, *The Awakening*, 1889

You see those charts that say if you put away $500 a year starting at age 20, by the time you're 50, you'd have a gazillion dollars? It just makes you ill that you didn't do it. —James Carville, quoted by Andrew Tobias, *Parade* (New York), 2002

... money ... is really the difference between men and animals, most of the things men feel animals feel and vice versa, but animals do not know about money, money is a purely human conception and that is very important to know very very important. —Gertrude Stein, *Everybody's Autobiography*, 1937

> "Dogs have no money. Isn't that amazing? They're broke their entire lives. But they get through. You know why dogs have no money? No pockets."
>
> —Jerry Seinfeld, stand-up routine

Money speaks sense in a language all nations understand. —Aphra Behn, *The Rover*, 1677

Our economic dependence depended on individual initiative. It depended on a belief in the free market; but it has also depended on our sense of mutual regard for each other, the idea that everybody has a stake in the country, that we're all in it together and everybody's got a shot at opportunity. —Barack Obama, commencement address, Knox College (Galesburg, Illinois), 2005

It's the economy, stupid. —James Carville, Clinton campaign slogan, 1992

The secret point of money and power in America is neither the things that money can buy nor power for power's sake … but absolute personal freedom, mobility, privacy. It is the instinct which drove America to the Pacific, all through the nineteenth century, the desire to be able to find a restaurant open in case you want a sandwich, to be a free agent, live by one's own rules. —Joan Didion, *Slouching Towards Bethlehem*, 1968

The stock market is a no-called-strike game. You don't have to swing at everything—you can wait for your pitch. The problem when you're a money manager is that your fans keep yelling, "Swing, you bum!" —Warren Buffett, Berkshire Hathaway annual meeting, 1999

Beautiful credit! The foundation of modern society. —Mark Twain (with Charles Dudley Warner), *The Gilded Age*, 1873

Man was lost if he went to a usurer, for the interest ran faster than a tiger upon him. —Pearl S. Buck, "The Frill," *First Wife and Other Stories*, 1933

What's breaking into a bank compared with founding a bank?

—Bertolt Brecht, *The Threepenny Opera*, 1928

Let's kill two birds with one loan! —Goodman Ace, *Easy Aces* radio show, 1930s–1940s

Neither a borrower nor a lender be: / For loan oft loses both itself and friend. —William Shakespeare, *Hamlet*, 1600

The banks have a new image. Now you have "a friend," your friendly bank. If the banks are so friendly, how come they chain down the pens? —Alan King, stand-up routine

The state of the union is that money talks and public policy is sold to the highest bidder. —Molly Ivins, newspaper column, "Creators Syndicate," 2003

No one would remember the Good Samaritan if he'd only had good intentions. He had money as well. —Margaret Thatcher, television interview, *The Times* (London), 1986

Money only appeals to selfishness and always tempts its owners irresistibly to abuse it. // Can anyone imagine Moses, Jesus, or Gandhi armed with the money-bags of Carnegie? —Albert Einstein, "Of Wealth" (1934), *The World As I See It*, 1949

The average family exists only on paper and its average budget is a fiction, invented by statisticians for the convenience of statisticians. —Sylvia Porter, *Sylvia Porter's Money Book*, 1975

When it comes to finances, remember that there are no withholding taxes on the wages of sin. —Mae West, *Mae West on Sex, Health and ESP*, 1975

The IRS sent back my tax return saying I owed $800. I said, "If you'll notice, I sent a paper clip with my return. Given what you've been paying for things lately, that should more than make up the difference." —Emo Philips, "A Fine How-Do-Ya-Do," 1985

… that's nothing but a tax dodge! … This is what the Internal Revenue Service expects. It's all part of the game. They play their part, we have to play ours. It's our duty as American citizens! —Muriel Resnik, *Any Wednesday*, 1963

> … I do want to get rich but I never want to do what there is to do to get rich.
>
> —Gertrude Stein, *Everybody's Autobiography*, 1937

I have only one thing to say to the tax increasers: Go ahead, make my day! —Ronald Reagan, speech, 1985

Keeping accounts, Sir, is of no use when a man is spending his own money, and has nobody to whom he is to account. You won't eat less beef today, because you have written down what it cost yesterday. —Samuel Johnson, quoted by James Boswell, *Life of Samuel Johnson*, 1791

I'm a middle-bracket person with a middle-bracket spouse / And we live together gaily in a middle-bracket house. / We've a fair-to-middlin' family; we take the middle view; / So we're manna sent from heaven to internal revenue. —Phyllis McGinley, "The Chosen People," *Times Three*, 1960

President Bush says he now wants to simplify the tax code. Only those in the blue states will pay. —David Letterman, *Jokes*, Getlen

New rule: If churches don't have to pay taxes, they also can't call the fire department when they catch fire. Sorry reverend, that's one of those services that goes along with paying in. I'll use the fire department I pay for. You can pray for rain. —Bill Maher, *Real Time with Bill Maher*, 2006

It's my absolute opinion that in our complex industrial society, no business enterprise can succeed without sharing the burden of the problems of other enterprises. —Ayn Rand, *Atlas Shrugged*, 1957

I've made it my business to make business my business. —Mae West, quoted by M. George Haddad, *Working Woman*, 1979

> Corporation, n. An ingenious device for obtaining individual profit without individual responsibility.
>
> —Ambrose Bierce, *The Devil's Dictionary*, 1906

What most people don't seem to realize is that there is just as much money to be made out of the wreckage of a civilization as from the upbuilding of one. —Margaret Mitchell, *Gone with the Wind*, 1936

Most of the rich people I've known have been fairly miserable. —Agatha Christie, *Endless Night*, 1967

Choosing wealth as a goal requires facing everything about your money bravely, honestly, with courage—which is a very, very hard thing for most of us to do. —Suze Orman, *The Courage to Be Rich*, 1999

... the impassable gulf that lies between riches and poverty. —Elizabeth Cady Stanton, *History of Woman Suffrage*, Anthony

It is very difficult for the prosperous to be humble. —Jane Austen, *Emma*, 1815

... a Man that wants Money thinks none can be unhappy that has it .... —Susanna Centlivre, *The Busie Body*, 1709

I do not value wealth or riches, / Wherefore I shall be ever more content / To bring more richness to my mind / And not to keep my mind on riches. —Juana Inés de la Cruz, "Oh World, Why do you thus pursue me?", *Spanish Poetry*, Muriel Kittel, tr.

> Money is like manure; it's not worth a thing unless it's spread around encouraging young things to grow.
>
> —Thornton Wilder, *The Matchmaker*, 1954

Until we end the masculinization of wealth, we will not end the feminization of poverty. —Gloria Steinem, speech, Women of Power Conference (Seattle), 2000

Another good thing about being poor is that when you are seventy your children will not have declared you legally insane in order to gain control of your estate. —Woody Allen, attributed

Come away! Poverty's catching. —Aphra Behn, *The Rover*, 1677

If a free society cannot help the many who are poor, it cannot save the few who are rich. —John F. Kennedy, *Inaugural Address* (Washington, D.C.), 1961

Could we have the vision of doing away in this great country with poverty? ... That would be one of the very best arguments against Communism that we could possibly have. —Eleanor Roosevelt, address, Democratic National Convention (Chicago), 1956

I am for lifting everyone off the social bottom. In fact, I am for doing away with the social bottom altogether. —Clare Boothe Luce, quoted in *Time* (New York), 1964

> You don't seem to realize that a poor person who is unhappy is in a better position than a rich person who is unhappy. Because the poor person has hope. He thinks money would help.
>
> —Jean Kerr, *Poor Richard,* 1963

When you're poor, you grow up fast. —Billie Holiday (with William Dufty), *Lady Sings the Blues*, 1956

No, not rich. I am a poor man with money, which is not the same thing. —Gabriel Gárcia Márquez, *Love in the Time of Cholera*, 1985

Money is better than poverty, if only for financial reasons. —Woody Allen, "The Early Essays," *Without Feathers*, 1975

Without frugality none can be rich, and with it very few would be poor. —Samuel Johnson, No. 57, *The Rambler*, 1750

The only value of stock forecasters is to make fortune tellers look good.

—Warren Buffett, chairman's letter to Berkshire Hathaway shareholders, 1999

Rich people plan for four generations. Poor people plan for Saturday night. —Gloria Steinem, attributed

Life is a game. Money is how we keep score. —Ted Turner, attributed

Now he disliked talking business with her as much as he had enjoyed it before they were married. —Margaret Mitchell, *Gone with the Wind*, 1936

You can be young without money but you can't be old without it. —Tennessee Williams, *Cat on a Hot Tin Roof*, 1955

It is better to live rich, than to die rich. —Samuel Johnson (1778), quoted by James Boswell, *The Life of Samuel Johnson*, 1791

Maybe wealth begins the day you are finally able to want what you have. —Leonard Pitts, column, *The Miami Herald* (Miami), 2002

Hollywood money isn't money. It's congealed snow, melts in your hand, and there you are. —Dorothy Parker, *Writers at Work*, Cowley

I knew so little about money I used to sign my check, "Love, Rita." —Rita Rudner, *Tickled Pink*, 2001

Thinking to get at once all the gold the goose could give, he killed it and opened it only to find—nothing. —Aesop, "The Goose with the Golden Eggs," *Fables*

Hi-Ho, It's Off to Work We Go

Vice President to CEO, secretary to junior exec, PFC to 1st Lieutenant, lawyer to partner—a new job, a raise, a promotion, or retirement, work is a major part of our lives. And moving up or over is always cause for a special congratulations.

• • •

He and I had an office so tiny that an inch smaller and it would have been adultery. —Dorothy Parker, attributed

There is perhaps one human being in a thousand who is passionately interested in his job for the job's sake. The difference is that if that one person in a thousand is a man, we say, simply, that he is passionately keen on his job; if she is a woman, we say she is a freak. —Dorothy L. Sayers, *Gaudy Nights*, 1936

> There are very few jobs that actually require a penis or vagina. All other jobs should be open to everybody.
>
> —Florynce Kennedy, quoted by John Brady, *Writer's Digest* (Cincinnati), 1974

Once lay down the rule that the job comes first, and you throw that job open to every individual … who is able to do that job better than the rest of the world. —Dorothy L. Sayers, *Gaudy Nights*, 1936

"People don't look for kinds of work anymore, ma'am," he answered impassively. "They just look for work." —Ayn Rand, *Atlas Shrugged*, 1957

My work is the only ground I've ever had to stand on. I seem to have a whole superstructure with no foundation—but I'm working on the foundation. —Marilyn Monroe, "Acting," *Marilyn Monroe In Her Own Words*, 1990

> I think crime pays. The hours are good, you meet a lot of interesting people, you travel a lot.
>
> —Woody Allen, *Take the Money and Run,* 1968

Committee—a group of men who individually can do nothing but as a group decide that nothing can be done. —Fred Allen, radio show

> A molehill man is a pseudo-busy executive who comes to work at 9 A.M. and finds a molehill on his desk. He has until 5 P.M. to make this molehill into a mountain. An accomplished molehill man will often have his mountain finished before lunch.
>
> —Fred Allen, *Treadmill to Oblivion,* 1954

You have to look at leadership through the eyes of the followers and you have to live the message. What I have learned is that people become motivated when you guide them to the source of their own power and when you make heroes out of employees who personify what you want to see in the organization. —Anita Roddick, *Body and Soul*, 1991

Busy work brings after ease; / Ease brings sport and sport brings rest; / For young and old, of all degrees, / The mingled lot is best. —Joanna Baillie, "Rhymes," *Fugitive Verses*, 1790

All work and no play makes Jack a dull boy, / All play and no work makes Jack a mere toy. —Maria Edgeworth, *Harry and Lucy*, 1801

The definition of women's work is shitwork. —Gloria Steinem, quoted by John Brady, *Writer's Digest* (Cincinnati), 1974

For a salesman, there is no rock bottom to life. He don't put a bolt to a nut, he don't tell you the law or give you medicine. He's a man way out there in the blue, riding on a smile and a shoeshine .... A salesman is got to dream, boy. It comes with the territory. —Arthur Miller, *Death of a Salesman*, 1949

> "I suppose I have a really loose interpretation of "work," because I think that just being alive is so much work at something you don't always want to do ... The machinery is always going. Even when you sleep."
>
> —Andy Warhol, *From A to B and Back Again*, 1975

I realized that selling was the greatest career a man could want. 'Cause what could be more satisfying than to be able to go, at the age of eighty-four, into twenty or thirty different cities, and pick up a phone, and be remembered and loved and helped by so many different people? —Arthur Miller, *Death of a Salesman*, 1949

I didn't want to work. It was as simple as that. I distrusted work, disliked it. I thought it was a very bad thing that the human race had unfortunately invented for itself. —Agatha Christie, *Endless Night*, 1967

Any single thing I have written can be paralleled or even surpassed by something someone else has done. However, my total corpus for quantity, quality and *variety* can be duplicated by no one else. That is what I want to be remembered for. —Isaac Asimov, *Yours*, 1973

The road to hell is paved with works-in-progress. —Philip Roth, quoted in *The New York Times Book Review* (New York), 1979

A person's work is her only signature; we forget this at our peril. It is to the work and the life we must turn. —Alice Walker, "How Long Shall They Torture Our Mothers?," *Anything We Love Can Be Saved*, 1997

I am afraid that the pleasantness of an employment does not always evince its propriety. —Jane Austen, *Sense and Sensibility*, 1811

You have much more power when you are working for the right thing than when you are working against the wrong thing. —Peace Pilgrim, *Her Life and Work*

His lordship may compel us to be equal upstairs, but there will never be equality in the servants' hall. —J. M. Barrie, *The Admirable Crichton*, 1903

> The world is full of willing people, some willing to work, the rest willing to let them.
>
> —Robert Frost, attributed

If it's a good script I'll do it. And if it's a bad script, and they pay me enough, I'll do it. —George Burns, quoted in *The International Herald Tribune* (Paris), 1988

I have nothing to offer but blood, toil, tears and sweat. —Winston Churchill, premier speech as Prime Minister, House of Commons (London), 1940

You can't eat eight hours a day nor drink for eight hours a day nor make love for eight hours—all you can do for eight hours is work. Which is the reason why man makes himself and everybody else so miserable and unhappy. —William Faulkner, interview, *Writers at Work*, Cowley

A career is born in public—talent in privacy. —Marilyn Monroe, quoted by Gloria Steinem, *Ms. Reader*, Klagsbrun

A man is not idle, because he is absorbed in thought. There is a visible labour and there is an invisible labour. —Victor Hugo, *Les Misérables*, 1864

Labor is work that leaves no trace behind it when it is finished, or if it does, as in the case of the tilled field, this product of human activity requires still more labor, incessant, tireless labor, to maintain its identity as a "work" of man. —Mary McCarthy, "The *Vita Activa*," *The New Yorker* (New York), 1958

> One machine can do the work of fifty ordinary men. No machine can do the work of one extraordinary man.
>
> —Elbert Hubbard, *The Roycroft Dictionary and Book of Epigrams*, 1923

Work is life, you know, and without it, there's nothing but fear and insecurity. —John Lennon, "Twenty-Four Hours," BBC-TV (London), 1969

The growth of entrepreneurial classes throughout the world is an asset in the promotion of human rights and individual liberty, and it should be understood and used as such. —Condoleezza Rice, article in *Foreign Affairs* (New York), 2000

Each morning sees some task begin, / Each evening sees it close / Something attempted, something done, / Has earned a night's repose. —Henry Wadsworth Longfellow, "The Village Blacksmith," 1842

And blessed are the horny hands of toil. —James Russell Lowell, "A Glance Behind the Curtain," 1843

If you don't want to work, you have to work to earn enough money so that you won't have to work. —Ogden Nash, "More About People," *Many Long Years Ago*, 1945

You take my life / When you do take the means whereby I live. —William Shakespeare, *The Merchant of Venice*, 1596

Do not hire a man who does your work for money, but him who does it for love of it. —Henry David Thoreau, "Life Without Principle," *The Atlantic Monthly* (Boston), 1863

If you don't work, what the hell do you do? Sit around and rot! The retirement age of 65 has killed *millions*. Luckily, I'm in an industry with no retirement. They only retire you if you don't make money for them. —Bette Davis, quoted by Dotson Rader, *Parade* (New York), 1983

> "Mandatory retirement ought to be illegal.
> —Maggie Kuhn, quoted by Carol Offen, "Profile of a Gray Panther," *Retirement Living*, December 1972"

Retirement is the most loathsome word in the English language. —Ernest Hemingway, attributed

The happiest people I know are the ones that are still working. The saddest are the ones who are retired. —George Burns, interview with Arthur Marx, *Cigar Aficionado* (New York), 1994

I don't deserve this award, but I have arthritis and I don't deserve that either. —Jack Benny, stand-up routine

Sooner or later I'm going to die, but I'm not going to retire. —Margaret Mead, attributed

Retirement at sixty-five is ridiculous. When I was sixty-five I still had pimples. —George Burns, attributed

The cross of the Legion of Honor has been conferred on me. However, few escape that distinction. —Mark Twain, *A Tramp Abroad*, 1880

A Flourish of Trumpets 10

Special accomplishments deserve special attention. From getting an A on a report card, to losing 20 pounds, to finishing a 5K run, to hitting par for the first time, there's nothing like getting a pat on the back (or a letter in your mailbox) to spur one on to even greater heights. Let your special someone know how proud you are of their accomplishments.

• • •

Self-trust is the first secret of success. —Ralph Waldo Emerson, "Success," *Society and Solitude*, 1870

There are two great rules in life, the one general and the other particular. The first is that every one can in the end get what he wants if he only tries. This is the general rule. The particular rule is that every individual is more or less of an exception to the general rule. —Samuel Butler, quoted by Henry Festing Jones, *A Memoir*, 1919

"You lose in the end unless you know how the wheel is fixed or can fix it yourself.
—Edna Ferber, *Saratoga Trunk*, 1941"

They just elected me Miss Phonograph Record of 1966. They discovered my measurements were 33⅓, 45, 78! —Phyllis Diller, *Women in Comedy*, Martin

To refuse awards … is another way of accepting them with more noise than is normal. —Peter Ustinov, quoted by David Shipman, *Marlon Brando*, 1989

Our deeds determine us, as much as we determine our deeds. —George Eliot, *Adam Bede*, 1859

Feeling and longing are the motive force behind all human endeavor and human creation, in however exalted a guise the latter may present themselves to us. —Albert Einstein, "Religion and Science," *The New York Times Magazine* (New York), 1930

If my mind can conceive it and my heart can believe it, I know I can achieve it. —Jesse Jackson, attributed

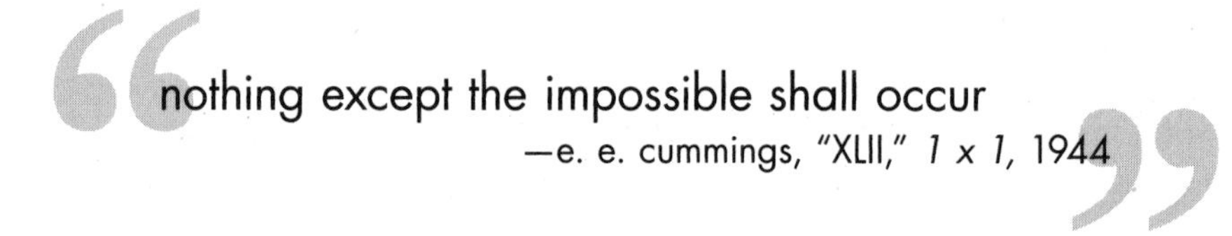

It's bad policy to speculate on what you'll do if a plan fails when you're trying to make a plan work. —Condoleezza Rice, testimony, Senate Foreign Relations Committee, 2007

Few things are impossible to diligence and skill. —Samuel Johnson, *The History of Rasselas, Prince of Abissinia*, 1759

Without passion, you don't have energy; without energy, you have nothing. Nothing great in the world has been accomplished without passion. —Donald Trump, interview, *Playboy* (Los Angeles), 1990

Process is the great happiness … while the highly advertised Achievement brings a certain emptiness since it is very hard to experience or even believe. —Mike Nichols, quoted by David Dudley, *AARP Magazine* (Washington, D.C.), 2004

Sometimes, fame means nobody places any limits on your behavior. And that's a dangerous thing. —Leonard Pitts, column, *The Miami Herald* (Miami), 2002

Excellence encourages one about life generally; it shows the spiritual wealth of the world. —George Eliot, *Daniel Deronda*, 1874–1876

In my opinion, most of the great men of the past were only there for the beer—the wealth, prestige and grandeur that went with the power. —A. J. P. Taylor, introduction in Peter Vansittart, *Voices, 1870–1914*, 1984

Twenty years from now you will be more disappointed by the things that you didn't do than by the ones you did do. So throw off the bow-lines. Sail away from the safe harbor. Catch the trade winds in your sails. Explore. Dream. Discover. —Mark Twain, attributed

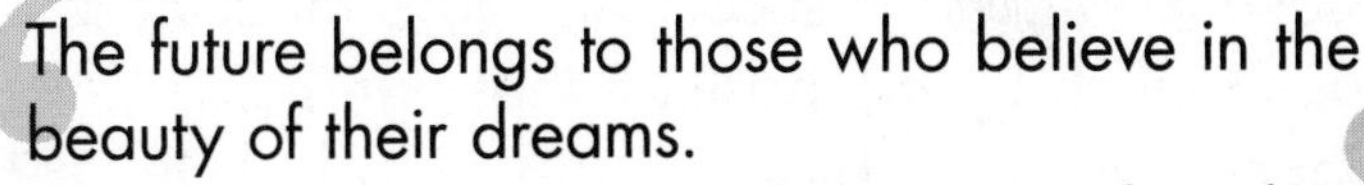

> The future belongs to those who believe in the beauty of their dreams.
>
> —Eleanor Roosevelt, attributed

The only limit to our realization of tomorrow will be our doubts of today. —Franklin D. Roosevelt, attributed

The most important single ingredient in the formula of success is knowing how to get along with people. —Theodore "Teddy" Roosevelt, attributed

But, if it be a sin to covet honour, / I am the most offending soul alive. —William Shakespeare, *Henry V*, 1599

Slow and steady wins the race. —Aesop, "The Hare and the Tortoise," *Fables*

It's them as take advantage that get advantage i' this world. —George Eliot, *Adam Bede*, 1859

Talent is luck. The important thing in life is courage. —Woody Allen, *Manhattan*, 1979

Hunger is the handmaid of genius. —Mark Twain, *Following the Equator*, 1897

The secret of a great success for which you are at a loss to account is a crime that has never been found out, because it was properly executed. —Honoré de Balzac, *Le Père Goriot*, 1835

One's religion is whatever he is most interested in, and yours is Success. —J. M. Barrie, *The Twelve-Pound Look*, 1910

> "I have learned that success is to be measured not so much by the position that one has reached in life as by the obstacles which he has overcome while trying to succeed."
> —Booker T. Washington, *Up From Slavery,* 1901

If A is a success in life, then A equals x plus y plus z. Work is x; y is play; and z is keeping your mouth shut. —Albert Einstein, quoted in *The Observer* (London), 1950

Try to become not a man of success, but try rather to become a man of value. —Albert Einstein, quoted in *Life* (New York), 1955

Success treads on every right step. —Ralph Waldo Emerson, address, "The American Scholar" Harvard University (Cambridge, Massachusetts), 1837

If you can meet with Triumph and Disaster / And treat those two imposters just the same. —Rudyard Kipling, "If—," *Reward and Fairies*, 1910

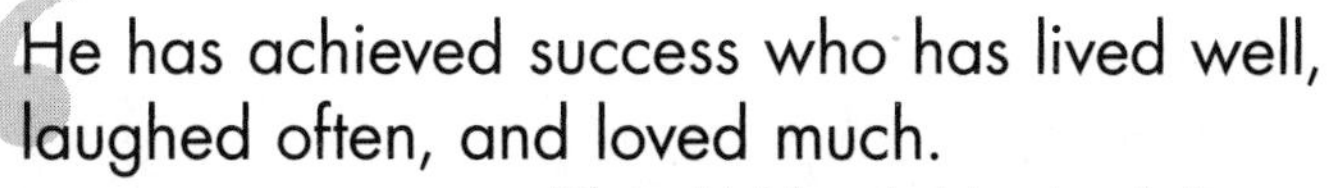

> He has achieved success who has lived well, laughed often, and loved much.
>
> —Elbert Hubbard, *Notebook*, Petrocelli

Always bear in mind that your own resolution to succeed is more important than any one thing. —Abraham Lincoln, letter, 5 November 1855

There is no limit to what a man can do or where he can go if he doesn't mind who gets the credit. —Ronald Reagan, *First Inaugural Address* (Washington, D.C.), 1981

The man with a new idea is a Crank until the idea succeeds. —Mark Twain, *Following the Equator*, 1897

When success happens to an English writer, he acquires a new type-writer. When success happens to an American writer, he acquires a new life. —Martin Amis, *Kurt Vonnegut, 1983*

The best augury of a man's success in his profession is that he thinks it the finest in the world. —George Eliot, *Daniel Deronda*, 1874–1876

The fly sat upon the axel-tree of the chariot-wheel and said, What a dust do I raise! —Aesop, "The Fly on the Wheel," *Fables*

People may oppose you, but when they realize you can hurt them, they'll join your side. —Condoleezza Rice, quoted by James Mann, *Rise of the Vulcans*, 2004

Excellence encourages one about life generally; it shows the spiritual wealth of the world. —George Eliot, *Daniel Deronda*, 1874–1876

The surest sign of fitness is success. —Olive Schreiner, *The Story of an African Farm*, 1883

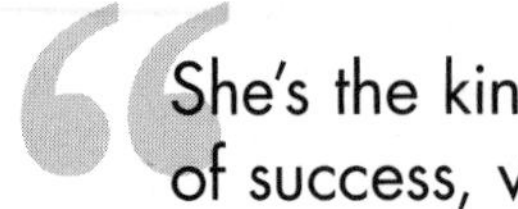

She's the kind of girl who climbed the ladder of success, wrong by wrong.
—Mae West, *I'm No Angel*, 1933

… with a good fortune, a brilliant position, and a weak, indulgent husband, what more could she desire? —Marguerite Blessington, "La Marquise Le Villeroi to Miss Montressor," *The Victims of Society*, 1837

EARTH has her usual delights—which can be met with six days out of the seven. But here and there upon grey earth there exist, like the flying of sunlight, celestial pleasures also—and one of these is the heaven of success. —Enid Bagnold, *The Happy Foreigner*, 1920

Nothing fails like success; nothing is so defeated as yesterday's triumphant Cause. —Phyllis McGinley, "How to Get Along with Men," *The Province of the Heart*, 1959

If people are highly successful in their professions they lose their senses. Sight goes. They have no time to look at pictures. Sound goes. They have no time to listen to music. Speech goes. They have no time for conversation. They lose their sense of proportion—the relations between one thing and another. Humanity goes …. —Virginia Woolf, *Three Guineas*, 1938

… it is a peaceful thing to be one succeeding. —Gertrude Stein, *Everybody's Autobiography*, 1937

How success changes the opinion of men! —Maria Edgeworth, *The Will*, 1800

Success can make you go one of two ways. It can make you a prima donna, or it can smooth the edges, take away the insecurities, let the nice things come out. —Barbara Walters, quoted in *Newsweek* (New York), 1974

Success has killed more men than bullets. —Texas Guinan, nightclub act

11 A Spoonful of Sugar

There's always someone important in your life, it seems, who's either under the weather, facing surgery, getting a face lift, or coping with a serious disease. Keep those cards and letters coming—they boost morale and the immune system, doing your special someone immeasurable good.

• • •

"Medicine seems to be all cycles," continued Mrs. Hartshorn. "That's the bone I pick with Sloan. Like what's his name's new theory of history. First we nursed our babies; then science told us not to. Now it tells us we were right in the first place. Or were we wrong then but would be right now? Reminds me of relativity, if I understand Mr. Einstein." —Mary McCarthy, *The Group*, 1954

My health is so often impaired that I begin to be as weary of it as mending old lace; when it is patched in one place, it breaks out in another. —Mary Wortley Montagu, *Letters*

"And how are you?" said Winnie-the-Pooh .... // "Not very how," he said. "I don't seem to have felt at all how for a long time."
—A. A. Milne, *Winnie the Pooh,* 1926

My sore throats are always worse than everyone's. —Jane Austen, *Persuasion*, 1818

Is not disease the rule of existence? There is not a lily pad floating on the river but has been riddled by insects. Almost every shrub and tree has its gall, oftentimes esteemed its chief ornament and hardly to be distinguished from the fruit. If misery loves company, misery has company enough. Now, at midsummer, find me a perfect leaf or fruit. —Henry David Thoreau, *Journals*, 1906

Next to gold and jewelry, health is the most important thing you can have. —Phyllis Diller, *Funny Women*, Unterbrink

We currently have a system for taking care of sickness. We do not have a system for enhancing and promoting health. —Hillary Rodham Clinton, speech, 1993

My HMO is so expensive, they charge me for a self-breast exam. It's a flat fee.

—Wendy Liebman, glee mail, wendyliebman.com, 2003

Human beings are divided into mind and body. The mind embraces all the nobler aspirations, like poetry and philosophy, but the body has all the fun. —Woody Allen, *Love and Death*, 1975

A woman watches her body uneasily, as though it were an unreliable ally in the battle for love. —Leonard Cohen, *The Favourite Game*, 1963

We are all sculptors and painters, and our material is our own flesh and blood and bones. Any nobleness begins at once to refine a man's features, any meanness or sensuality to imbrute them. —Henry David Thoreau, *Walden*, 1854

Men's bodies are the most dangerous things on earth. —Margaret Atwood, "Making a Man," *Good Bones and Simple Murders*, 1994

If God made the body and the body is dirty, the fault lies with the manufacturer. —Lenny Bruce, quoted by Stephen Robb, BBC News (London), 2006

Numbing the pain for a while will make it worse when you finally feel it. —J. K. Rowling, *Harry Potter and the Goblet of Fire*, 2000

I think of my illness as a school, and finally I've graduated. —Gilda Radner, quoted in *Life* (New York), 1988

Illness sets the mind free sometimes to roam and surmise. —Alice B. Toklas, *The Alice B. Toklas Cook Book*, 1954

Back in my rummy days, I would tremble and shake for hours upon arising. It was the only exercise I got. —W. C. Fields, *The Temperance Lecture*, 1944

The first time I see a jogger smiling, I'll consider it. —Joan Rivers, attributed

> "The mind and the heart sometimes get another chance, but if anything happens to the poor old human frame, why, it's just out of luck, that's all."
>
> —Katherine Anne Porter, *Pale Horse, Pale Rider,* 1939

As in a theater and circus the statues of the king must be kept clean by him to whom they have been entrusted, so the bathing of the body is a duty of man, who was created in the image of the almighty King of the world. —Hillel, quoted in *Midrash*

The basic Female body comes with the following accessories: garter belt, panti-girdle, crinoline, camisole, bustle, brassiere, stomacher, chemise, virgin zone, spike heels, nose ring, veil, kid gloves, fishnet stockings, fichu, bandeau, Merry Widow, weepers, chokers, barrettes, bangles, beads, lorgnette, feather boa, basic black, compact, Lycra stretch one-piece with modesty panel, designer peignoir, flannel nightie, lace teddy, bed, head. —Margaret Atwood, "The Female Body," *Michigan Quarterly Review* (Ann Arbor), 1990

Children show scars like medals. Lovers use them as secrets to reveal. A scar is what happens when the word is made flesh. —Leonard Cohen, *The Favourite Game*, 1963

Personal size and mental sorrow have certainly no necessary proportions. A large bulky figure has as good a right to be in deep affliction as the most graceful set of limbs in the world. But, fair or not fair, there are unbecoming conjunctions, which… taste cannot tolerate—which ridicule will seize. —Jane Austen, *Persuasion*, 1818

I think it's time for a real woman who has led a real life to re-design Barbie …. Her hips could start out at a normal size and then quietly expand over the years while she remained powerless to do anything about it …. Are you listening, Mattel? —Rita Rudner, "Waist Management," ritafunny.com, 2003

The moon lives in the lining of your skin. —Pablo Neruda, "Ode to a Beautiful Nude," Nathaniel Tarn, tr., *Nuevas Odas Elementales*, 1956

I don't know what my mother-in-law's measurements are. We haven't had her surveyed yet. —Phyllis Diller, *Funny Women*, Unterbrink

> It used to be said that by a certain age a man had the face that he deserved. Nowadays, he has the face he can afford.
>
> —Martin Amis, *Visiting Mrs. Nabokov and Other Excursions*, 1993

What was my body to me? A kind of flunkey in my service. Let but my anger wax hot, my love grow exalted, my hatred collect in me, and that boasted solidarity between me and my body was gone. —Antoine de Saint-Exupéry, *Flight to Arras*, 1942

I pick up the magazines. I buy into the ideal. I believe that blond, flat girls have the secret. What is far more frightening than narcissism is the zeal for self-mutilation that is spreading, infecting the world. —Eve Ensler, preface, *The Good Body*, 2004

Be bold and LOVE YOUR BODY. STOP FIXING IT. It was never broken. —Eve Ensler, *The Good Body*, 2004

Don't worry about your heart, it will last you as long as you live. —W. C. Fields, quoted by Ronald J. Fields, *W. C. Fields: A Life on Film*, 1984

We are so fond of one another, because our ailments are the same. —Jonathan Swift, *Journal to Stella*, 1711

The least you can do is recuperate! —Goodman Ace, *Easy Aces* radio show, 1930s–1940s

> A doctor's reputation is made by the number of eminent men who die under his care.
>
> —George Bernard Shaw, quoted by Hesketh Pearson, *George Bernard Shaw: His Life and Personality*, 1942

Every affliction has its own rich lesson to teach, if we would learn it. —Mohandas Gandhi, quoted by D. G. Tendulkar, *Mahatma*, 1960

A junky runs on junk time. When his junk is cut off, the clock runs down and stops. All he can do is hang on and wait for non-junk time to start. —William S. Burroughs, *Junkie*, 1953

In those days, all I did, when I wasn't taking pills (speed, Ritalin especially) all day, was drink all night. —Eve Babitz, *Black Swans*, 1993

All sin tends to be addictive, and the terminal point of addiction is what is called damnation. —W. H. Auden, "Hell," *A Certain World*, 1970

Every form of addiction is bad, no matter whether the narcotic be alcohol or morphine or idealism. —Carl Jung, *Memories, Dreams, Reflections*, Aniela Jaffé, ed., 1963

Why, if it wasn't for psychoanalysis you'd never find out how wonderful your own mind is! —Susan Glaspell, *Suppressed Desires*, 1914

Incidentally, why was it that none of all the pious ever discovered psycho-analysis? Why did it have to wait for a completely godless Jew? —Sigmund Freud, letter (1818), *Psycho-Analysis and Faith*, 1963

Psychotherapy can be one of the greatest and most rewarding adventures, it can bring with it the deepest feelings of personal worth, of purpose and richness in living. —Eda J. Le Shan, *How to Survive Parenthood*, 1965

> "My therapist told me the way to achieve true inner peace is to finish what I start. So far today, I have finished two bags of M&M's and a chocolate cake. I feel better already."
>
> —Dave Barry, *Jokes*, Getlen

Psychotherapy, unlike castor oil, which will work no matter how you get it down, is useless when forced on an uncooperative patient. —Abigail Van Buren, "Dear Abby," newspaper column, 1974

Schizophrenia may be a necessary consequence of literacy. —Marshall McLuhan, *The Gutenberg Galaxy*, 1962

He had been in analysis for seven years and he regarded life as a long disease, alleviated by little fifty-minute bloodlettings of words from the couch. —Erica Jong, *How to Save Your Own Life*, 1977

You can be down, you can even be broken, but there's always a way to mend. —Oprah Winfrey, quoted by Robert Waldron, *Oprah!*, 1987

It is through suppression that hells are formed in us. —Susan Glaspell, *Suppressed Desires*, 1914

Before I went into analysis, I told everyone lies—but when you spend all that money, you tell the truth.... —Jane Fonda, quoted by Thomas Kiernan, *Jane: An Intimate Biography of Jane Fonda*, 1973

The last four years of psychoanalysis are a waste of money. —Nora Ephron, *I Feel Bad About My Neck*, 2006

The doctor should be opaque to his patients and, like a mirror, should show them nothing but what is shown to him. —Sigmund Freud, "Recommendations to Physicians Practising Psycho-Analysis," 1912

Psychotherapy has taught us that in the final reckoning it is not knowledge, not technical skill, that has a curative effect, but the personality of the doctor. —Carl Jung, "The Gifted Child" (1942), *The Development of Personality*, R. F. C. Hull, tr., 1954

We serve the patient in various functions, as an authority and a substitute for his parents, as a teacher and educator. —Sigmund Freud, *An Outline of Psychoanalysis*, James Strachey, tr., 1940

I am always running into peoples' unconscious. —Marilyn Monroe, quoted by Norman Mailer, *Marilyn*, 1973

Sunday—the doctor's paradise! Doctors at country clubs, doctors at the seaside, doctors with mistresses, doctors with wives, doctors in church, doctors in yachts, doctors everywhere resolutely being people, not doctors. —Sylvia Plath, *The Bell Jar*, 1963

> He must have killed a lot of men to have made so much money.
>
> —Molière, *The Imaginary Invalid*, 1673

He who advises a sick man, whose manner of life is prejudicial to health, is clearly bound first of all to change his patient's manner of life. —Plato, *Epistles*, John Harward, tr., 1932

Besides the obstinancy of the nurse, I had the ignorance of the physicians to contend with. —Elizabeth Cady Stanton, *Eighty Years and More*, 1902

No *man*, not even a doctor, ever gives any other definition of what a nurse should be than this—"devoted and obedient." This definition would do just as well for a porter. It might even do for a horse. It would not do for a policeman. —Florence Nightingale, *Notes on Nursing*, 1859

Man seems to be a rickety poor sort of a thing, any way you take him; a kind of British Museum of infirmities and inferiorities. He is always undergoing repairs. A machine that was as unreliable as he is would have no market. —Mark Twain, *Letters from the Earth*, Bernard DeVoto, ed., 1962

> After two days in hospital, I took a turn for the nurse.
>
> —W. C. Fields, radio show

The Long Goodbye 12

We all suffer losses, the death of loved one being the mightiest. But heartbreak is a loss, too. Even the loss of a thing you hold dear can be a terrible blow. When those you care about go through great sorrow, you may feel at a loss for words. This chapter can help you find the right ones … and even use a little levity for leavening.

• • •

The planet's tyrant, dotard Death, had held his gray mirror before them for a moment and shown them the image of things to come. —Dorothy L. Sayers, *The Unpleasantness at the Bellona Club*, 1928

One always dies too soon—or too late. —Jean-Paul Sartre, *No Exit*, 1945

"life's not a paragraph / And death i think is no parenthesis

—e. e. cummings, "Four VII," *is 5*, 1926"

Dawn comes slowly but dusk is rapid. —Alice B. Toklas, *Staying On Alone*, Edward Burns, ed., 1973

I shall die, but that is all that I shall do for Death; I am not on his pay-roll. —Edna St. Vincent Millay, "Conscientious Objector," *Wine from These Grapes*, 1934

Pardon me for not getting up. —Ernest Hemingway, proposed epitaph for himself, quoted in *Cassell Dictionary of Humorous Quotations*, Nigel Rees, ed., 1998

So few people achieve the final end. *Most* are caught napping. —Enid Bagnold, *The Chinese Prime Minister*, 1964

> It is the unknown we fear when we look upon death and darkness, nothing more.
>
> —*Harry Potter and the Half-Blood Prince,* 2005
>
> To the well-organized mind, death is but the next great adventure.
>
> —*Harry Potter and the Sorcerer's Stone,* 1997
>
> —J. K. Rowling

On the death of a friend, we should consider that the fates through confidence have devolved on us the task of a double living, that we have henceforth to fulfill the promise of our friend's life also, in our own, to the world. —Henry David Thoreau, journal entry, 28 February 1840

Nothing is more difficult than to understand the dead, I've found; but nothing is more dangerous than to ignore them. —Margaret Atwood, *The Blind Assassin*, 2000

Death unites as well as separates; it silences all paltry feeling. —Honoré de Balzac, "Letters of Two Brides," *La Press*, 1841–1842

I can remember how when I was young I believed death to be a phenomenon of the body; now I know it to be merely a function of the mind—and that of the minds who suffer the bereavement. The nihilists say it is the end; the fundamentalists, the beginning; when in reality it is no more than a single tenant or family moving out of a tenement or a town. —William Faulkner, *As I Lay Dying*, 1930

I used to think getting old was about vanity—but actually it's about losing people you love. Getting wrinkles is trivial. —Joyce Carol Oates, interview, *The Guardian* (London), 1989

Those who have been immersed in the tragedy of massive death during wartime, and who have faced it squarely, never allowing their senses and feelings to become numbed and indifferent, have emerged from their experiences with growth and humanness greater than that achieved through almost any other means. —Elizabeth Kübler-Ross, *Death: The Final Stage of Growth*, 1975

> Cowards die many times before their deaths; / The valiant never taste of death but once.
>
> —*Julius Caesar,* 1599
>
> Now cracks a noble heart. Good-night, sweet prince; / And flights of angels sing thee to thy rest!
>
> —*Hamlet,* 1600
>
> Fear no more the heat o' th' sun, / Nor the furious winter's rages. / Thou thy worldly task hast done, / Home art gone and ta'en thy wages.
>
> —*Cymbeline,* 1609
>
> —William Shakespeare

There is no Death! What seems so is transition; / This life of mortal breath / Is but a suburb of the life Elysian, / Whose portal we call Death. —Henry Wadsworth Longfellow, "Resignation," 1849

I am, and always have been, pro-death. I'm pro-death penalty; I'm pro-choice; I'm pro-assisted suicide; I'm pro-regular suicide—I'm for anything that gets the freeway moving faster. —Bill Maher, *Jokes*, Getlen

Death … / … suddenly breathes out: / it blows out a mournful sound that swells the sheets, / and the beds go sailing toward a port / where death is waiting, dressed like an admiral. —Pablo Neruda, "Nothing But Death," *Neruda & Vallejo: Selected Poems*, Robert Bly, ed. and tr., 1993

Against you I will fling myself, unvanquished and unyielding, O Death! —Virginia Woolf, *The Waves*, 1931

Down you mongrel, Death! / Back into your kennel! —Edna St. Vincent Millay, "The Poet and His Book," *Second April*, 1921

He whispered craftily to me, for the hundredth, the thousandth time, that now was the time to help him die. —M. F. K. Fisher, *Stay Me, Oh Comfort Me*, 1993

> "How do men act, when they together stand, on the last perch of this swiftly-sinking wreck? / Do they not bravely give their parting cheer, / And make their last voice loud and boldly sound / Amidst the hollow roarings of the storm?"
>
> —Joanna Baillie, *Constantine Paleologus,* 1804

You haven't lived until you've died in California. —Mort Sahl, stand-up routine

Death seems to provide the minds of the Anglo-Saxon race with a greater fund of amusement than any other single subject. —Dorothy L. Sayers, introduction, *The Third Omnibus of Crime*, 1935

After all, there are worse things in life than death. If you've ever spent an evening with an insurance salesman, you know what I'm talking about. —Woody Allen, *Love and Death*, 1975

Death is the final stage of growth in this life. There is no total death. Only the body dies. The self or spirit, or whatever you may wish to label it, is eternal. —Elizabeth Kübler-Ross, *Death: The Final Stage of Growth*, 1975

It is so hard for us little human beings to accept this deal that we get. It's really crazy, isn't it? We get to live, then we have to die. What we put into every moment is all we have. —Gilda Radner, *It's Always Something*, 1989

I will leave behind me the dark ravine, and climb up gentler slopes toward that spiritual mesa where at last a wide light will fall upon my days. From there I will sing words of hope, without looking into my heart. As one who was full of compassion wished: I will sing to console men. —Gabriela Mistral, introduction, *Tala*, 1938

> I reason, Earth is short— / And Anguish—absolute— / And many hurt, / But, what of that?
>
> —No. 301
>
> Because I could not stop for Death— / He kindly stopped for me
>
> —No. 712
>
> Death is a Dialogue between, / The Spirit and the Dust.
>
> —No. 976
>
> Parting is all we know of heaven, / And all we need of hell.
>
> —No. 1732
>
> —Emily Dickinson, *Poems*, Johnson

There is no solution to death … Life intends to kill us. —Dorothy L. Sayers, "Problem Picture," *The Mind of the Maker*, 1941

I suppose there is no man who to-day loves his country who has not perceived that in the life of the nation, as in the life of the individual, the hour of external success may be the hour of irrevocable failure, and that the hour of death, whether to nations or individuals, is often the hour of immortality. —Olive Schreiner, *The English South African's View of the Situation*, c. 1899

The child had been like a strap that held them close. Now, unbuckled, they had to struggle to keep together. —Faye Moskowitz, "A Leak in the Heart," *Shaking Eve's Tree*, Niederman

How replace the life of a loved lost child with a dream? —Daphne du Maurier, *Don't Look Now*, 1970

It's a terrible thing to die young. Still, it saves a lot of time. —Grace Paley, *Just As I Thought*, 1998

"Childhood is the Kingdom Where Nobody Dies" —Poem title, Edna St. Vincent Millay, *Wine from These Grapes*, 1934

There is no lonelier man in death … than that man who has lived many years with a good wife and then outlived her. If two people love each other there can be no happy end to it. —Ernest Hemingway, *Death in the Afternoon*, 1932

Life, in my estimation, is a biological misadventure that we terminate on the shoulders of six strange men whose only objective is to make a hole in one with you. —Fred Allen, *Forbes* (New York), 1967

> "We are all cremated equal.
> —Goodman Ace, *Easy Aces* radio show, 1930s–1940s"

Always go to other peoples' funerals otherwise they won't go to yours. —Yogi Berra, "Yogi-isms," YogiBerra.com

I've a great fancy to see my own funeral afore I die. —Maria Edgeworth, *Castle Rackrent*, 1800

The woman is perfected / Her dead / Body wears the smile of accomplishment. —Sylvia Plath, "Edge," 1963

Let's talk of graves, of worms, and epitaphs. —William Shakespeare, *Richard II*, 1595

Their lives are in my heart / but my love grows as I see more / the roots of their wrongs and hopes. —Burton Witkovsky, "Aspects of Clutter," 1997

No one seems to have said that it was an appropriate death though we know that all deaths are appropriate. —Joyce Carol Oates, *Cybele*, 1980

A grave is such a quiet place. —Edna St. Vincent Millay, "Renascence," *Renascence and Other Poems*, 1917

It is not the end of the physical body that should worry us. Rather, our concern must be to *live* while we're alive—to release our inner selves from the spiritual death that comes with living behind a façade designed to conform to external definitions of who and what we are. —Elizabeth Kübler-Ross, *Death: The Final Stage of Growth*, 1975

> "... it's wrong what they say about the past, I've learned, about how you can bury it. Because the past claws its way out."
>
> —Khaled Hosseini, *The Kite Runner*, 2003

I tell you the past is a bucket of ashes. —Carl Sandburg, "Prairie," 1918

For those who live neither with religious consolations about death nor with a sense of death (or of anything else) as natural, death is the obscene mystery, the ultimate affront, the thing that cannot be controlled. It can only be denied. —Susan Sontag, *Illness As Metaphor*, 1978

She was no longer wrestling with the grief, but could sit down with it as a lasting companion and make it a sharer in her thoughts. —George Eliot, *Middlemarch*, 1871–1872

Where a blood relation sobs, an intimate friend should choke up, a distant acquaintance should sigh, a stranger should merely fumble sympathetically with his handkerchief. —Mark Twain, *Letters from the Earth*, Bernard DeVoto, ed., 1962

He was my North, my South, my East and West, / My working week and my Sunday rest, / My noon, my midnight, my talk, my song. —W. H. Auden, "Funeral Blues," 1937

Not with a Club, the Heart is broken / Nor with a Stone— / A Whip so small you could not see it / I've known / To lash the Magic Creature / Till it fell. —Emily Dickinson, No. 1304, *Poems*, Johnson

It's not that I'm afraid to die, I just don't want to be there when it happens. —Woody Allen, *Without Feathers*, 1976

I have never thought there was much to be said in favour of dragging on long after all one's friends were dead. —Murasaki Shikibu, *The Tale of Genji*, 1001–1015

> If my doctor told me I had only six minutes to live, I wouldn't brood. I'd type a little faster.
>
> —Isaac Asimov, quoted in *Life* (New York), 1984

Trust not thyself till the day of thy death. —Hillel, quoted in *Sayings of the Fathers*

The years seem to rush by now, and I think of death as a fast approaching end of a journey—double and treble reason for loving as well as working while it is day. —George Eliot, letter (1861), *George Eliot's Life as Related in Her Letters and Journals*, J. W. Cross, ed., 1900

The reports of my death are greatly exaggerated. —Mark Twain, cable from London to the Associated Press in New York, 1897

I contemplate death as though I were continuing after its arrival. I, therefore, survive since I can contemplate myself afterward as well as before. —Pearl S. Buck, *The Goddess Abides*, 1972

Death, when it approaches, ought not to take one by surprise. It should be part of the full expectancy of life. —Muriel Spark, *Memento Mori*, 1959

Just like those who are incurably ill, the aged know everything about their dying except exactly when. —Philip Roth, *The Facts: A Novelist's Autobiography*, 1988

Now twilight lets her curtain down / And pins it with a star. —Lydia Maria Child, quoted in an obituary for MacDonald Clark, 1842

Dying seems less sad than having lived too little. —Gloria Steinem, *Outrageous Acts and Everyday Rebellion*, 1983

Let us endeavor so to live that when we come to die even the undertaker will be sorry. —Mark Twain, *Pudd'n'head Wilson*, 1894

Oh, everything is gorgeous once it's gone. —Gregory Maguire, *Wicked*, 1995

… all that she had had, and all that she had missed, were lost together, and were twice lost in this landslide of remembered losses. —Katherine Anne Porter, "Theft," *Flowering Judas and Other Stories*, 1930

> The heart once broken is a heart no more, / And is absolved from all a heart must be.
> —"Fatal Interview," 1931
>
> Spring will not ail nor summer falter; / Nothing will know that you are gone ….
> —"Elegy Before Death," *Second April,* 1921
> —Edna St. Vincent Millay

Think not that I have come in quest of common flowers; but rather to bemoan the loss of one whose scent has vanished from the air. —Murasaki Shikibu, *The Tale of Genji*, 1001–1015

Mostly only loss teaches us about the value of things. —Arthur Schopenhauer, *Essays and Aphorisms* (1851), R. J. Hollingdale, tr., 1970

In loss itself / I find assuagement: / having lost the treasure, / I've nothing to fear. —Juana Inés de la Cruz, "Disillusionment," *A Sor Juana Anthology*, Alan S. Trueblood, tr., 1988

It will take mind and memory months and possibly years to gather together the details and thus learn and know the whole extent of the loss. —Mark Twain, *Autobiography*, Charles Neider, ed., 1959

We lose not only through death, but also by leaving and being left, by changing and letting go and moving on. And our losses include not only our separations and departures from those we love, but our conscious and unconscious losses of romantic dreams, impossible expectations, illusions of freedom and power, illusions of safety—and the loss of our own younger self, the self that thought it would always be unwrinkled and invulnerable and immortal. —Judith Viorst, introduction, *Necessary Losses*, 1986

… I was never one to leave anything. I had trouble parting with our old '78 Buick. —Fran Drescher, *Cancer Schmancer*, 2002

Rocky Roads

Life isn't like ice cream. Those lumps and bumps don't just melt away. The only way to lick 'em is to stay the course. And sometimes we need a lot of help to do so. Caring friends, family, and mentors will find words of inspiration to help those they care about deal with life's unexpected changes.

• • •

Little by little does the trick. —Aesop, "The Crow and the Pitcher," *Fables*

I had rather die in the adventure of noble achievements, than live in obscure and sluggish security. —Margaret Cavendish, *The Description of a New World Called the Blazing World*, 1666

There is no such thing as security. There never has been …. Security is when everything is settled, when nothing can happen to you; security is the denial of life. —Germaine Greer, *The Female Eunuch*, 1971

Beliefs are what divide people. Doubt unites them.

—Peter Ustinov, quoted by James A. Haught, *2000 Years of Disbelief*

That was our clowning achievement. —Goodman Ace, *Easy Aces* radio show, 1930s–1940s

God writes a lot of comedy ... the trouble is, he's stuck with so many bad actors who don't know how to play funny. —Garrison Keillor, attributed

Those who are animated by hope can perform what would seem impossibilities to those who are under the depressing influence of fear. —Maria Edgeworth, *The Grateful Negro*, 1802

The point of living, and of being an optimist, is to be foolish enough to believe the best is yet to come. —Peter Ustinov, attributed

Hold fast to dreams / For if dreams die / Life is a broken-winged bird / That cannot fly. —Langston Hughes, "Dreams," *Golden Slippers: An Anthology of Negro Poetry for Young Readers*, 1941

We live in the midst of alarms; anxiety beclouds the future; we expect some new disaster with each newspaper we read. —Abraham Lincoln, speech (Bloomington, Illinois), 1856

The natural condition is one of insurmountable obstacles on the road to imminent disaster. —Tom Stoppard and Marc Norman, *Shakespeare in Love*, 1998

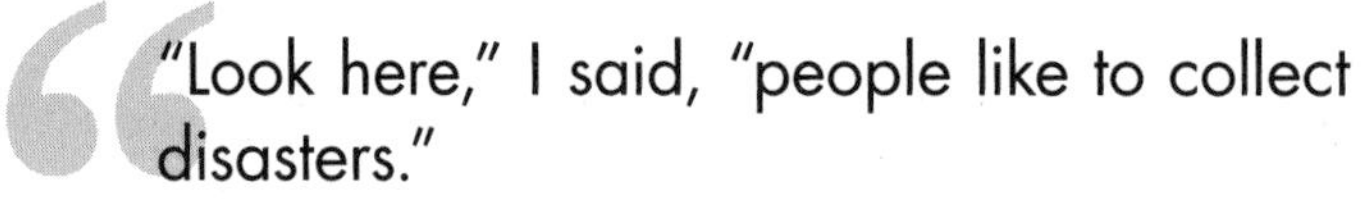

"Look here," I said, "people like to collect disasters."

—Agatha Christie, *Endless Night*, 1967

In the absence of a natural disaster we are left again to our own uneasy devices. —Joan Didion, quoted in *Life* (New York), 1969

Perhaps catastrophe is the natural human environment, and even though we spend a good deal of energy trying to get away from it, we are programmed for survival amid catastrophe. —Germaine Greer, *Sex and Destiny*, 1984

Between two evils, I always pick the one I never tried before. —Mae West, *Klondike Annie*, 1936

People could survive their natural trouble all right if it weren't for the trouble they make for themselves. —Ogden Nash, "Little Miss Muffet Sat on a Prophet—And Quite Right," *I'm a Stranger Here Myself*, 1938

Truly the suffering is great, here on earth. We blunder along, shredded by our mistakes, bludgeoned by our faults. Not having a clue where the dark path leads us. But on the whole, we stumble along bravely, don't you think? —Alice Walker, *By the Light of My Father's Smile*, 1998

Life, that can shower you with so much splendour, is unremittingly cruel to those who have given up. —Stephen Fry, *Moab is My Washpot*, 1997

If life gives you lemons, make some sort of fruity juice. —Conan O'Brien, *Jokes*, Getlen

> "Troubles grow by recounting them.
> —Elbert Hubbard, *Note Book*"

Double, double toil and trouble; / Fire burn and cauldron bubble. —William Shakespeare, *Macbeth*, 1605

This became a credo of mine … attempt the impossible in order to improve your work. —Bette Davis, *Mother Goddamn*, 1974

A woman is like a teabag. You can't tell how strong she is until you put her in hot water. —Nancy Pelosi, quoted by Hillary Rodham Clinton, interview, ABC News (New York), 2006

Trouble is a great equalizer. No matter what our differences, in time of trouble the differences fade, and we become brothers and sisters. We want to reach out and help one another. —Ann Landers, column, *Seattle Post-Intelligencer* (Seattle), 17 November 1998

a man who had fallen among thieves / lay by the roadside on his back / dressed in fifteenthrate ideas / wearing a round jeer for a hat —e. e. cummings, "One XXVIII," *is 5*, 1926

Though the snow-drifts of Yoshino were heaped across his path, doubt not that whither his heart is set, his footsteps shall tread out their way. —Murasaki Shikibu, *The Tale of Genji*, 1001–1015

"What makes the desert beautiful," says the little prince, "is that somewhere it hides a well." —Antoine de Saint-Exupéry, *The Little Prince*

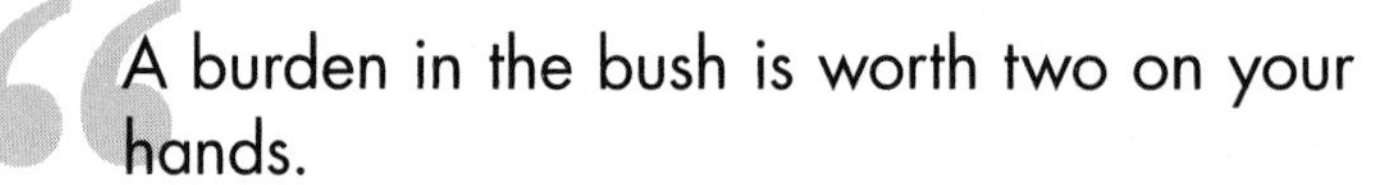

A burden in the bush is worth two on your hands.

—James Thurber, *Fables for Our Time*, 1940

The worst walls are never the ones you find in your way. The worst walls are the ones you put there—you build yourself. Those are the high ones, the thick ones, the ones with no doors in. —Ursula K. Le Guin, "The Stone Ax and the Muskoxen," *The Language of the Night*, 1979

You were once wild here. Don't let them tame you! —Isadora Duncan, curtain speech, Symphony Hall (Boston), 1922

I always write a good first line, but I have trouble in writing the others. —Molière, *Les Précieuses Ridicules*, 1659

Man needs difficulties; they are necessary for health. —Carl Jung, "The Transcendent Function" (1916), *The Structure and Dynamics of the Psyche*, R. F. C. Hull, tr., 1960

But I don't know how to fight. All I know how to do is stay alive. —Alice Walker, *The Color Purple*, 1982

Jesus said the meek would inherit the earth, but so far all we've gotten is Minnesota and North Dakota. —Garrison Keilor, "When I'm 64," Salon.com, 8 August 2006

Someone has to stand up for wimps. —Barbara Ehrenreich, "Wimps," *The Worst Years of Our Lives*, 1991

I got anything I want to have; but I'll never have anything at all if trouble makes me go and give up! —Ruth Gordon, *Years Ago*, 1946

I generally avoid temptation unless I can't resist it. —Mae West, *My Little Chickadee*, 1940

> Failure after long perseverance is much grander than never to have a striving good enough to be called a failure.
> —George Eliot, *Middlemarch*, 1871–1872

If failure, then another long beginning. / Why hope, / Why think that Spring must bring relenting. —Amy Lowell, "A Legend of Porcelain," *Legends*, 1921

tomorrow is our permanent address / and there they'll scarcely find us (if they do, / we'll move away still further: into now —e. e. cummings, "XXXIX," *1 x 1*, 1944

Thank goodness you're a failure—it's why I so distinguish you! Anything else to-day is too hideous. Look about you—look at the successes. Would you be one, on your honour? —Henry James, *The Ambassadors*, 1903

I think success has no rules, but you can learn a great deal from failure. —Jean Kerr, *Mary, Mary*, 1960

You can be down, you can even be broken, but there's always a way to mend. —Oprah Winfrey, quoted by Robert Waldron, *Oprah!*, 1987

It is better to be looked over than overlooked. —Mae West, *Belle of the Nineties*, 1934

He had discovered a great law of human action, without knowing it—namely, that in order to make a man or a boy covet a thing, it is only necessary to make the thing difficult to obtain. —Mark Twain, *The Adventures of Tom Sawyer*, 1976

We must open the doors of opportunity. But we must also equip our people to walk through those doors. —Lyndon B. Johnson, attributed

People do not live nowadays—they get about ten percent out of life. —Isadora Duncan, *This Quarter* (Paris), Autumn 1929

> Too much of a good thing can be wonderful.
> —Mae West, *Wit and Wisdom*, Weintraub

It ain't no sin if you crack a few laws now and then just so long as you don't break any. —Mae West, *Every Day's a Holiday*, 1937

The troubles of our proud and angry dust / Are from eternity, and shall not fail. / Bear them we can, and if we can we must. / Shoulder the sky, my lad, and drink your ale. —A. E. Housman, No. IX, *Last Poems*, 1922

We will not tire; we will not falter, and we will not fail. —George W. Bush, address, joint session of Congress (Washington, D.C.), 20 September 2001

Press on. Nothing in the world can take the place of persistence. Talent will not; nothing in the world is more common than unsuccessful men with talent. Genius will not; unrewarded genius is a proverb. Education will not; the world is full of educated derelicts. Persistence and determination alone are omnipotent. —Calvin Coolidge, statement upon retirement as president of board of directors of New York Life Insurance Company, 1933

He who hesitates is last. —Mae West, *Wit and Wisdom*, Weintraub

I believe in pulling yourself up by your own bootstraps. I believe it is possible—I saw this guy do it once in Cirque du Soleil. It was magical. —Stephen Colbert, speech, White House Correspondents' Association Dinner (Washington, D.C.), 2006

Never give in—never, never, never, never, in nothing great or small, large or petty, never give in except to convictions of honour and good sense. —Winston Churchill, speech, Harrow School (London), 1941

You have enemies? Why, it is the story of every man who has done a great deed or created a new idea. It is the cloud which thunders around everything that shines. Fame must have enemies, as light must have gnats. Do not bother yourself about it; disdain. —Victor Hugo, *Villemain*, 1845

It is not the style of clothes one wears, neither the kind of automobile ne drives, nor the amount of money one has in the bank, that counts. These mean nothing. It is simply service that measures success. —George Washington Carver, newspaper column, "Professor Carver's Advice," 1920s

There can be no deep disappointment where there is not deep love. —Martin Luther King Jr., "Letter from Birmingham City Jail" 1963

What happens to a dream deferred? // Does it dry up / like a raisin in the sun? —Langston Hughes, "Harlem," *A Dream Deferred*, 1951

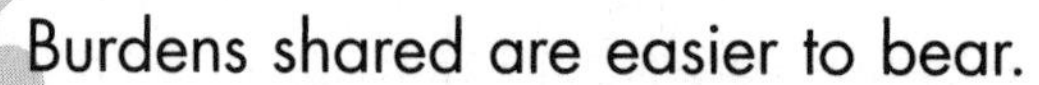

—Jesse Jackson, address, Democratic National Convention (Chicago), 26 August 1996

We are such stuff / As dreams are made on; and our little life / Is rounded with a sleep. —William Shakespeare, *The Tempest*, 1610

The great thing about attaining some level of success in your life is being spiritually in a place where you accept it and feel good about it … and not be afraid that tomorrow it's going to end. —Oprah Winfrey, quoted by Robert Waldron, *Oprah!*, 1987

You have to be a bastard to make it, and that's a fact. And the Beatles are the biggest bastards on earth. —John Lennon, *Lennon Remembers*, Jann Wenner, ed., 1970

My strength has not equaled my mad ambition. I have remained obscure; I have done worse—I have touched success, and allowed it to escape me. —George Sand, *The Marquise*, 1869

… people seldom see the halting and painful steps by which the most insignificant success is achieved. —Annie Sullivan, letter (1887), quoted by Helen Keller, *The Story of My Life*, 1903

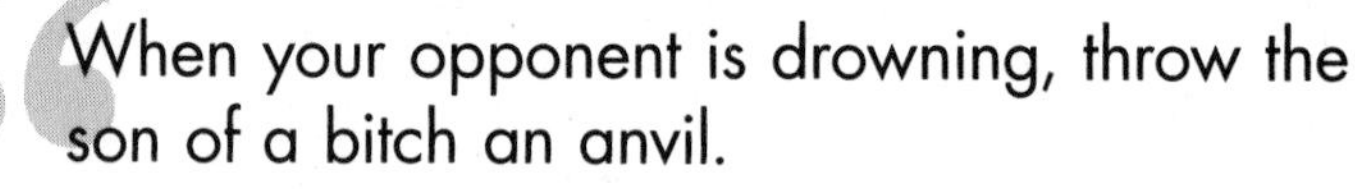

—James Carville, motto

Success is counted sweetest / By those who ne'er succeed. —Emily Dickinson, No. 67, *Poems*, Johnson

If you can keep your head when all about you / Are losing theirs—and blaming it on you. —Rudyard Kipling, "If–," *Reward and Fairies*, 1910

14 Nothing Ventured ...

Life is an adventure. Each event is cause for celebration. That long-ago planned road trip is finally happening: celebrate! You're embarking on new studies: celebrate! Even mistakes and misadventures can be blessings in disguise—getting lost, appearing on the wrong day, and so on. These quotes help you mark each occasion. Ready. Set. Action!

• • •

I saw that all beings are fated to happiness: action is not life, but a way of wasting some force, an ennervation. —Jean-Paul Sartre, *Une Saison en Enfer*, 1874

Up and the world is your oyster! This time you can't miss! Whack comes down the old shillaly and you're down again bitin' the dust! Can't face it! Screeching into your pillow nights! Put back your smile in the morning, trampin' to managers' offices! Home again in the evenin' ready to give up the ghost. Somebody come by, to tell you: "Go see Frohman nine-thirty sharp!" Luck's turned, you're on the trolley again! Curl up your ostrich feathers! Sponge off the train of your skirt! Because it's all aboard tomorrow .... —Ruth Gordon, *The Leading Lady*, 1948

He's a ragged individualist. —Goodman Ace, *Easy Aces* radio show, 1930s–1940s

Be nobody's darling; / Be an outcast. —Alice Walker, "Be Nobody's Darling," *Revolutionary Petunias and Other Poems*, 1973

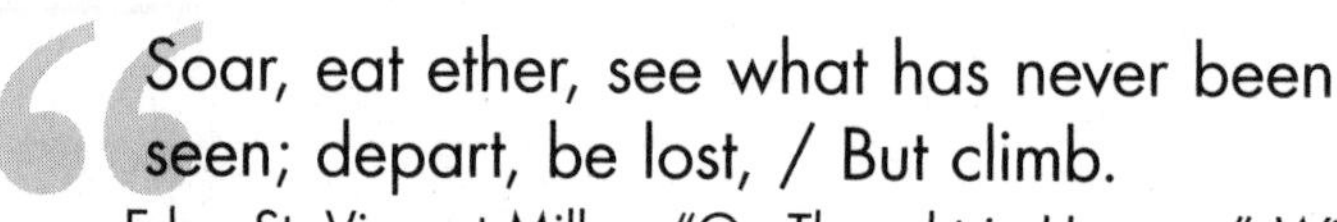

Soar, eat ether, see what has never been seen; depart, be lost, / But climb.
—Edna St. Vincent Millay, "On Thought in Harness," *Wine from These Grapes*, 1934

… inventiveness is childish, practice sublime. —Germaine de Staël, *Reflections on Internal Peace*, 1795 training

I hate a fellow whom pride or cowardice or laziness drives into a corner, and who does nothing when he is there but sit and *growl.* Let him come out as I do, and *bark.* —Samuel Johnson, *Anecdotes*, Piozzi

When action grows unprofitable, gather information; when information grows unprofitable, sleep. —Ursula K. Le Guin, *The Left Hand of Darkness*, 1969

I find that the great thing in this world is not so much where we stand as in what direction we are moving: To reach the port of heaven, we must sail sometimes with the wind and sometimes against it—but we must sail, and not drift, nor lie at anchor. —Oliver Wendell Holmes, *The Autocrat of the Breakfast Table*, 1858

The greatest happiness is to transform one's feelings into actions. —Germaine de Staël, letter (1796), *Madame de Staël*, de Pange

Don't agonize. Organize. —Florynce Kennedy, quoted by Gloria Steinem, *Ms.* (New York), 1973

Imagining something is better than remembering something. —John Irving, *The World According to Garp*, 1988

So I never lose an opportunity of urging a practical beginning, however small, for it is wonderful how often in such matters the mustard-seed germinates and roots itself. —Florence Nightingale, "Health Missionaries for Rural India," *India*, 1896

Know ye not, each thing we prize / Does from small beginnings rise? —Mary Ann Lamb, "The Brother's Reply," *Poetry for Children*, 1809

Is there ever any particular spot where one can put one's finger and say, "It all began that day, at such a time and such a place, with such an incident." —Agatha Christie, *Endless Night*, 1967

> Never confuse movement with action.
>
> —Ernest Hemingway, quoted by Marlene Dietrich, *Papa Hemingway*, 1966

But once I had set out, I was already far on my way. —Colette, "The Photographer's Missus", 1944

To stroll is a science, it is the gastronomy of the eye. To walk is to vegetate, to stroll is to live .... —Honoré de Balzac, "Meditation Number III," *Physiology of Marriage*, 1829

I love walking my feet off. Gimme a map and a box of Band-Aids and I'm all set! —Fran Drescher, *Cancer, Schmancer*, 2002

"I admit that I have no fixed income like your friend, and I have no desire for it," he said to Faye. "I like adventure. I don't dare prophesy where my liking for adventure will lead." —Joyce Carol Oates, *Them*, 1969

> The greatest mistake you can make in life is to be continually fearing you will make one.
>
> —Elbert Hubbard, *Note Book*

New York is full of people on this kind of leave of absence, of people with a feeling for the tangential adventure, the risk adventure, the interlude that's not likely to end in any double-ring ceremony. —Joan Didion, *Mademoiselle*, 1961

He had never outgrown the feeling that a quest for information was a series of maneuvers in a game of espionage. —Mary McCarthy, "Winter Visitors," *Birds of America*, 1965

Action is at bottom a swinging and flailing of the arms to regain one's balance and keep afloat. —Eric Hoffer, *The Passionate State of Mind: And Other Aphorisms*, 1954

The power of doing anything with quickness is always much prized by the possessor, and often without any attention to the imperfection of the performance. —Jane Austen, *Pride and Prejudice*, 1813

Nothing is accidental in the universe—this is one of my Laws of Physics—except the entire universe itself, which is Pure Accident, pure divinity. —Joyce Carol Oates, "The Summing Up: Meredith Dawe," *Do with Me What You Will*, 1970

Accident is veiled necessity. —Maria von Ebner Eschenbach, *Aphorisms*, 1905

I intend to do everything that frightens me. —Gilda Radner, *Funny Women*, Unterbrink

Learn to get in touch with silence within yourself and know that everything in this life has a purpose. There are no mistakes, no coincidences; all events are blessings given to us to learn from. —Elizabeth Kübler-Ross, speech (1976), quoted by Lennie Kronisch, *Yoga Journal* (San Francisco), 1976

Action limits us; whereas in the state of contemplation we are endlessly expansive. —Henri-Frédéric Amiel, journal entry (1868), *Journal Intime*

Commit actions and the ideas will follow. —Tom Stoppard, *The Coast of Utopia: Shipwreck*, 2002

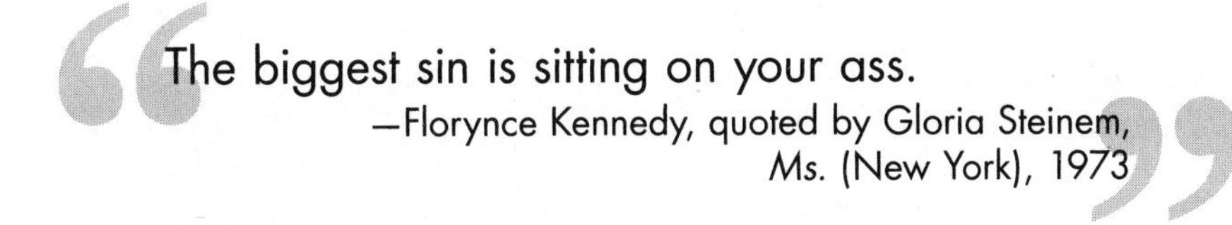

The biggest sin is sitting on your ass.
—Florynce Kennedy, quoted by Gloria Steinem, Ms. (New York), 1973

The ancestor of every action is a thought. —Ralph Waldo Emerson, "Spiritual Laws," *Essays: First Series*, 1841

A Deed knocks first at Thought / And then—it knocks at Will— / That is the manufacturing spot. —Emily Dickinson, No. 1216, *Poems*, Johnson

One of the marks of a truly vigorous society is the ability to dispense with passion as a midwife of action—the ability to pass directly from thought to action. —Eric Hoffer, *Reflections on the Human Condition*, 1973

Every man feels instinctively that all the beautiful sentiments in the world weigh less than a single lovely action. —James Russell Lowell, *North American Review* (Cedar Falls, Iowa), July 1867

An ounce of performance is worth pounds of promises.
—Mae West, *Wit and Wisdom*, Weintraub

No, Ernest, don't talk about action ... It is the last resource of those who know not how to dream. —Oscar Wilde, *The Critic as Artist*, 1891

To meditate is to labour; to think is to act. —Victor Hugo, *Les Misérables*, 1864

Man can do as he will, but not will as he will. —Arthur Schopenhauer, attributed by Albert Einstein

Now this is not the end. It is not even the beginning of the end. But it is, perhaps, the end of the beginning. —Winston Churchill, speech (London), 10 November 1942

To promise not to do a thing is the surest way in the world to make a body want to go and do that very thing. —Mark Twain, *The Adventures of Tom Sawyer*, 1876

Life is risky. You can decide to live your life afraid of that happening, or you can decide to live your life the way Americans live their lives, which is unafraid. There's no reason to have this increased fear. —Rudolph Giuliani, speech, 2001

… men seldom risk their lives where an escape is without hope of recompense. —Fanny Burney, *Cecilia*, 1782

If we didn't live venturously, plucking the wild goat by the beard, and trembling over precipices, we should never be depressed, I've no doubt; but already should be faded, fatalistic and aged. —Virginia Woolf, diary entry (1924), *A Writer's Diary*, Leonard Woolf, ed., 1954

I tasted—careless—then— / I did not know the Wine / Came once a World—Did you? —Emily Dickinson, No. 296, *Poems*, Johnson

> We shall not cease from exploration / And the end of all our exploring / Will be to arrive where we started / And know the place for the first time.
>
> —T. S. Eliot, "Little Gidding," *Four Quartets*, 1943

The test of an adventure is that when you're in the middle of it, you say to yourself, "Oh, now I've got myself into an awful mess; I wish I were sitting quietly at home." And the sign that something's wrong with you is when you sit quietly at home wishing you were out having lots of adventure. —Thornton Wilder, *The Matchmaker*, 1954

In my writing I am acting as a map maker, an explorer of psychic areas ... a cosmonaut of inner space, and I see no point in exploring areas that have already been thoroughly surveyed. —William S. Burroughs, Remark (1964), quoted by Eric Mottram, *William Burroughs: The Algebra of Need*, 1977

What is there that confers the noblest delight? What is that which swells a man's breast with pride above that which any other experience can bring to him? Discovery! To know that you are walking where none others have walked; that you are beholding what human eye has not seen before; that you are breathing a virgin atmosphere. To give birth to an idea, to discover a great thought—an intellectual nugget, right under the dust of a field that many a brain-plough had gone over before. To find a new planet, to invent a new hinge, to find a way to make the lightnings carry your messages. To be the first—that is the idea. —Mark Twain, *The Innocents Abroad*, 1869

But we are not known for our ability to follow through on our unearned discoveries. We are top-of-the-water adventurers, who limit our opinions of the icebergs to what we can see. —John Irving, *Trying to Save Piggy Sneed*, 1996

Undermining experience, embellishing experience, rearranging and enlarging experience into a species of mythology. —Philip Roth, *The Facts: A Novelist's Autobiography*, 1988

If a man knew anything, he would sit in a corner and be modest; but he is such an ignorant peacock, that he goes bustling up and down, and hits on extraordinary discoveries. —Ralph Waldo Emerson, "Cockayne," *English Traits*, 1856

There are no signposts in the sky to show a man has passed that way before. There are no channels marked. The flier breaks each second into new uncharted seas. —Anne Morrow Lindbergh, *North to the Orient*, 1935

"I was a-trembling, because I'd got to decide, forever, betwixt two things, and I knowed it. I studied a minute, sort of holding my breath, and then says to myself, "All right, then, I'll GO to hell.""

—Mark Twain, *The Adventures of Huckleberry Finn,* 1885

I feel about airplanes the way I feel about diets. It seems to me that they are wonderful things for other people to go on. —Jean Kerr, *The Snake Has All the Lines*, 1958

Writing and travel broaden your ass if not your mind and I like to write standing up. —Ernest Hemingway, letter (1950), *Selected Letters*, Carlos Baker, ed., 1981

The fabric of my faithful love / No power shall dim or ravel / Whilst I stay here—but oh, my dear, / If I should ever travel! —Edna St. Vincent Millay, "To the Not Impossible Him," *A Few Figs from Thistles*, 1920

Life on board a pleasure steamer violates every moral and physical condition of healthy life except fresh air …. It is a guzzling, lounging, gambling, dog's life. The only alternative to excitement is irritability. —George Bernard Shaw, letter (1899), *Collected Letters*, 1972

Traveling is a fool's paradise. Our first journeys discover to us the indifference of places. —Ralph Waldo Emerson, "Self-Reliance," *Essays: First Series*, 1841

I am not much an advocate for traveling, and I observe that men run away to other countries because they are not good in their own, and run back to their own because they pass for nothing in the new places. —Ralph Waldo Emerson, "Culture," *The Conduct of Life*, 1860

If you don't know where you're going, you'll wind up somewhere else. —Yogi Berra, "Yogi-isms," yogiberra.com

Forget Takeout! 15

Whether you're cooking up a storm for a special occasion or taking it easy and dining out, food is a major occasion for everyone at some time. For some people, it's a major occasion all the time! From gustatory pleasures to dietary concerns, from choosing fine wines to having a drop too much, one of the quotes that follows should taste just right.

• • •

Without such a thing as fast food there would be no need for slow food .... —Michael Pollan, *The Omnivore's Dilemma*, 2006

> She is convinced there is no civilization without bialys, a bialy being a sort of Brooklyn tortilla.
> —Molly Ivins, column, *The Texas Observer* (Austin), 1977

Why does man kill? He kills for food. And not only food—frequently, there must be a beverage. —Woody Allen, *Jokes*, Getlen

But the fruit that will fall without shaking, / Indeed is too mellow for me. —Mary Wortley Montagu, "To a Lady Making Love; or, answered for Lord Hamilton," *Poetical Works*, 1768

As life's pleasures go, food is second only to sex. Except for salami and eggs. Now that's better than sex, but only if the salami is thickly sliced. —Alan King, stand-up routine

It's a lot easier to slap a health claim on a box of sugary cereal than on a potato or carrot, with the perverse result that the most healthful foods in the supermarket sit there quietly in the produce section, silent as stroke victims, while a few aisles over, the Cocoa Puffs and Lucky Charms are screaming about their newfound whole-grain goodness. —Michael Pollan, "Unhappy Meals," *The New York Times Magazine* (New York), 2007

Who has told you that the fruit belies the flower? For the fruit you have not tasted, and the flower you know but by report. —Murasaki Shikibu, *The Diary of Murasaki Shikibu*, c. 994–1010

Oats—A grain which in England is generally given to horses, but in Scotland supports the people. —Samuel Johnson, *A Dictionary of the English Language*, 1755

I do not like green eggs and ham. / I do not like them Sam I Am. —Dr. Seuss, *Green Eggs and Ham*, 1960

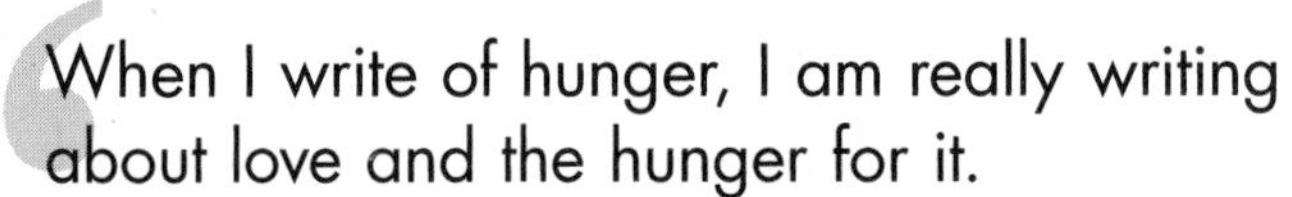

"When I write of hunger, I am really writing about love and the hunger for it.
—M. F. K. Fisher, *The Gastronomical Me*, 1943"

Having someone else peel your potatoes can be habit-forming. —Letty Cottin Pogrebin, *Deborah, Golda, and Me*

A hungry man is not a free man. —Adlai Stevenson, speech (Kasson, Minnesota), 1952

Ever notice on a box of cookies it says, "Open here." What do they think you're gonna do—move to Hong Kong to open their cookies? —George Carlin, *Jokes*, Getlen

Too many cooks may spoil the broth, but it only takes one to burn it. —Julia Child, quoted by Madeleine Bingham, *Something's Burning: The Bad Cook's Guide*, 1968

Four of the five basic French sauces are certainly unknown even by name to half the population of France. —Alice B. Toklas, *The Alice B. Toklas Cook Book*, 1954

I read recipes the same way I read science fiction. I get to the end and think, "Well, that's not going to happen." —Rita Rudner, ritafunny.com, 2003

Usually one's cooking is better than one thinks it is. —Julia Child (with Alex Prud'homme), *My Life in France*, 2006

"I probably couldn't learn to cook creole food, anyway. It's too complicated." // "Sheeit. Ain't nothing but onions, green peppers and garlic. Put that in everything and you got creole food." —Maya Angelou, *Gather Together in My Name*, 1974

I hereby affirm my own right as a Jewish American feminist to make chicken soup, even though I sometimes take it out of a can. —Betty Friedan, quoted in *Tikkun*, 1988

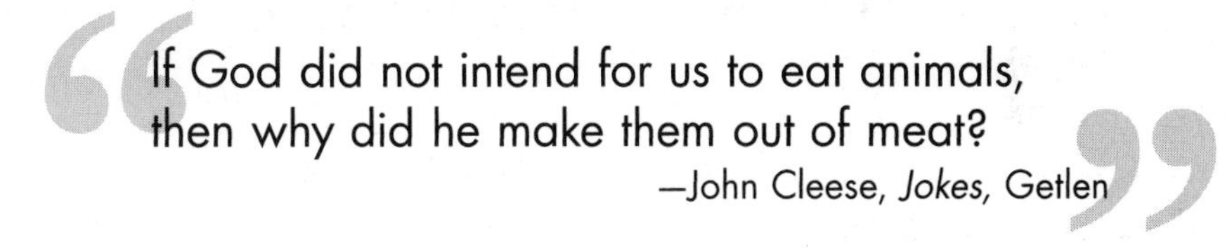

Remember, you are alone in the kitchen, and no one can see you. —Julia Child, "The French Chef" TV show

What is sauce for the goose may be sauce for the gander, but it is not necessarily sauce for the chicken, the duck, the turkey, or the guinea hen. —Alice B. Toklas, *The Alice B. Toklas Cook Book*, 1954

A cookbook is only as good as its worst recipe. —Julia Child, quoted by Regina Schrambling, *The New York Times Book Review* (New York), 2004

This is a book for the servantless American cook who can be unconcerned on occasion with budgets, waistlines, time schedules, children's meals, the parent-chauffeur-den mother syndrome or anything else which might interfere with the enjoyment of producing something wonderful to eat. —Julia Child, *Mastering the Art of French Cooking*, 1983

Comparing the cooking of a dish to the painting of a picture, it has always seemed to me that however much the cook or painter did to cover any weakness would not in the least avail. Such devices would only emphasize the weakness. —Alice B. Toklas, *The Alice B. Toklas Cook Book*, 1954

The best doctors in the world are Dr Diet, Dr Quiet, and Dr Merryman. —Jonathan Swift, *Polite Conversation*, 1738

Diets, like clothes, should be tailored to you. —Joan Rivers, quoted in *Los Angeles Times* (Los Angeles), 1974

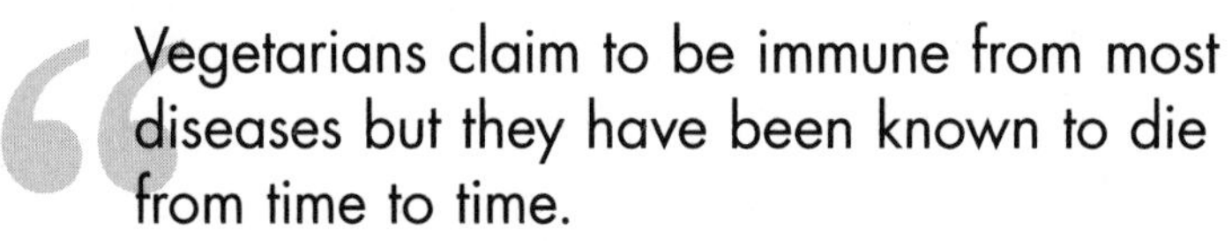

Vegetarians claim to be immune from most diseases but they have been known to die from time to time.

—George Bernard Shaw, quoted by Hesketh Pearson, *George Bernard Shaw: His Life and Personality,* 1942

One farmer says to me, "You cannot live on vegetable food solely, for it furnishes nothing to make bones with"; and so he religiously devotes a part of his day to supplying his system with the raw material of bones; walking all the while he talks behind his oxen, which, with vegetable-made bones, jerk him and his lumbering plow along in spite of every obstacle. —Henry David Thoreau, *Walden*, 1854

She's got this real funny idea about a diet: you don't get fat if no one sees you eating. —Gloria Naylor, *Linden Hills*, 1985

I'm so compulsive about losing weight, I weigh myself after I cough. —Elayne Boosler, *Women in Comedy*, Martin

Upscale people are fixated with food simply because they are now able to eat so much of it without getting fat, and the reason they don't get fat is that they maintain a profligate level of calorie expenditure. The very same people whose evenings begin with melted goats cheese … get up at dawn to run, break for a mid-morning aerobics class, and watch the evening news while racing on a stationary bicycle. —Barbara Ehrenreich, "Food Worship," *The Worst Years of Our Lives*, 1991

It is wonderful, if we choose the right diet, what an extraordinary small quantity would suffice. —Mohandas Gandhi, quoted by D. G. Tendulkar, *Mahatma*, 1960

I have found it to be the most serious objection to coarse labors long continued, that they compelled me to eat and drink coarsely also. —Henry David Thoreau, *Walden*, 1854

"'Tis an ill cook that cannot lick his own fingers.
—William Shakespeare, *Romeo and Juliet*, 1594"

"How long does getting thin take?" Pooh asked anxiously. —A. A. Milne, *Winnie the Pooh*, 1926

Give me a dozen such heart-breaks, if that would help me to lose a couple of pounds. —Colette, *Cheri*, 1920

'Tis a superstition to insist on a special diet. All is made at last of the same chemical atoms. —Ralph Waldo Emerson, *The Conduct of Life*, 1860

I have no doubt that it is a part of the destiny of the human race, in its gradual improvement, to leave off eating animals, as surely as the savage tribes have left off eating each other when they came in contact with the more civilized. —Henry David Thoreau, *Walden*, 1854

A man of my spiritual intensity does not eat corpses. —George Bernard Shaw, quoted by Hesketh Pearson, *George Bernard Shaw: His Life and Personality*, 1942

Learn how to cook! That's the way to save money. You don't save it buying hamburger helpers, and prepared food; you save it buying fresh foods in season or in large supply, when they are cheapest and usually best, and you prepare them from scratch at home. Why pay for someone else's work, when if you know how to do it, you can save all that money for yourself? —Julia Child, *Julia Child's Kitchen*, 1975

Burning dinner is not incompetence but war. —Marge Piercy, "What's That Smell in the Kitchen?" *Stone, Paper, Knife*, 1983

A man can live and be healthy without killing animals for food; therefore, if he eats meat, he participates in taking animal life merely for the sake of his appetite. And to act so is immoral. —Leo Tolstoy, *Writings on Civil Disobedience and Nonviolence*, 1987

> "But, lady, as women, what wisdom may be ours if not the philosophies of the kitchen? … I often say, when observing these trivial details: had Aristotle prepared victuals, he would have written more."
>
> —Juana Inés de la Cruz, "Reply to Sister Philotea: 1691," *A Woman of Genius*, Margaret Sayers Peden, tr., 1982

It is my view that the vegetarian manner of living by its purely physical effect on the human temperament would most beneficially influence the lot of mankind. —Albert Einstein, letter, quoted in *Vegetarian Watch-Tower*, 1930

Sharing food with another human being is an intimate act that should not be indulged in lightly. —M. F. K. Fisher, *An Alphabet for Gourmets*, 1949

There is a communion of more than our bodies when bread is broken and wine is drunk. And that is my answer when people ask me: Why do you write about hunger, and not wars or love? —M. F. K. Fisher, quoted by Mimi Sheraton, *Time* (New York), 1987

To a waitress in a restaurant: I didn't squawk about the steak, dear. I merely said I didn't see that old horse that used to be tethered outside here. —W. C. Fields, *Never Give a Sucker an Even Break*, 1941

Bread that must be sliced with an ax is bread that is too nourishing. —Fran Lebowitz, "Food for Thought and Vice Versa," *Metropolitan Life*, 1978

Can one be inspired by rows of prepared canned meals? Never. One must get nearer to creation to be able to create, even in the kitchen. —Alice B. Toklas, *The Alice B. Toklas Cook Book*, 1954

From supper to bedtime is twice as long as from breakfast to supper. —Edna Ferber, *Roast Beef, Medium*, 1911

He showed me his bill of fare to tempt me to dine with him; said I, I value not your bill of fare, give me your bill of company. —Jonathan Swift, *Journal to Stella*, 1711

An empty stomach is not a good political adviser. —Albert Einstein, attributed

Tell me what you eat, and I shall tell you what you are. —M. F. K. Fisher, quoted by Michiko Kakutani, *The New York Times Book Review* (New York), 1983

Part of the secret of success in life is to eat what you like and let the food fight it out inside. —Mark Twain, attributed

After a good dinner one can forgive anybody, even one's own relations. —Oscar Wilde, *A Woman of No Importance*, 1893

It's a scientific fact that your body will not absorb cholesterol if you take it from another person's plate.

—Dave Barry, *Jokes*, Getlen

He who distinguishes the true savor of his food can never be a glutton; he who does not cannot be otherwise. —Henry David Thoreau, attributed

What a nuisance! Why should one have to eat? And what shall we eat this evening? —Colette, *My Mother's House*, 1922

There is small danger of being starved in our land of plenty; but the danger of being stuffed is imminent. —Sara Josepha Hale, *Traits of American Life*, 1835

One of the stupidest things in an earnest but stupid school of culinary thought is that each of the three daily meals should be "balanced." Of course, where countless humans are herded together, as in military camps or schools or prisons, it is necessary to strike what is ironically called the happy medium. In this case, what kills the least number with the most ease is the chosen way. —M. F. K. Fisher, *How to Cook a Wolf*, 1942

Indigestion is charged by God with enforcing morality on the stomach. —Victor Hugo, *Les Misérables*

One cannot think well, love well, sleep well, if one has not dined well. —Virginia Woolf, *A Room of One's Own*, 1929

I'm willing to eat animals without faces, such as mollusks, on the theory that they're not sufficiently sentient to suffer. No, this isn't "facist" of me …. —Michael Pollan, *The Omnivore's Dilemma*, 2006

How easy for those who do not bulge / To not overindulge! —Ogden Nash, "A Necessary Dirge," *I'm a Stranger Here Myself*, 1938

A crust eaten in peace is better than a banquet partaken in anxiety. —Aesop, "The Town Mouse and the Country Mouse," *Fables*

We never repent of having eaten too little. —Thomas Jefferson, "A Decalogue of Canons for Observation in Practical Life," 1825

One must eat to live, and not live to eat. —Molière, *L'Avare*, 1668

Malt does more than Milton can / To justify God's ways to man. —A. E. Houseman, No. 62, *A Shropshire Lad*, 1896

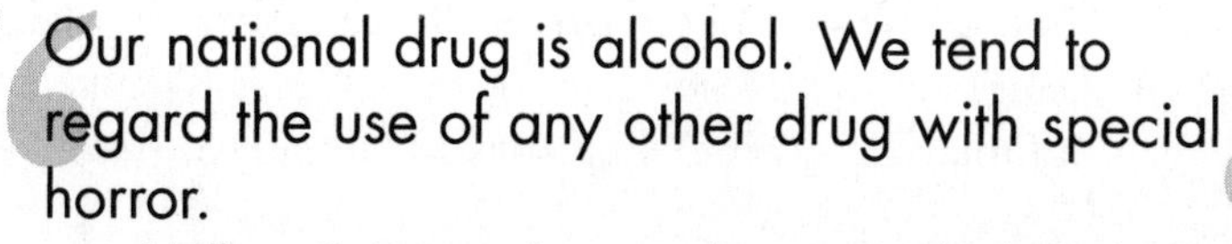

> Our national drug is alcohol. We tend to regard the use of any other drug with special horror.
>
> —William S. Burroughs, introduction, *Naked Lunch*, 1959

Claret is the liquor for boys; port for men; but he who aspires to be a hero must drink brandy. —Samuel Johnson, quoted by James Boswell, *The Life of Samuel Johnson*, 1791

O thou invisible spirit of wine, if thou hast no name / to be known by, let us call thee devil. —William Shakespeare, *Othello*, 1604

Give an Irishman lager for a month, and he's a dead man. An Irishman is lined with copper, and the beer corrodes it. But whiskey polishes the copper and is the saving of him, sir. —Mark Twain, *Life on the Mississippi*, 1883

Scientists announced that they have located the gene for alcoholism. They found it at a party, talking way too much. —Conan O'Brien, *Jokes*, Getlen

Better belly burst than good liquor be lost. —Jonathan Swift, *Polite Conversation*, 1738

Don't you hate people who drink white wine? I mean, my dear, every alcoholic in town is getting falling-down drunk on white wine. They think they aren't drunks because they only drink wine. Never, never trust anyone who asks for white wine. It means they're phonies. —Bette Davis, quoted by Dotson Rader, *Parade* (New York), 1983

> Even though a number of people have tried, no one has yet found a way to drink for a living.
> —Jean Kerr, *Poor Richard,* 1963

You know, my Friends, with what a brave Carouse / I made a Second Marriage in my house; / Divorced old barren Reason from my Bed, / And took the Daughter of the Vine to Spouse. —Omar Khayyám, "The Rubáiyát of Omar Khayyám," Edward FitzGerald, tr., 1859

Candy / Is Dandy / But liquor / Is quicker.—Ogden Nash, "Reflections on Ice-Breaking," *Hard Lines*, 1931

> Wine makes a man more pleased with himself. I do not say that it makes him more pleasing to others.
> —Samuel Johnson, quoted by James Boswell, *The Life of Samuel Johnson,* 1791

Ale, man, ale's the stuff to drink / For fellows whom it hurts to think. —A. E. Houseman, No. 62, *A Shropshire Lad*, 1896

I believe, if we take habitual drunkards as a class, their heads and their hearts will bear an advantageous comparison with those of any other class. There seems ever to have been a proneness in the brilliant and warm-blooded to fall into this vice. —Abraham Lincoln, speech, Washingtonian Temperance Society (Springfield, Illinois), 1842

Abstainer, n. A weak person who yields to the temptation of denying himself a pleasure. —Ambrose Bierce, *The Devil's Dictionary*, 1906

Good Times

Everyone likes to have a good time—and everyone's idea of a good time is different: fishing, golf, partying, dancing, loafing. Sometimes we need to remind others to go out (or stay in) and have some fun. Or thank them for having made fun for us. A quick quip shows your appreciation of what's to come, or what's been done.

• • •

You can have it all. You just can't have it all at once. —Oprah Winfrey, attributed

What are the means and the causes that lead a man into a merry spirit! Truly, in my best judgment, it seems that there are good sports and honest games in which a man takes pleasure without any repentance afterward. —Juliana Berners, *The Treatise of Fishing With an Angle*, 1496

> “When life hands you lemons, make whisky sours.”
>
> —W. C. Fields, radio show

Nothing is so good as it seems beforehand. —George Eliot, *Silas Marner*, 1861

Life is like a mirror. Smile at it and it smiles back at you. —Peace Pilgrim, *Her Life and Work*

… in recent years it has sometimes seemed that [sports] officials might as well simply hang a calculator around the neck of the winner. —Anna Quindlen, column, *The New York Times* (New York), 1993

I think most people think I am like the mother of modern sports … I happened to come along at a time when the world was ready for some change. —Billie Jean King, interview with Barbara Walters, *ABC News* (New York), 1999

Karate is a form of martial arts in which people who have had years and years of training can, using only their hands and feet, make some of the worst movies in the history of the world. —Dave Barry, *Jokes*, Getlen

The motto of professional athletics has been clear for some time—it isn't how you play the game, it's whether you win. —Anna Quindlen, column, *The New York Times* (New York), 1993

If you watch a game, it's fun. If you play it, it's recreation. If you work at it, it's golf. —Bob Hope, quoted in *Reader's Digest* (Pleasantville, New York), 1958

> When a man wants to murder a tiger, he calls it sport; when a tiger wants to kill him, he calls it ferocity.
>
> —George Bernard Shaw, "Maxims for Revolutionists," *Man and Superman*, 1903

When one is hunting, the air has another, more exquisite feel as it glides over the skin or enters the lungs, the rocks acquire a more expressive physiognomy, and the vegetation becomes loaded with meaning. —José Ortega y Gassett, *Meditations on Hunting*, Howard B. Westcott, tr., 1972

No humane being, past the thoughtless age of boyhood, will wantonly murder any creature which holds its life by the same tenure that he does. —Henry David Thoreau, *Walden*, 1854

I will now choose among four good sports and honorable pastimes—to whit, among hunting, hawking, fishing and fowling. The best, in my simple judgment, is fishing, called angling, with a rod and a line and a hook. —Juliana Berners, *The Treatise of Fishing With an Angle*, 1496

Fishing is boring, unless you catch an actual fish—then it is disgusting. —Dave Barry, *Jokes*, Getlen

Fly fishing may be a very pleasant amusement; but angling or float fishing I can only compare to a stick and a string, with a worm at one end and a fool at the other. —Samuel Johnson, quoted by Peter Hawker, *Instructions to Young Sportsmen*, 1824

Fishing … is a sport invented by insects and you are the bait. —P. J. O'Rourke, *Republican Party Reptile*, 1987

Exercise is the yuppie version of bulimia. —Barbara Ehrenreich, "Food Worship," *The Worst Years of Our Lives*, 1991

> My candle burns at both its ends; / It will not last the night; / But oh, my foes, and oh, my friends / It gives a lovely light.
>
> —Edna St. Vincent Millay, "First Fig," *A Few Figs from Thistles*, 1920

"A desire to have all the fun," he says, "is nine-tenths of the law of chivalry." —Dorothy L. Sayers, *Gaudy Night*, 1936

There is no such thing as "fun" for the whole family. —Jerry Seinfeld, stand-up routine

… fun was all the truth we needed. —Eve Babitz, *Black Swans*, 1993

Everything that's fun in life is dangerous. —P. J. O'Rourke, *Republican Party Reptile*, 1987

Pleasure is very seldom found where it is sought. Our brightest blazes of gladness are commonly kindled by unexpected sparks. —Samuel Johnson, No. 58, *The Idler*, 1759

Pleasure that isn't paid for is as insipid as everything else that's free. —Anita Loos, *Kiss Hollywood Good-by*, 1974

Here with a Loaf of Bread beneath the Bough, / A Flask of Wine, a Book of Verse—and Thou / Beside me singing in the Wilderness. —Omar Khayyám, "The Rubáiyát of Omar Khayyám," Edward FitzGerald, tr., 1859

It's true Heaven forbids some pleasures, but a compromise can usually be found. —Molière, *Tartuffe*, 1664

One way of getting an idea of our fellow-countrymen's miseries is to go and look at their pleasures. —George Eliot, *Felix Holt, The Radical*, 1866

My advice to you is not to inquire why or whither, but just enjoy your ice cream while it's on your plate—that's my philosophy. —Thornton Wilder, *The Skin of Our Teeth*, 1942

It is better to have loafed and lost, than never to have loafed at all. —James Thurber, *Fables for Our Time*, 1940

Cut if you will, with Sleep's dull knife, / Each day to half its length, my friend,— / The years that time takes off my life, / He'll take from off the other end! —Edna St. Vincent Millay, "Midnight Oil," *A Few Figs from Thistles*, 1920

How pleasant to sit on the beach, / On the beach, on the sand, in the sun, / With ocean galore within reach, / And nothing at all to be done! —Ogden Nash, "Pretty Halcyon Days"

I don't generally feel anything until noon, then it's time for my nap. —Bob Hope, quoted in *The International Herald Tribune* (Paris), 1990

> "They exchanged one or two universal if minor truths—pleasure was so often more exhausting than the hardest work ...."
> —Katherine Anne Porter, *Ship of Fools*, 1962

Business was his aversion; pleasure was his business. —Maria Edgeworth, *The Contrast*, 1801

You do too much. Go and do nothing for a while. Nothing. —Lillian Hellman, *Toys in the Attic*, 1959

There can be no education without leisure, and without leisure education is useless. —Sarah Josepha Hale, *Godey's Lady's Book*, 1837–1877

Horse sense is the thing a horse has which keeps it from betting on people. —W. C. Fields, *Never Give a Sucker an Even Break*, 1941

Tango is such torture that I was glad to discover the Texas two-step, which was much more fun. —Eve Babitz, interview with Ron Hogan, *Beatrice Interview*, 2000

The Oscars is really I guess the one night of the year when you can see all your favorite stars without having to donate any money to the Democratic Party. —Jon Stewart, Academy Awards presentation, 2006

Show business is the best possible therapy for remorse. —Anita Loos, *Kiss Hollywood Good-by*, 1974

One cannot have too large a party. A large party secures its own amusement. —Jane Austen, *Emma*, 1815

Hostesses who entertain much must make up their parties as ministers make up their cabinets, on grounds other than personal liking. —George Eliot, *Daniel Deronda*, 1874–1876

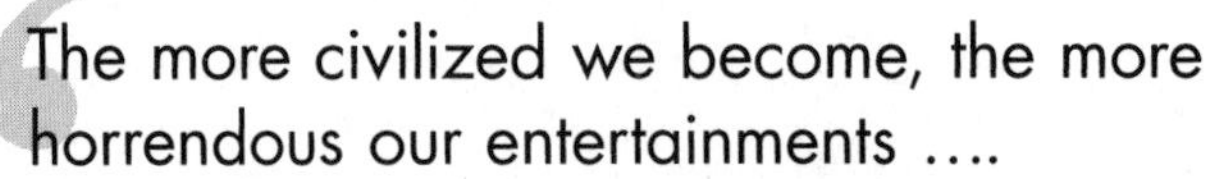

> The more civilized we become, the more horrendous our entertainments ....
>
> —Gregory Maguire, *Wicked*, 1995

Last year my husband decided a mere television was no longer enough for us. We needed surround sound. It was imperative we go into immediate debt over two side-speakers, a center speaker, and a subwoofer. A man who doesn't listen to anything I say wanted to hear strangers talk to him from four different angles. —Rita Rudner, "Speaker of the House," ritafunny.com, 2003

If I'd taken my doctor's advice and quit smoking when he advised me to, I wouldn't have lived to go to his funeral. —George Burns, interview with Arthur Marx, *Cigar Aficionado* (New York), 1994

A woman is an occasional pleasure but a cigar is always a smoke. —Groucho Marx, *A Day at the Races*, 1937

There's nothing quite like tobacco: it's the passion of decent folk, and whoever lives without tobacco doesn't deserve to live. —Molière, *Don Juan*, 1665

Our nation has withstood many divisions—North and South, black and white, labor and management—but I do not know if the country can survive division into smoking and non-smoking sections. —P. J. O'Rourke, *Republican Party Reptile*, 1987

Once … in the wilds of Afghanistan, I lost my corkscrew, and we were forced to live on nothing but food and water for days. —W. C. Fields, *My Little Chickadee*, 1940

You know a little drink now and then never hurt nobody, but when you can't git started without asking the bottle, you in trouble. —Alice Walker, *The Color Purple*, 1982

> I love to drink Martinis, / Two at the very most / Three, I'm under the table; / Four, I'm under the host.
>
> —Dorothy Parker, *The New Yorker*

I exercise extreme self control. I never drink anything stronger than gin before breakfast. —W. C. Fields, *His Follies and Fortunes*, Taylor drinking

When I was in England I experimented with marijuana a time or two—and didn't like it—and didn't inhale and never tried inhaling again. —Bill Clinton, TV interview, quoted in *The New York Times* (New York), 1992

The seven dwarfs were each on different little trips. Happy was into grass and grass alone … Sleepy was into reds. Grumpy. Too much speed. Sneezy was a full blown coke freak. Doc was a connection. Dopey was into everything. Any old orifice will do for Dopey. He's always got his arm out and his leg up. And then, the one we always forget, because he was, Bashful. Bashful didn't use drugs. He was paranoid on his own. Didn't need any help on that ladder. —George Carlin, "Nursery Rhymes," *Toledo Window Box*, 1974

Drugs are very much a part of professional sports today, but when you think about it, golf is the only sport where the players aren't penalized for being on grass. —Bob Hope, stand-up routine

Chemically induced hallucinations, delusions and raptures may be frightening or wonderfully gratifying; in either case they are in the nature of confidence tricks played on one's own nervous system. —Arthur Koestler, "Return Trip to Nirvana," article in *The Sunday Telegraph* (London), 1967

… products that people really want need no hard-sell or soft-sell TV push. / Why not? / Look at pot. —Ogden Nash, "Most Doctors Recommend or Yours for Fast Fast Fast Relief," *The Old Dog Barks Backwards*, 1972

Jamaica. They would never make an Atomic Bomb; they may make an Atomic Bong. But I'd rather fight a war with an Atomic Bong. Cuz when the Atomic Bomb goes off there's devastation and radiation. When the Atomic Bong goes off there's celebration! —Robin Williams, *Live On Broadway*, 2002

> Every generation finds the drug it needs.
> —P. J. O'Rourke, *Republican Party Reptile*, 1987

… I used to think that communing with nature was a healing, positive thing. Now, I think I'd like to commune with other things—like room service and temperature control. —Roseanne Barr, *My Life as a Woman*, 1989

Travel is fatal to prejudice, bigotry, and narrow-mindedness, and many of our people need it sorely on these accounts. —Mark Twain, *The Innocents Abroad*, 1869

It is true that when we travel we are in search of distance. But distance is not to be found. It melts away. And escape has never led anywhere. —Antoine de Saint-Exupéry, *Flight to Arras*, 1942

But travel is by no means a prerequisite to getting lost. —Eve Ensler, *Insecure At Last*, 2006

Travel broadens, they say. My personal experience has been that, in the short term at any rate, it merely flattens, aiming its steam-roller of deadlines and details straight at one's daily life, leaving a person flat and gasping at its passage. —Laurie R. King, *The Game*, 2004

Being abroad makes you conscious of the whole imitative side of human behavior. The ape in man. —Mary McCarthy, "Epistle from Mother Carey's Chicken," *Birds of America*, 1965

I have found out that there ain't no surer way to find out whether you like people or hate them than to travel with them. —Mark Twain, *Tom Sawyer Abroad*, 1894

> To put it rather bluntly, I am not the type who wants to go back to the land; I am the type who wants to go back to the hotel.
>
> —Fran Lebowitz, *Social Studies,* 1981

Have people lost their minds? Can someone possibly think that sitting out on a stinking, floating Vegas hotel for five days, running into the same people all day, could be interpreted as a vacation? —Sandra Bernhard, *May I Kiss You on the Lips, Miss Sandra?*, 1998

Get your own entry in an encyclopedia. In the media age, everybody was famous for 15 minutes. In the Wikipedia age, everybody can be an expert in five minutes. Special bonus: You can edit your own entry to make yourself seem even smarter. —Stephen Colbert, quoted in *Wired* (San Francisco), 2006

> "Pleasing for a moment," said Helen, smiling, "is of some consequence; for, if we take care of the moments, the years will take care of themselves, you know."
>
> —Maria Edgeworth, *Mademoiselle Panache,* 1795

We have belittled the son of man by giving him foolish and degrading toys, a world of idleness where he is suffocated by a badly conceived discipline. —Maria Montessori, *The Montessori Method*, Anne Everett George, tr., 1912

One half of the world cannot understand the pleasures of the other. —Jane Austen, *Emma*, 1816

Ah, make the most of what we yet may spend, / Before we too into the Dust descend. —Omar Khayyám, "The Rubáiyát of Omar Khayyám," Edward FitzGerald, tr., 1859

Laughter isn't even the other side of tears. It is tears turned inside out. —Alice Walker, *By the Light of My Father's Smile*, 1998

Drink, and dance and laugh and lie, / Love the reeling midnight through, / For tomorrow we shall die! / (But, alas, we never do.) —Dorothy Parker, "The Flaw in Paganism," 1936

Most people don't know how to have a good time, any more than spoiled children. I show them. I spend their money for them, and they're grateful for it. I've got nothing to lose, because I live by my wits. They can't take that away from me. —Edna Ferber, *Saratoga Trunk*, 1941

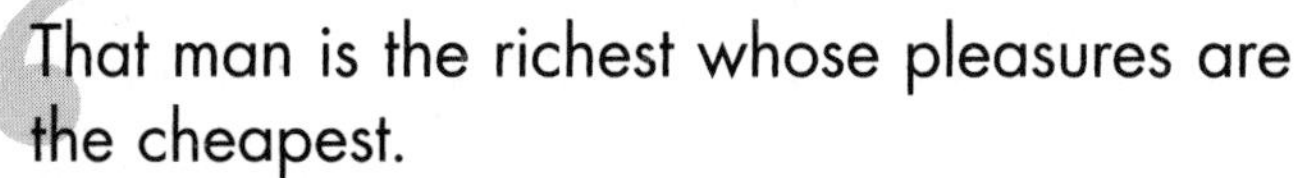

> That man is the richest whose pleasures are the cheapest.
>
> —Henry David Thoreau, journal entry, 11 March 1856

Those who try to make life one long holiday find that they need a holiday from that too. —George Bernard Shaw, *The Intelligent Woman's Guide to Socialism, Capitalism, Sovietism and Fascism*, 1928

There is only one way to achieve happiness / on this terrestrial ball, / And that is to have either a clear conscience, or none at all. —Ogden Nash, "Interoffice Memorandum," *I'm a Stranger Here Myself*, 1938

Happiness [is] prosperity combined with virtue. —Aristotle, *Rhetoric*, W. Rhys Roberts, tr., 1954

A large income is the best recipe for happiness I ever heard of. —Jane Austen, *Mansfield Park*, 1816

17 You Gotta Have Friends

Getting a note or card or email from a special friend for absolutely no reason other than to let that person how special she or he is to you is the best kind of note of all.

• • •

A friend may well be reckoned the masterpiece of nature. —Ralph Waldo Emerson, "Friendship," *Essays: First Series*, 1841

Friendless, adj. Having no favors to bestow. Destitute of fortune. Addicted to utterance of truth and common sense. —Ambrose Bierce, *The Devil's Dictionary*, 1906

Loneliness is never more cruel than when it is felt in close propinquity with someone who has ceased to communicate. —Germaine Greed, *The Female Eunuch*, 1971

"Are we not like the two volumes of one book?
—Marceline Desbordes-Valmore, *Memoirs*"

In answer to the query, "What is a friend?": A single soul dwelling in two bodies. —Aristotle, quoted by Diogenes Laertius, *Lives of Eminent Philosophers*

The truth is I now find that I have not the slightest pleasure in the society of any but a few indispensable friends. They must be people who really interest me, with whom I can talk seriously on serious subjects, and with whom I am brought into contact without effort on my side in the natural course of everyday existence. —Murasaki Shikibu, *The Diary of Murasaki Shikibu*, c. 994–1010

My true friends have always given me that supreme proof of devotion, a spontaneous aversion for the man I loved. —Colette, *Break of Day*, 1928

> I do not believe that friends are necessarily the people you like best, they are merely the people who got there first.
>
> —Peter Ustinov, *Dear Me*, 1977

The only reward of virtue is virtue; the only way to have a friend is to be one. —Ralph Waldo Emerson, "Friendship," *Essays: First Series*, 1841

Surely we ought to prize those friends on whose principles and opinions we may constantly rely—of whom we may say in all emergencies, "I know what they would think." —Hannah Farnham Lee, *The Log-Cabin; or, the World Before You*, 1844

… one may be my very good friend, and yet not of my opinion. —Margaret Cavendish, "Letter XVI," *Sociable Letters*, 1664

What a wretched lot of old shriveled creatures we shall be by-and-by. Never mind—the uglier we get in the eyes of others, the lovelier we shall be to each other; that has always been my firm faith about friendship. —George Eliot, letter, *George Eliot's Life as Related in Her Letters and Journals*, J. W. Cross, ed., 1885–1886

Your friend is the man who knows all about you, and still likes you. —Elbert Hubbard, *A Thousand and One Epigrams*, 1911

One friend in a lifetime is much, two are many, three are hardly possible. Friendship needs a certain parallelism of life, a community of thought, a rivalry of aim. —Henry Adams, *The Education of Henry Adams*, 1907

Best friend, my well-spring in the wilderness! —George Eliot, *The Spanish Gypsy*, 1868

A friend is a second self. —Aristotle, *Nicomachean Ethics*, c. 325 B.C.E.

Bloody noses had made them friends, but giving sound to the bruised places in their hearts made them brothers. —Gloria Naylor, *Linden Hills*, 1985

One can be a brother only *in* something. Where there is no tie that binds men, men are not united but merely lined up. —Antoine de Saint-Exupéry, *Flight to Arras*, 1942

> Four be the things I am wiser to know: / Idleness, sorrow, a friend, and a foe.
> —Dorothy Parker, "Inventory," *Enough Rope*, 1927

I don't have trouble with men. There are plenty of neurotic contemporaries of mine still around. —Selma Diamond, *Funny Women*, Unterbrink

Friendship is constant in all other things, / Save in the office and affairs of love. —William Shakespeare, *Much Ado About Nothing*, 1600

If a stranger taps you on the ass and says, "How's the little lady today!" you will probably cringe. But if he's an American, he's only being friendly. —Margaret Atwood, interview, *Conversations*, Earl G. Ingersoll, ed., 1990

A relationship, I think, is like a shark, you know? It has to constantly move forward or it dies. And I think what we got on our hands is a dead shark. —Woody Allen and Marshall Brickman, *Annie Hall*, 1977

No man can be friends with a woman he finds attractive. He always wants to have sex with her. Sex is always out there. Friendship is ultimately doomed and that is the end of the story. —Nora Ephron, *When Harry Met Sally*, 1989

A dog will stay stupid. That's why we love them so much. —Jerry Seinfeld, stand-up routine

Animals are such agreeable friends—they ask no questions, they pass no criticisms. —George Eliot, *Scenes of Clerical Life*, 1857

How sad it is that a turtle can live to 150, or a parrot can live as long as a human, but man's best friend can only live for a decade or two. With some things there's little justice. —Fran Drescher, *Cancer, Schmancer*, 2002

I think dogs are the most amazing creatures; they give unconditional love. For me they are the role model for being alive. —Gilda Radner, *It's Always Something*, 1989

> "Dogs are the leaders of the planet. If you see two life forms, one of them's making a poop, the other one's carrying it for him, who would you assume is in charge?"
>
> —Jerry Seinfeld, stand-up routine

Cats are intended to teach us that not everything in nature has a purpose. —Garrison Keillor, attributed

Then if my friendships break and bend, / There's little need to cry / The while I know that every foe / Is faithful till I die. —Dorothy Parker, "The Heel"

My friends, there are no friends. —Coco Chanel, quoted by Marcel Haedrich, *Coco Chanel, Her Life, Her Secrets*, 1971

To let friendship die away by negligence and silence, is certainly not wise. It is voluntarily to throw away one of the greatest comforts of this weary pilgrimage. —Samuel Johnson, quoted by James Boswell, *The Life of Samuel Johnson*, 1791

Now a Frende I have Founde / That I woll nother banne ne curse, / But of all frendes in felde or towne / Ever, gramercy, myn own purse. —Juliana Berners, "Song," *Boke of Saint Albans*, 1486

The holy passion of Friendship is of so sweet and steady and loyal and enduring a nature that it will last through a whole lifetime, if not asked to lend money. —Mark Twain, *Pudd'n'head Wilson*, 1894

Business, you know, may bring money, but friendship hardly ever does. —Jane Austen, *Emma*, 1815

A friend in power is a friend lost. —Henry Adams, *The Education of Henry Adams*, 1907

Misfortune shows those who are not really friends. —Aristotle, *Eudemian Ethics*, c. 325 B.C.E.

I've been barbecued, stewed, screwed, tattooed, and fried by people claiming to be my friends. The human race has gone backward, not forward, since the days we were apes swinging through the trees. —W. C. Fields, quoted by Carlotta Monti (with Cy Rice), *W. C. Fields & Me*, 1971

She is probably by this time as tired of me, as I am of her; but as she is too polite and I am too civil to say so, our letters are still as frequent and affectionate as ever, and our Attachment as firm and sincere as when it first commenced. —Jane Austen, *Lesley Castle*, 1792

Those whom we support hold us up in life. —Maria von Ebner Eschenbach, *Aphorisms*, 1905

> Everyone wants to ride with you in the limo, but what you need is someone who will take the bus with you when the limo breaks down.
> —Oprah Winfrey, attributed

I have no patience with anyone born after World War II. You have to explain *everything* to these people. —Selma Diamond, *Funny Women*, Unterbrink

It's very important when making a friend to check and see if they have a private plane. People think a good personality trait in a friend is kindness or a sense of humor. No, in a friend a good personality trait is a Gulfstream. —Fran Lebowitz, quoted in *Travel + Leisure* (New York), 1994

There's a kind of emotional exploration you plumb with a friend that you don't really do with your family. —Bette Midler, quoted by Tom Seligson, *Parade* (New York), 1989

Every time a man unburdens his heart to a stranger he reaffirms the love that unites humanity. —Germaine Greed, *The Female Eunuch*, 1971

Women are quite mad when it comes to hospitality. —Laurie R. King, *The Moor*, 1998

In a bad marriage, friends are the invisible glue. If we have enough friends, we may go on for years, intending to leave, talking about leaving—instead of actually getting up and leaving. —Erica Jong, "A Day in the Life …," *How to Save Your Own Life*, 1977

Grief can take care of itself; but to get the full value of a joy you must have somebody to divide it with. —Mark Twain, *Following the Equator*, 1897

Without friends no one would choose to live, though he had all other goods. —Aristotle, *Nicomachean Ethics*, c. 325 B.C.E.

> Sometimes people come into your life for a season and other times for a lifetime.
>
> —Fran Drescher, TV.com

There are very few honest friends—the demand is not particularly great. —Marie von Ebner-Eschenbach, *Aphorisms*, 1880–1905

Happy is the house that shelters a friend! —Ralph Waldo Emerson, "Friendship," *Essays: First Series*, 1841

> "My idea of good company, Mr. Elliot, is a company of clever, well-informed people, who have a great deal of conversation; that is what I call good company." // "You are mistaken," said he, gently, "that is not good company; that is the best."
>
> —Jane Austen, *Persuasion*, 1818

They cherish each other's hopes. They are kind to each other's dreams. —Henry David Thoreau, "Wednesday," *A Week on the Concord and Merrimack Rivers*, 1849

I think I have learned that the best way to lift one's self up is to help someone else. —Booker T. Washington, *The Story of My Life and Work*, vol. I, 1900

A friend I can trust is the one who will let me have my death. / The rest are actors who want me to stay and further the plot. —Adrienne Rich, untitled poem, *Poems: Selected and New (1950–1974)*, 1974

It is wise to apply the oil of refined politeness to the mechanism of friendship. —Colette, *Pure and the Impure*, 1933

Friends are self-elected. Reverence is a great part of it. —Ralph Waldo Emerson, "Friendship," *Essays: First Series*, 1841

> "Quarrel? Nonsense; we have not quarreled. If one is not to get into a rage sometimes, what is the good of being friends?"
>
> —George Eliot, *Middlemarch*, 1871–1872

Friends love misery, in fact. Sometimes, especially if we are too lucky or too successful or too pretty, our misery is the only thing that endears us to our friends. —Erica Jong, *How to Save your Own Life*, 1977

It is not time or opportunity that is to determine intimacy; it is disposition alone. Seven years would be insufficient to make some people acquainted with each other, and seven days are more than enough for others. —Jane Austen, *Sense and Sensibility*, 1811

When the sun shines on you, you see your friends. Friends are the thermometers by which one may judge the temperature of our fortunes. —Marguerite Blessington, *Commonplace Book*

Good friends, good books, and a sleepy conscience: this is the ideal life. —Mark Twain, 1898, *Mark Twain's Notebook*, Albert Bigelow Paine, ed., 1935

… that perfect tranquility of life, which is nowhere to be found but in retreat, a faithful friend, a good library …. —Aphra Behn, *The Lucky Mistake*, 1689

18 Yakkity-Yak, Please Talk Back

Often we let too much time drift between contacting someone we care about. Whether you go by Skype or cell phone, snail mail or e-mail, or even if you live in the same house, communication is essential to staying in touch. If you need to remind any overscheduled family members, taciturn friends, or long-lost relatives to keep in touch, you'll find help in this chapter.

• • •

Can we talk? —Joan Rivers, catchphrase

There are many tongues to talk, and but few heads to think. —Victor Hugo, *Les Misérables*, 1864

> It was hard to communicate with you. You were always communicating with yourself. The line was busy.
>
> —Jean Kerr, *Mary, Mary*, 1960

Transport of the mails, transport of the human voice, transport of flickering pictures—in this century as in others our highest accomplishments still have the single aim of bringing men together. —Antoine de Saint-Exupéry, *Wind, Sand, and Stars*, 1939

Well, people change and forget to tell each other. Too bad—causes so many mistakes. —Lillian Hellman, *Toys in the Attic*, 1959

I used to tell my husband that, if he could make *me* understand something, it would be clear to all the other people in the country. —Eleanor Roosevelt, "My Day," newspaper column, 1947

One true self speaks to another, using the language of the heart, and in that bond a person is healed. —Deepak Chopra, *Unconditional Life*, 1991

… the natural itch of talking and lying …. —Aphra Behn, *The Dutch Lover*, 1673

> The opposite of talking isn't listening. The opposite of talking is waiting.
>
> —Fran Lebowitz, "People," *Social Studies*, 1982

If only her brain worked as well as her jaws! —Colette, *Gigi*, 1944

It is not what we learn in conversation that enriches us. It is the elation that comes of swift contact with tingling currents of thought. —Agnes Repplier, "The Luxury of Conversation," *Compromises*, 1904

To be misunderstood even by those whom one loves is the cross and bitterness of life. —Henri-Frédéric Amiel, journal entry (1849), *Journal Intime*

Don't write anything you can phone. Don't phone anything you can talk. Don't talk anything you can whisper. Don't whisper anything you can smile. Don't smile anything you can nod. Don't nod anything you can wink. —Earl K. Long, advice to his older brother, Huey Long

Language is the source of misunderstandings. —Antoine de Saint-Exupéry, *The Little Prince*

Basil Fawlty to Manuel: Oh, I could spend the rest of my life having this conversation—look—please try to understand before one of us dies. —John Cleese, *Fawlty Towers*, 1975

Galinda didn't often stop to consider whether she believed in what she said or not; the whole point of conversation was *flow*. —Gregory Maguire, *Wicked*, 1995

... the more fools speak the more people will despise them. —Joanna Baillie, *The Trial*, 1798

Conversation is but carving! / Give no more to every guest / Than he's able to digest. —Jonathan Swift, *Polite Conversation*, 1738

Ultimately, the bond of all companionship, whether in marriage or friendship, is conversation. —Oscar Wilde, *De Profundis*, 1905

Brevity is the soul of wit. —William Shakespeare, *Hamlet*, 1600

> He's a wonderful talker, who has the art of telling you nothing in a great harangue.
> —Molière, *Le Misanthrope*, 1666

... one never discusses anything with anybody who can understand, one discusses things with people who cannot understand .... —Gertrude Stein, *Everybody's Autobiography*, 1937

'Tis better to be brief than tedious. —William Shakespeare, *Richard III*, 1592

I often quote myself. It adds spice to my conversation. —George Bernard Shaw, quoted in *Reader's Digest* (Pleasantville, New York), June 1943

Don't confuse being stimulating with being blunt. —Barbara Walters, *How to Talk with Practically Anybody About Practically Anything*, 1970

Conversation is the socializing instrument par excellence, and in its style one can see reflected the capacities of a race. —José Ortega y Gassett, *Invertebrate Spain*, 1922

A human being, Hastings, cannot resist the opportunity to reveal himself and express his personality which conversation gives him. Every time he will give himself away. —Agatha Christie, *The ABC Murders*, 1936

Table talk and lovers' talk equally elude the grasp; lovers' talk is clouds, table talk is smoke. —Victor Hugo, *Les Misérables*, 1864

… when a conversation becomes a monologue, poked along with tiny cattle-prod questions, it isn't a conversation any more. —Barbara Walters, *How to Talk with Practically Anybody About Practically Anything*, 1970

> "We have to face the fact that either all of us are going to die together or we are going to learn to live together and if we are to live together we have to talk."
>
> —Eleanor Roosevelt, quoted by A. David Gurewitsch, *The New York Times*, (New York), 1960

A good compromise … is like a good sentence; or a good piece of music. Everybody can recognize it. They say, "Huh. It works. It makes sense." —Barack Obama, quoted in *The New Yorker* (New York), 2004

Buffet, ball, banquet, quilting bee, / Wherever conversation's flowing, / Why must I feel it falls on me / To keep things going? —Phyllis McGinley, "Reflections at Dawn," *Times Three*, 1960

To use many words to communicate few thoughts is everywhere the unmistakable sign of mediocrity. To gather much thought into few words stamps the man of genius. —Arthur Schopenhauer, *Essays*

There can be no doubt that distrust of words is less harmful than unwarranted trust in them. —Václav Havel, acceptance address, Nobel Peace Prize (Stockholm), 1989

A flow of words is a sure sign of duplicity. —Honoré de Balzac, "Letters of Two Brides," *La Press*, 1841–1842

Words calculated to catch everyone may catch no one. —Adlai Stevenson, address, Democratic National Convention (Chicago), 1952

I read for the part of Elizabeth, the virgin queen. I thought they said they were looking for a virgin from Queens. Whatever, the only virgin in my house is the olive oil. —Fran Drescher, perfectpeople.com, 2003

I really do inhabit a system in which words are capable of shaking the entire structure of government, where words can prove mightier than ten military divisions. —Václav Havel, acceptance address, Nobel Peace Prize (Stockholm), 1989

The first principle of a free society is an untrammeled flow of words in an open forum. —Adlai Stevenson, interview, *The New York Times* (New York), 1962

Arguments are like fire-arms which a man may keep at home but should not carry about with him. —Samuel Butler, *Samuel Butler's Notebooks*, 1912

> "There is no good in arguing with the inevitable. The only argument available with an east wind is to put on your overcoat."
> —James Russell Lowell, *Democracy and Other Addresses,* 1887

Using insult instead of argument is the sign of a small mind .... —Laurie R. King, *O Jerusalem*, 1999

Many words have no legal meaning. Others have a legal meaning very unlike their ordinary meaning. For example, the word "daffy-down-dilly." It is a criminal libel to call a lawyer a "daffy-down-dilly." Ha! Yes, I advise you never to do such a thing. No, I certainly advise you *never* to do it. —Dorothy L. Sayers, *Unnatural Death*, 1955

The difficult part in an argument is not to defend one's opinion, but rather to know it. —André Maurois, quoted in *A Little Book of Aphorisms*, Frederic B. Wilcox, ed., 1947

I dislike arguments of any kind. They are always vulgar, and often convincing. —Oscar Wilde, *The Importance of Being Ernest*, 1895

There's no procrastination on TV. —John Irving, *The Fourth Hand*, 2001

Email has made sending regular mail such a chore. "Wait, I stick it in an envelope and now I gotta go outside? What am I, a triathelete?" —Jim Gaffigan, *Beyond the Pale*, 2006

Nowadays, when you get a handwritten letter in the mail you're like, "What? Has someone been kidnapped!?" "Well, I'm not opening it, it's probably filled with anthrax." —Jim Gaffigan, *Beyond the Pale*, 2006

A person who can write a long letter with ease, cannot write ill. —Jane Austen, *Pride and Prejudice*, 1813

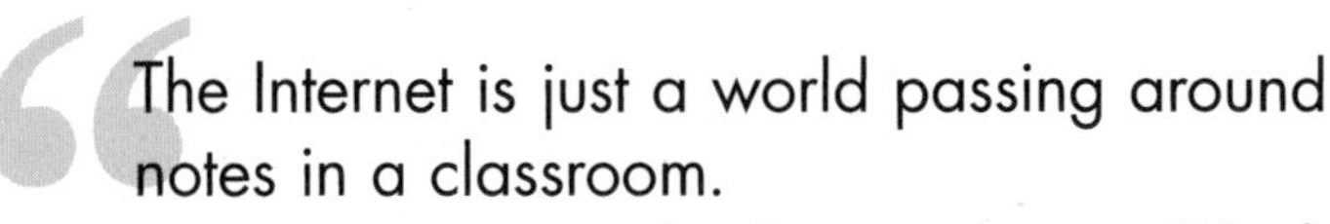

The Internet is just a world passing around notes in a classroom.

—Jon Stewart, interview, *Wired,* 2005

The Internet is not a rising tide, it's a tidal wave! —Bill Gates, attributed

The new electronic interdependence recreates the world in the image of a global village. —Marshall McLuhan, *Gutenberg Galaxy*, 1962

Languages never stand still. Modern spelling crystallizes lost pronunciations: the visual never quite catches up with the aural. —Anthony Burgess, *A Mouthful of Air*, 1992

We are tied down to a language which makes up in obscurity what it lacks in style. —Tom Stoppard, *Rosencrantz & Guildenstern Are Dead*, 1966

Did Cicero say anything? // Ay, he spoke Greek. // To what effect? // Nay … those that understood him smiled at one another, and shook their heads; but, for mine own part, it was Greek to me. —William Shakespeare, *Julius Caesar*, 1599

Language is power …. Language can be used as a means of changing reality. —Adrienne Rich, "Teaching Language in Open Admissions" (1972), *On Lies, Secrets, and Silence: Selected Prose 1966–1978*, 1979

In Paris they just simply opened their eyes and stared when we spoke to them in French! We never did succeed in making those idiots understand their own language. —Mark Twain, *The Innocents Abroad*, 1869

… slang … the home-made language of the ruled, not the rulers, the acted upon, the used, the used up. It is demotic poetry emerging in flashes of ironic insight. —Anthony Burgess, A *Mouthful of Air*, 1992

> Eloquence is the power to translate a truth into language perfectly intelligible to the person to whom you speak.
>
> —Ralph Waldo Emerson, "Eloquence," *Letters and Social Aims*, 1876

If one does not understand a person, one tends to regard him as a fool. —Carl Jung, *Mysterium Coniunctionis*, 1955

I love talking about nothing, father. It is the only thing I know anything about. —Oscar Wilde, *An Ideal Husband*, 1895

It is always observable that silence propagates itself, and that the longer talk has been suspended, the more difficult it is to find any thing to say. —Samuel Johnson, No. 85, *The Adventurer*, 1753

Silence is the universal refuge, the sequel to all dull discourses and all foolish acts, a balm to our every chagrin, as welcome after satiety as after disappointment …. —Henry David Thoreau, *A Week on the Concord and Merrimac Rivers*, 1849

Three Silences there are: the first of speech, / The second of desire, the third of thought. —Henry Wadsworth Longfellow, "The Three Silences of Molionos," 1878

We all arrive by different streets, / by unequal languages, at Silence. —Pablo Neruda, *Still Another Day*, William O'Daly, tr., 1984

The silence often of pure innocence persuades when speaking fails. —William Shakespeare, *The Winter's Tale*, 1610

> "In times like the present, men should utter nothing for which they would not willingly be responsible through time and in eternity."
> —Abraham Lincoln, *Second Annual Message to Congress* (Washington, D.C.), 1 December 1862

The saying is true, "The empty vessel makes the greatest sound." —William Shakespeare, *Henry V*, 1598

Politics and Poker 19

The singular act of voting makes us citizens of our government. Many of us go beyond that and are involved in the workings of our government at a local, state, national, or even international level. I call myself an armchair activist, signing online petitions, writing to my local and national representatives, composing letters to the editor. It can really help to have some handy-dandy quotes by persons of influence to illustrate one's point. Caveat: like many politicians, this chapter is a tad long-winded.

• • •

… one of the most important developments in modern politics has been the unprecedented phenomenon of masses of people organizing, not just against those who violently oppress them, but against the oppression of others—and even against the use of violence itself. —Riane Eisler, *Sacred Pleasure*, 1996

Agitators are a set of interfering, meddling people, who come down to some perfectly contented class of the community and sow the seeds of discontent amongst them. That is the reason why agitators are so absolutely necessary. Without them, in our incomplete state, there would be no advance towards civilisation. —Oscar Wilde, article in *The Fortnightly Review* (London), 1891

I am for keeping the thing going while things are stirring. Because if we wait till it is still, it will take a great while to get it going again. —Sojourner Truth, speech, American Equal Rights Association Convention, 1867

> Can there be a higher desire than to change the world? Not to draw Utopian blueprints, but really to order change? To revise the misshapen, reshape the mistaken, to justify the margins of this ragged error of a universe?
> —Gregory Maguire, *Wicked,* 1995

Every reform movement has a lunatic fringe. —Theodore "Teddy" Roosevelt, speech, *An Autobiography*, 1913

A society which is clamouring for choice, which is filled with many articulate groups, each urging its own brand of salvation, its own variety of economic philosophy, will give each new generation no peace until all have chosen or gone under, unable to bear the conditions of choice. —Margaret Mead, *Coming of Age in Samoa*, 1928

You may trod me in the very dirt / But still, like dust, I'll rise. —Maya Angelou, "Still I Rise," 1978

'Tis not enough to help the feeble up, / But to support him after. —William Shakespeare, *Timon of Athens*, 1607

Our responsibility is much greater than we might have supposed, because it involves all mankind. —Jean-Paul Sartre, *Existentialism and Human Emotions*, 1957

Nutopia has no land, no boundaries, no passports, only people. Nutopia has no laws other than cosmic. All people of Nutopia are ambassadors of the country. Citizenship of the country can be obtained by declaration of your awareness of Nutopia. —John Lennon and Yoko Ono, declaration, 1973

> Wall, childern, whar dar is so much racket dar must be somethin' out o' kilter.
> —Sojourner Truth, speech, Ohio Women's Rights Convention (Akron, 1851), *History of Women Suffrage,* Anthony

"You hate America, don't you?" she said. // "That would be as silly as loving it," I said. "It's impossible for me to get emotional about it, because real estate doesn't interest me. It's no doubt a great flaw in my personality, but I can't think in terms of boundaries. Those imaginary lines are as unreal to me as elves and pixies." —Kurt Vonnegut, *Mother Night*, 1961

The ballot is stronger than the bullet. —Abraham Lincoln, speech (Bloomington, Illinois), 1856

The fate of the country does not depend on ... what kind of paper you drop into the ballot-box once a year, but on what kind of man you drop from your chamber into the street every morning. —Henry David Thoreau, speech, "Slavery in Massachusetts" (Farmingham), 4 July 1854

The virtue of patriotism has been extolled most loudly and publicly by nations that are in the process of conquering others .... —W. H. Auden, *Forewords and Afterwords*, 1973

It requires philosophy and heroism to rise above the opinion of the wise men of all nations and races .... —Elizabeth Cady Stanton, *History of Woman Suffrage*, Anthony

Never do anything against conscience even if the state demands it. —Albert Einstein, quoted by Virgil Henshaw, *Albert Einstein: Philosopher Scientist*, 1949

"I will not cease from mental fight," Blake wrote. Mental fight means thinking against the current, not with it. The current flows fast and furious. It issues a spate of words from the loudspeakers and the politicians. —Virginia Woolf, article in *The New Republic* (Washington, D.C.), 1940

It is not always the same thing to be a good man and a good citizen. —Aristotle, *Nicomachean Ethics*, c. 325 B.C.E.

If every day a man takes orders in silence from an incompetent superior, if every day he solemnly performs ritual acts which he privately finds ridiculous … it still does not mean that he has entirely lost the use of one of the basic human senses, namely, the sense of humiliation. —Václav Havel, letter (1975), *Living in Truth*, 1986

Each of us is a citizen of a common planet, bound to a common destiny. So connected are we, that each of us has the power to be the eyes of the world, the voice of the world, the conscience of the world, or the end of the world. And as each one of us chooses, so becomes the world. —Dennis J. Kucinich, speech, House of Representatives (Washington, D.C.), 2002

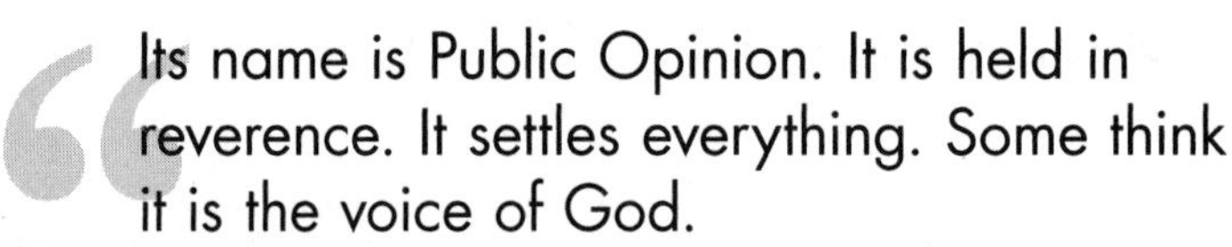

Its name is Public Opinion. It is held in reverence. It settles everything. Some think it is the voice of God.
—Mark Twain, "Europe and Elsewhere," *Corn Pone Opinions*, 1923

With public sentiment, nothing can fail; without it nothing can succeed. —Abraham Lincoln, first Lincoln-Douglas debate (Ottawa, Illinois), 1858

… public opinion is a giant which has frightened stouter-hearted Jacks on bigger beanstalks than hers. —Louisa May Alcott, *Little Women*, 1868

Standing up to your government can mean standing up for your country. —Bill Moyers, speech, National Conference for Media Reform (St. Louis), 2005

The victories that the 60's generation brought about … have made America a far better place for all its citizens. But what has been lost in the process, and has yet to be replaced, are those shared assumptions—that quality of trust and fellow feeling—that bring us together as Americans. —Barack Obama, *The Audacity of Hope*, 2006

We hold these truths to be self-evident, that all men are created equal; that they are endowed by their Creator with inherent and inalienable rights; that among these, are life, liberty, and the pursuit of happiness .... —Thomas Jefferson, Declaration of Independence (Philadelphia), 4 July 1776

We hold these truths to be self-evident: that all men and women are created equal .... // The history of mankind is a history of repeated injuries and usurpations on the part of man toward woman, having in direct object the establishment of an absolute tyranny over her. —Elizabeth Cady Stanton, Declaration of Sentiments, First Woman's Rights Convention (Seneca Falls, New York), 19 July 1848

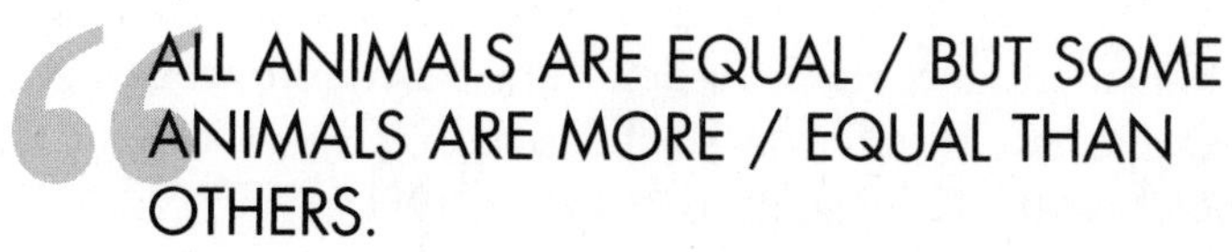

ALL ANIMALS ARE EQUAL / BUT SOME ANIMALS ARE MORE / EQUAL THAN OTHERS.

—George Orwell, *Animal Farm*, 1946

It is by the goodness of God that in our country we have those three unspeakably precious things: freedom of speech, freedom of conscience, and the prudence never to practice either. —Mark Twain, *Following the Equator*, 1897

... the authority of any governing institution must stop at its citizen's skin. —Gloria Steinem, "Night Thoughts of a Media-Watcher," *Ms.* (New York), November 1981

And what authority even the creases in a suit can convey. —Doris Lessing, *The Summer Before the Dark*, 1973

Every time a new nation...advances toward civilization, the human race perfects itself; every time an inferior class emerges from enslavement and degradation, the human race again perfects itself. —Germaine de Staël, *The Influence of Literature upon Society*, 1800

Civility is not a tactic or a sentiment. It is the determined choice of trust over cynicism, of community over chaos. —George W. Bush, *First Inaugural Address* (Washington, D.C.), 2001

It is impossible for one class to appreciate the wrongs of another. —Elizabeth Cady Stanton, *History of Woman Suffrage*, Anthony

Primitiveness and civilization are degrees of the same thing. If civilization has an opposite, it is war. Of these two things, you have either one, or the other. Not both. —Ursula K. Le Guin, *The Left Hand of Darkness*, 1969

More than any other time in history, mankind faces a crossroads. One path leads to despair and utter hopelessness. The other, to total extinction. Let us pray we have the wisdom to choose correctly. —Woody Allen, "My Speech to the Graduates," *Side Effects*, 1981

… another existence swallowed up in the fearful rush of what is called civilization, but is very like chaos. —Marceline Desbordes-Valmore, *Memoirs of Madame Desbordes-Valmore*, Sainte-Beuve

Civilization is the process of setting man free from men. —Ayn Rand, *The Fountainhead*, 1943

> "The … mass of mankind has not been born with saddles on their backs, nor a favored few booted and spurred, ready to ride them legitimately, by the grace of God."
>
> —Thomas Jefferson, letter to Roger C. Weightman, 24 June 1826.

You think we build a world; I think we leave / Only these tools, wherewith to strain and grieve. —Edna St. Vincent Millay, "Count them unclean …," *Huntsman, What Quarry?*, 1939

How do you feel about women's rights? I like either side of them. —Groucho Marx, www.Grouch-Marx.com, 2007

The Universal Declaration of Human Rights ... is the first code of ethical conduct that was not a product of one culture, or one sphere of civilization only, but a universal creation, shaped and subscribed to by representatives of all humankind. —Václav Havel, speech, 50th anniversary of the United Nations Universal Declaration of Human Rights (Prague), 1998

Declaration of Sentiments: Resolved: That the same amount of virtue, delicacy, and refinement of behavior that is required of woman in the social station, should also be required of man, and the same transgressions should be visited with equal severity on both man and woman. —Elizabeth Cady Stanton, *History of Woman Suffrage*, Anthony

Holy is the hand that works for peace and for justice, / holy is the mouth that speaks for goodness / holy is the foot that walks toward mercy. —Marge Piercy, interpretation of the She'ma, *The Art of Blessing the Day*, 1999

> "Den dat little man in black dar, he say women can't have as much rights as men, 'cause Christ wasn't a woman! ... Whar did your Christ come from? From God and a woman. Man had notin' to do wid Him."
>
> —Sojourner Truth, speech, Ohio Women's Rights Convention (Akron, 1851), *History of Women Suffrage*, Anthony

As a nation, we began by declaring that "all men are created equal." We now practically read it "all men are created equal, except negroes." When the Know-Nothings get control, it will read "all men are created equal, except negroes, and foreigners, and catholics." When it comes to this I should prefer emigrating to some country where they make no pretence of loving liberty—to Russia, for instance, where despotism can be taken pure, and without the base alloy of hypocracy [sic]. —Abraham Lincoln, letter to Joshua Speed, 24 August 1855

I was never so naïve or foolish as to think that if you merely believe in something it happens. You must struggle for it. —Golda Meir, quoted by Claire Price-Groff, *Twentieth-Century Women Political Leaders*, 1998

Every era of renaissance has come out of new freedoms for peoples. The coming renaissance will be greater than any in human history, for this time all the peoples of the earth will share in it. —Pearl S. Buck, *What America Means to Me*, 1942

I remember when I was a boy and I heard repeated time and time again the phrase, "My country, right or wrong, my country!" How absolutely absurd is such an idea. How absolutely absurd to teach this idea to the youth of the country. —Mark Twain, speech, "True Citizenship at the Children's Theater," 1907

When a whole nation is roaring Patriotism at the top of its voice, I am fain to explore the cleanness of its hands and purity of its heart. —Ralph Waldo Emerson, journal entry, 1824

Patriotism is the last refuge of a scoundrel. —Samuel Johnson (1775), quoted by James Boswell, *The Life of Samuel Johnson*, 1791

> Patriotism means to stand by the country. It does not mean to stand by the president or any other public official, save exactly to the degree in which he himself stands by the country.
>
> —Theodore "Teddy" Roosevelt, speech

My kind of loyalty was loyalty to one's country, not to its institutions or its officeholders … institutions are extraneous, they are its mere clothing, and clothing can wear out, become ragged, cease to be comfortable, cease to protect the body from winter, disease, and death. —Mark Twain, *A Connecticut Yankee in King Arthur's Court*, 1889

A nation that continues year after year to spend more money on military defense than on programs of social uplift is approaching spiritual death. —Martin Luther King Jr., sermon, Riverside Church (New York), 4 April 1967

A soldier is a yahoo hired to kill in cold blood as many of his own species, who have never offended him, as possibly he can. —Jonathan Swift, *Gulliver's Travels*, 1726

We had forgotten that wars were fought by babies. When I saw those freshly shaved faces, it was a shock. My God, my God—I said to myself, "It's the Children's Crusade." —Kurt Vonnegut, *Slaughterhouse-Five*, 1969

> "He had grown up in a country run by politicians who sent the pilots to man the bombers to kill the babies to make the world safe for children to grow up in."
>
> —Ursula K. Le Guin, *The Lathe of Heaven,* 1971

Because no battle is ever won, he said. They are not even fought. The field only reveals to man his own folly and despair, and victory is an illusion of philosophers and fools. —William Faulkner, *The Sound and the Fury*, 1929

I believe that man will not merely endure: he will prevail. He is immortal, not because he alone among creatures has an inexhaustible voice, but because he has a soul, a spirit capable of compassion and sacrifice and endurance. —William Faulkner, acceptance address, Nobel Prize in Literature (Stockholm), 10 December 1950

Is a shift from a system leading to chronic wars, social injustice, and ecological imbalance to one of peace, social justice, and ecological balance a realistic possibility? —Riane Eisler, *The Chalice and the Blade*, 1988

To punish me for my contempt of authority, Fate has made me an authority myself. —Albert Einstein, letter (1930), quoted by Banesh Hoffman and Helen Dukas, *Albert Einstein: Creator and Rebel*, 1988

The ability of a special interest group to secretly insert provisions into law for its own narrow benefit and to the detriment of the public interest raises fundamental questions about the integrity of our government. —Dennis J. Kucinich, quoted by Arianna Huffington, *Tribune Media Services*, 2002

Politics is about power: about who has it, how it is defined, and how it is exercised. —Riane Eisler, *Sacred Pleasure*, 1996

The pursuit of politics is religion, morality, and poetry all in one. —Germaine de Staël, quoted by J. Christopher Herold, *Mistress to an Age*, 1958

When he laughed, respectable senators burst with laughter, / And when he cried the little children died in the streets. —W. H. Auden, "Epitaph on a Tyrant," 1939

While I was sleeping in my bed in there, things were happening in this world that directly concerned me—and nobody asked me, consulted me—they just went out and did things—and changed my life. —Lorraine Hansberry, *A Raisin in the Sun*, 1958

> If you can't beat them, arrange to have them beaten.
>
> —George Carlin, *Jokes*, Getlen

The people always have some champion whom they set over them and nurse into greatness .... This and no other is the root from which a tyrant springs; when he first appears he is a protector. —Plato, *The Republic*

A tyrant must put on the appearance of uncommon devotion to religion. Subjects are less apprehensive of illegal treatment from a ruler whom they consider god-fearing and pious. —Aristotle, *Politics*

The ruling class isn't dissatisfied: they are healthy, well-fed, live in beauty, enjoy their own importance: fun-loving cannibals. —Marge Piercy, "The Grand Coolie Damn," Article in *Sisterhood Is Powerful*, Robin Morgan, ed., 1970

Morality must guide calculation, and calculation must guide politics. —Germaine de Staël, *The Influence of Literature upon Society*, 1800

The highest moral law is that we should unremittingly work for the good of mankind. —Mohandas Gandhi, *Ethical Religion*, 1930

Without freedom there can be no morality. —Carl Jung (1928), *Two Essays on Analytical Psychology*, R. F. C. Hull, tr., 1953

> If American politics are too dirty for women to take part in, there's something wrong with American politics.
>
> —Edna Ferber, *Cimarron*, 1929

We mean by "politics" the people's business—the most important business there is. —Adlai Stevenson, speech (Chicago), 1955

I am in politics because of the conflict between good and evil, and I believe that in the end good will triumph. —Margaret Thatcher, quoted in *The Guardian* (London), 1990

The Senate seems like the place where smart people go to die. —Jon Stewart, quoted by David Sirota, *The Nation* (New York), 2006

Persuasion is often more effectual than force. —Aesop, "The Wind and the Sun," *Fables*

In politics women … type the letters, lick the stamps, distribute the pamphlets and get out the vote. Men get elected. —Clare Boothe Luce, quoted in *Saturday Review/World* (New York), 1974

… the new women in politics seem to be saying that we already know how to lose, thank you very much. Now we want to learn how to win. —Gloria Steinem, quoted in *Ms.* (New York), 1974

To put a woman on the ticket would challenge the loyalty of women everywhere to their sex, because it would be made to seem that the defeat of the ticket meant the defeat for a hundred years of women's chance to be truly equal with men in politics. —Clare Boothe Luce, quoted in *New York World-Telegram* (New York), 1948

> Politics is supposed to be the second oldest profession. I have come to realize that it bears a very close resemblance to the first.
>
> —Ronald Reagan, remarks at a business conference (Los Angeles), 1977

Will Rogers … used to come out with a newspaper and pretend he was a yokel criticizing the intellectuals who ran the government. I come out with a newspaper and pretend I'm an intellectual making fun of the yokels running the government. —Mort Sahl, *American Masters*, PBS

Professional intellectuals are the voice of a culture and are, therefore, its leaders, its integrators and its bodyguards. —Ayn Rand, *For the New Intellectual*, 1961

No man should be in politics unless he would honestly rather not be there. —Henry Adams, letter to Henry Cabot Lodge, 1881

Whether elected or appointed / He considers himself the Lord's anointed, / And indeed the ointment lingers on him / So thick you can't get your fingers on him. —Ogden Nash, "The Politician," *I'm a Stranger Here Myself*, 1938

Washington could not tell a lie; Nixon could not tell the truth; Reagan cannot tell the difference. —Mort Sahl, *Jokes*, Getlen

A politician is a statesman who approaches every question with an open mouth. —Adlai Stevenson, quoted by Leon Harris, *The Fine Art of Political Wit*, 1964

One of the things being in politics has taught me is that men are not a reasoned or reasonable sex. —Margaret Thatcher, interview, BBC (London), 1972

If we could harness the destructive energy of disagreements over politics, we wouldn't need the bomb. —Barbara Walters, *How to Talk with Practically Anybody About Practically Anything*, 1970

Politics, as a practice, whatever its professions, has always been the systematic organization of hatred. —Henry Adams, *The Education of Henry Adams*, 1907

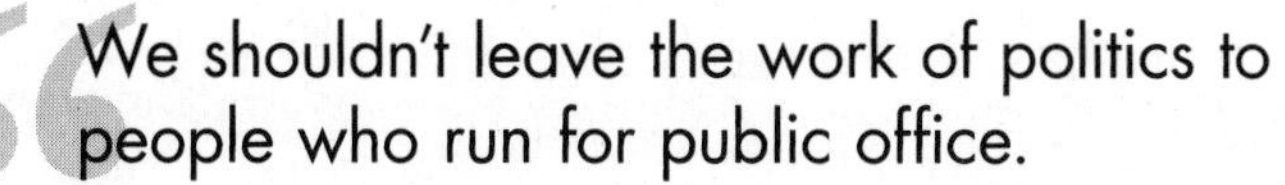

We shouldn't leave the work of politics to people who run for public office.

—Hillary Rodham Clinton (with Claire G. Osborne), *The Unique Voice of Hillary Rodham Clinton, 1997*

Conservative, n. A statesman enamored of existing evils, as opposed to a Liberal, who wants to replace them with new ones. —Ambrose Bierce, *The Devil's Dictionary*, 1906

Practical politics consists in ignoring facts. —Henry Adams, *The Education of Henry Adams*, 1907

I always cheer up immensely if an attack is particularly wounding because I think, well, if they attack one personally, it means they have not a single political argument left. —Margaret Thatcher, quoted in *The Daily Telegraph* (London), 1986

There is always a certain meanness in the argument of conservatism, joined with a certain superiority in its fact. —Ralph Waldo Emerson, lecture, "The Conservative" (Boston), 9 December 1841

For me party discipline is a sacred matter, not just lust for power as some people claim .... —Golda Meir, resignation statement, 1974

What is needed in politics is not the ability to lie but rather the sensibility to know when, where, how and to whom to say things. —Václav Havel, quoted in *The International Herald Tribune* (Paris), 1991

In politics, it seems, retreat is honorable if dictated by military considerations and shameful if even *suggested* for ethical reasons. —Mary McCarthy, *Vietnam*, 1967

Politics is the art of looking for trouble, finding it everywhere, diagnosing it incorrectly, and applying the wrong remedies. —Groucho Marx, *Jokes*, Getlen

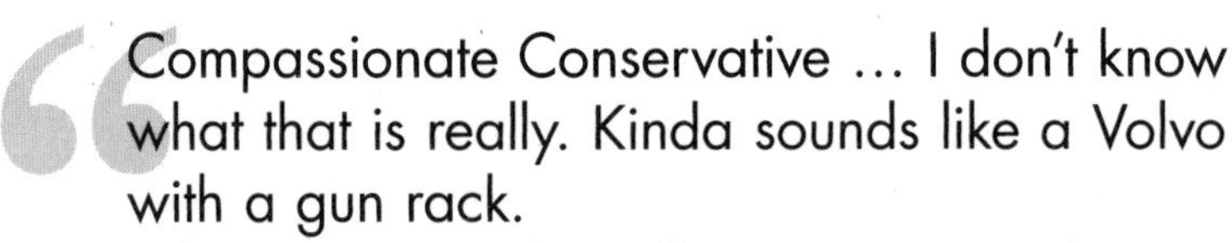

Democracy isn't just about deducing what the people want. Democracy is leading the people as well. —Margaret Thatcher, quoted by Claire Price-Groff, *Twentieth-Century Women Political Leaders*, 1998

Idiot, n. A member of a large and powerful tribe whose influence in human affairs has always been dominant and controlling. —Ambrose Bierce, *The Devil's Dictionary*, 1906

Each fool turns politician now, and wears / A formal face, and talks of state-affairs. —Aphra Behn, prologue, *The Feigned Courtezans*, 1679

Well, there are people who eat the earth and eat all the people on it like in the Bible with the locusts. And other people who stand around and watch them eat it. —Lillian Hellman, *The Little Foxes*, 1939

Our society is run by insane people for insane objectives .... I think we're being run by maniacs for maniacal ends ... and I think I'm liable to be put away as insane for expressing that. That's what's insane about it. —John Lennon, interview, BBC-TV (London), 1968

Treat bad men exactly as if they were insane. —Oliver Wendell Holmes, *Elsie Venner*, 1859

You can bind my body, tie my hands, govern my actions: you are the strongest, and society adds to your power; but with my will, sir, you can do nothing. God alone can restrain it and curb it. Seek then a law, a dungeon, an instrument of torture, by which you can hold it, it is as if you wished to grasp the air, and seize vacancy. —George Sand, preface, *Indiana*, 1832

I've always thought the American eagle needed a left wing and a right wing. The right wing would see to it that economic interests had their legitimate concerns addressed. The left wing would see to it that ordinary people were included in the bargain. Both would keep the great bird on course. But with two right wings or two left wings, it's no longer an eagle and it's going to crash. —Bill Moyers, speech, National Conference for Media Reform (St. Louis), 2005

> "The Scarecrow was now the ruler of the Emerald City, and although he was not a Wizard the people were proud of him. "For," they said, "there is not another city in all the world that is ruled by a stuffed man." And, so far as they knew, they were quite right."
>
> —L. Frank Baum, *The Wonderful Wizard of Oz,* 1900

Most of the stone a nation hammers goes toward its tomb only. It buries itself alive. —Henry David Thoreau, *Walden*, 1854

I'm seeing there is a new way, the third way. It's not left or right. It's not Democrat or Republican. It's a third way. And the third way to me is a shift in these principles where dominance, occupation, invasion and violence are the tools on which the whole planet turns and operates. The new tools would be cooperation, invitation, dialogue, and care. Care would be fundamental to the principles of the world. —Eve Ensler, quoted by Marianne Schnall, www.feminist.com, 2006

I know that it is hard for one who has held the reins for so long to give up; it cuts like a knife. It will feel all the better when it closes up again. —Sojourner Truth, speech, Annual Meeting of Equal Rights Convention (New York, 1867), *History of Woman Suffrage*, Anthony

Where we can find common ground on the economy, and on other domestic issues, we shall seek it .... Where we cannot find common ground, we must stand our ground. —Nancy Pelosi, quoted by David Espo, Associated Press, 2002

Capitalism used to be like an eagle, but now it's more like a vulture.

—Malcolm X, speech (1965), *Malcolm X Speaks: Selected Speeches and Statements,* George Breitman, ed., 1965

No nation keeps its word. A nation is a big, blind worm, following what? Fate perhaps. A nation has no honor, it has no word to keep. —Carl Jung, interview with Ernst Hanfstaengl

... the life of the nation is long; and it is longer, and stronger, more vigorous and more knit, if it grows slowly and spontaneously than if formed by violence or fraud. —Olive Schreiner, *Thoughts on South Africa*, 1892

Liberty, n. One of imagination's most precious possessions. —Ambrose Bierce, *The Devil's Dictionary*, 1906

We want a society where people are free to make choices, to make mistakes, to be generous and compassionate. This is what we mean by a moral society; not a society where the state is responsible for everything, and no one is responsible for the state. —Margaret Thatcher, speech, 1977

The liberty we prize is not America's gift to the world, it is God's gift to humanity. —George W. Bush, State of the Union Address (Washington, D.C.), January 2003

The liberty of the individual is no gift of civilization. It was greatest before there was any civilization. —Sigmund Freud, *Civilization and Its Discontents*, 1930

> In politics, if you want anything said, ask a man. If you want anything done, ask a woman.
> —Margaret Thatcher, quoted in *People* (New York), 1975

I don't believe civilization can do a lot more than educate a person's senses. —Grace Paley, *Enormous Changes at the Last Minute*, 1960

If liberty means anything at all, it means the right to tell people what they do not want to hear. —George Orwell, preface, *Animal Farm*, 1946

Every government is a parliament of whores. The trouble is, in a democracy the whores are us. —P. J. O'Rourke, *Parliament of Whores*, 1991

One set of messages of the society we live in is: Consume. Grow. Do what you want. Amuse yourselves. —Susan Sontag, *AIDS and Its Metaphors*, 1989

History, despite its wrenching pain, / Cannot be unlived, and if faced / With courage, need not be lived again. —Maya Angelou, "A Rock, A River, A Tree," *On The Pulse of Morning*, 1993

Giving money and power to government is like giving whiskey and car keys to teenage boys. —P. J. O'Rourke, *Parliament of Whores*, 1991

The punishment which the wise suffer who refuse to take part in the government, is to live under the government of worse men. —Plato, quoted by Ralph Waldo Emerson, "Eloquence," *Society and Solitude*, 1870

Government is not the solution to our problem. Government is the problem. —Ronald Reagan, *First Inaugural Address* (Washington, D.C.), 1981

The care of human life and happiness, and not their destruction, is the first and only legitimate object of good government. —Thomas Jefferson, letter to the Republican Citizens of Washington County (Maryland), 1809

For our democracy has been marred by imperialism, and it has been enlightened only by individual and sporadic efforts at freedom. —Pearl S. Buck, speech, "Freedom for All" (New York), 1942

> "Government's view of the economy could be summed up in a few short phrases: If it moves, tax it. If it keeps moving, regulate it. And if it stops moving, subsidize it."
>
> —Ronald Reagan, remarks to White House Conference on Small Business (Washington, D.C.), 1986

If liberty and equality, as is thought by some are chiefly to be found in democracy, they will be best attained when all persons alike share in the government to the utmost. —Aristotle, *Politics*

Democracy means that anyone can grow up to be president, and anyone who doesn't grow up can be vice president. —Johnny Carson, *The Tonight Show*

It has been said that democracy is the worst form of government except all those other forms that have been tried from time to time. —Winston Churchill, speech, House of Commons (London), 1947

I believe democracy is our greatest export. At least until China figures out a way to stamp it out of plastic for three cents a unit. —Stephen Colbert, speech, White House Correspondents' Association Dinner (Washington, D.C.), 2006

One of the strengths of democracy is the ability of the people to regularly demand changes in leadership and to fire a failing leader and hire a new one with the promise of hopeful change. —Al Gore, speech, MoveOn.org PAC (NYU), 2004

Indeed, the ideal for a well-functioning democratic state is like the ideal for a gentleman's well-cut suit—it is not noticed. —Arthur Koestler, quoted in *The New York Times* (New York), 1943

As I would not be a slave, so I would not be a master. This expresses my idea of democracy. Whatever differs from this, to the extent of the difference, is no democracy. —Abraham Lincoln, fragment (c. 1858), *The Collected Works of Abraham Lincoln*, Roy P. Basler, ed., 1953

The Republican Party makes even its young men seem old; the Democratic Party makes even its old men seem young. —Adlai Stevenson, speech, quoted by Earl Mazo, *Richard Nixon: A Political and Personal Portrait*, 1959

> It's not the voting that's democracy, it's the counting.
>
> —Tom Stoppard, *Jumpers*, 1972

There are few things wholly evil, or wholly good. Almost every thing, especially of governmental policy, is an inseparable compound of the two; so that our best judgment of the preponderance between them is continually demanded. —Abraham Lincoln, speech, House of Representatives (Washington, D.C.), 1848

I prefer an accommodating vice / To an obstinate virtue. —Molière, *Amphitryon*, 1666

The government has failed us; you can't deny that. Anytime you live in the twentieth century, 1964, and you walkin' around here singing "We Shall Overcome," the government has failed us. This is part of what's wrong with you—you do too much singing. Today it's time to stop singing and start swinging. —Malcolm X, speech, "The Bullet or the Ballot," 1964

The wickedness of men is that their power breeds stupidity and blindness. —Gregory Maguire, *Wicked*, 1995

I said to God, "What are they doing?" // God said, "Making pitfalls into which their fellows may sink." // I said to God, "Why do they do it?" // God said, "Because each thinks that when his brother falls he will rise." —Olive Schreiner, *Dreams*, 1890

We are arrant knaves all; believe none of us. —William Shakespeare, *Hamlet*, 1600

They were unable to bribe the members of Congress, and on the date stipulated by law the left calmly came to power. And on that date the right began to stockpile hatred. —Isabel Allende, *The House of the Spirits*, Magda Bogin, tr., 1982

Virtue itself turns vice, being misapplied; / And vice sometimes by action dignified. —William Shakespeare, *Romeo and Juliet*, 1597

... virtue that transgresses is but patched with sin; and sin that amends is but patched with virtue. —William Shakespeare, *Twelfth Night*, 1601

> There are many humorous things in the world; among them, the white man's notion that he is less savage than the other savages.
>
> —Mark Twain, *Following the Equator*, 1897

Power! ... You may dam up the fountain of water, and make it a stagnant marsh, or you may let it run free and do its work; but you cannot say whether it shall be there; it is there. And it will act, if not openly for good, then covertly for evil; but it will act. —Olive Schreiner, *The Story of an African Farm*, 1883

[Women] are not more moral, we are only less corrupted by power. —Gloria Steinem, quoted in *The New York Times Book Review* (New York), 1971

> The political and commercial morals of the United States are not merely food for laughter, they are an entire banquet.
>
> —Mark Twain, attributed

Power should not be concentrated in the hands of so few, and powerlessness in the hands of so many. —Maggie Kuhn, quoted in *Ms.* (New York), 1975

Power is poison. Its effect on Presidents had always been tragic. —Henry Adams, *The Education of Henry Adams*, 1907

There is a kind of physical pleasure in resisting an iniquitous power. —Germaine de Staël, quoted by J. Christopher Herold, *Mistress to an Age*,1958

Leverage is everything,—was what I used to say;—don't begin to pry till you have got the long arm on your side. —Oliver Wendell Holmes, *Elsie Venner*, 1859

The quality of the will to power is, precisely, growth .... The vaster the power gained, the vaster the appetite for more. —Ursula K. Le Guin, *The Lathe of Heaven*, 1971

The louder he talked of his honor, the faster we counted our spoons. —Ralph Waldo Emerson, "Worship," *The Conduct of Life*, 1860

The whole notion of loyalty inquisitions is a national characteristic of the police state, not of democracy …. We must not burn down the house to kill the rats. —Adlai Stevenson, speech in opposition to the Internal Security Act of 1950

How haughtily he cocks his nose, / To tell what every schoolboy knows. —Jonathan Swift, *The Country Life*, 1727

We shall squeeze you empty and then we shall fill you with ourselves. —George Orwell, *Nineteen Eighty-Four*, 1948

For years—decades—perhaps centuries—women have been complaining about men's lack of sensitivity, their unkindness, but no sooner have women acquired power than they permit, even sanctify, some of the nastiest manifestations of human nature. —Doris Lessing, *Walking in the Shade*, 1997

An appeaser is one who feeds a crocodile, hoping it will eat him last.
—Winston Churchill, quoted in *Reader's Digest* (Pleasantville, New York), 1954

Beware the wolf in sheep's clothing. —Aesop, "The Wolf in Sheep's Clothing," *Fables*

To tell a voice that's genuinely good / From one that's base but merely has succeeded. —W. H. Auden, "Base words are uttered," 1940

There is nothing more agreeable in life than to make peace with the Establishment—and nothing more corrupting. —A. J. P. Taylor, "William Cobbett," *New Statesman* (London), 1953

Never fight fair with a stranger, boy. You'll never get out of the jungle that way. —Arthur Miller, *Death of a Salesman*, 1949

I'll Never Do It Again 20

Making mistakes is inevitable, and often unavoidable. Lying is avoidable but often inevitable. Apologizing for one's errant ways is another matter. As is forgiving someone for screwing up. It takes a lot of self-examination. And when at last you've got yourself to the point of apologizing or forgiving, you may have trouble expressing it. Some mighty minds have come with verbiage to give us a hand.

• • •

But after all the punishment that misconduct can bring, it is still not less misconduct. Pain is no expiation. —Jane Austen, *Emma*, 1815

> The only one who makes no mistakes is one who never does anything!
>
> —Theodore "Teddy" Roosevelt, inscribed on the Theodore Roosevelt Birthplace National Historic Site (New York)

Every great mistake has a halfway moment, a split second when it can be recalled and perhaps remedied. —Pearl S. Buck, *What America Means to Me*, 1942

Mistakes are, after all, the foundations of truth, and if a man does not know what a thing is, it is at least an increase in knowledge if he knows what it is not. —Carl Jung, *Aion*, 1951

For what do we live, but to make sport for our neighbours, and laugh at them in our turn? —Jane Austen, *Pride and Prejudice*, 1813

It is the public scandal that offends; to sin in secret is no sin at all. —Molière, *Tartuffe*, 1669

Learn to get in touch with silence within yourself and know that everything in this life has a purpose. There are no mistakes, no coincidences; all events are blessings given to us to learn from. —Elizabeth Kübler-Ross, quoted by Lennie Kronisch, *Yoga Journal* (San Francisco), 1976

An error is the more dangerous in proportion to the degree of truth which it contains. —Henri-Frédéric Amiel, journal entry (1852), *Journal Intime*

Of all follies there is none greater than wanting to make the world a better place. —Molière, *Le Misanthrope*, 1666

Prophecy is the most gratuitous form of error. —George Eliot, *Middlemarch*, 1871–1872

I find the pain of a little censure, even when it is unfounded, is more acute than the pleasure of much praise. —Thomas Jefferson, letter, 1789

> Surgeons must be very careful / When they take the knife! / Underneath their fine incisions / Stirs the Culprit—Life!
>
> —Emily Dickinson, No. 108, *Poems*, Johnson

Life is a quest and love a quarrel …. —Edna St. Vincent Millay, "Weeds," *Second April*, 1921

On an occasion of this kind it becomes more than a moral duty to speak one's mind. It becomes a pleasure. —Oscar Wilde, *The Importance of Being Earnest*, 1895

Nobody can tell what I suffer! But it is always so. Those who do not complain are never pitied. —Jane Austen, *Pride and Prejudice*, 1813

The man who insists upon seeing with perfect clearness before he decides, never decides. Accept life, and you must accept regret. —Henri-Frédéric Amiel, journal entry (1856), *Journal Intime*

She had spent the golden time in grudging its going. —Dorothy Parker, "The Lovely Leave," *Laments for the Living*, 1929

Jealousy is never satisfied with anything short of an omniscience that would detect the subtlest fold of the heart. —George Eliot, *The Mill on the Floss*, 1860

Sorrow is tranquility remembered in emotion. —Dorothy Parker, "Sentiment," *The Portable Dorothy Parker*, 1944

> "Maybe all one can do is hope to end up with the right regrets."
>
> —Arthur Miller, *The Ride Down Mount Morgan,* 1991

There are some cases … in which the sense of injury breeds—not the will to inflict injuries and climb over them as a ladder, but—a hatred of all injury. —George Eliot, *Daniel Deronda*, 1874–1876

Nothing is more deceitful than the appearance of humility. It is often only carelessness of opinion, and sometimes an indirect boast. —Jane Austen, *Pride and Prejudice*, 1813

Believe me, every heart has its secret sorrow which the world knows not; and oftentimes we call a man cold, when he is only sad. —Henry Wadsworth Longfellow, *Hyperion: A Romance*, 1839

When sorrows come, they come not single spies, / But in battalions. —William Shakespeare, *Hamlet*, 1600

Pure and complete sorrow is as impossible as pure and complete joy. —Leo Tolstoy, *War and Peace*, 1865–1869

There is much pain that is quite noiseless; and vibrations that make human agonies are often a mere whisper in the roar of hurrying existence. —George Eliot, *Felix Holt, The Radical*, 1866

All skins are shed at length, remorse, even shame. —Edna St. Vincent Millay, "Time, that renews the tissues of this frame," *Wine from These Grapes*, 1934

Time wounds all heels.

—Goodman Ace, *Easy Aces* radio show, 1930s–1940s

Her mind lives tidily, apart / From cold and noise and pain, / And bolts the door against her heart, / Out wailing in the rain. —Dorothy Parker, "Interior," *Sunset Gun*, 1928

I had a little Sorrow, / Born of a little Sin. —Edna St. Vincent Millay, "The Penitent," *A Few Figs from Thistles*, 1920

To fight aloud is very brave, / But *gallanter*, I know, / Who charge within the bosom / The Cavalry of Woe. —Emily Dickinson, No. 126, *Poems*, Johnson

Many an inherited sorrow that has marred a life has been breathed into no human ear. —George Eliot, *Felix Holt, The Radical*, 1866

Pity me that the heart is slow to learn / What the swift mind beholds at every turn. —Edna St. Vincent Millay, "Pity me not because the light of day," *The Harp-Weaver and Other Poems*, 1923

It's but a little good you'll do a-watering the last year's crop. —George Eliot, *Adam Bede*, 1859

Yesterday is yesterday. If we try to recapture it, we will only lose tomorrow. —Bill Clinton, State of the Union Address (Washington, D.C.), 1999

Memories of the past are not memories of facts but memories of your imaginings of the facts. —Philip Roth, *The Facts: A Novelist's Autobiography*, 1988

Never explain—your friends do not need it and your enemies will not believe you anyway. —Elbert Hubbard, *The Motto Book*, 1907

Assent—and you are sane—, / Demur—you're straightway dangerous—, / And handled with a Chain—. —Emily Dickinson, No. 435, *Poems*, Johnson

To apologize is to lay the foundation for a future offense. —Ambrose Bierce, *The Devil's Dictionary*, 1906

Forgive but never forget. —John F. Kennedy, quoted by Theodore Sorensen, *Kennedy*, 1965

The quality of mercy is not strained. / It droppeth as the gentle rain from heaven. —William Shakespeare, *The Merchant of Venice*, 1596

Sweet mercy is nobility's true badge. —William Shakespeare, *Titus Andronicus*, 1593

Selfishness must always be forgiven, you know, because there is no hope of a cure. —Jane Austen, *Mansfield Park*, 1814

> You had best be quick, if you are ever going to forgive me at all; life does not last forever.
> —Murasaki Shikibu, *The Tale of Genji*, 1001–1015

There must be acceptance and the knowledge that sorrow fully accepted brings its own gifts. For there is an alchemy in sorrow. It can be transmuted into wisdom .... —Pearl S. Buck, *The Child Who Never Grew*, 1950

One minute of reconciliation is worth more than a whole life of friendship. —Gabriel Gárcia Márquez, *One Hundred Years of Solitude*, Gregory Rabassa, tr., 1967

More helpful than all wisdom is one draught of simple human pity that will not forsake us. —George Eliot, *The Mill on the Floss*, 1860

You ought certainly to forgive them as a Christian, but never admit them in your sight, or allow their names to be mentioned in your hearing. —Jane Austen, *Pride and Prejudice*, 1813

Even a stopped clock is right twice a day. —Maria von Ebner Eschenbach, *Aphorisms*, 1905

> "Do not be too moral. You may cheat yourself out of much life. Aim above morality. Be not simply good, be good for something."
> —Henry David Thoreau, letter, 1848

They [men] forgive us—oh! for many things, but not for the absence in us of their own feelings. —Colette, *Gigi*, 1944

Laughter always forgives. —Martin Amis, lecture, "Political Correctness: Robert Bly and Philip Larkin," Harvard University (Cambridge, Massachusetts), 1997

Would not love see returning penitence afar off, and fall on its neck and kiss it? —George Eliot, *Middlemarch*, 1871–1872

The preoccupation with what should be is estimable only when the respect for what is has been exhausted. —José Ortega y Gasset, *Meditations on Hunting*, Howard B. Westcott, tr., 1972

I wondered if that was how forgiveness budded, not with the fanfare of epiphany, but with pain gathering its things, packing up, and slipping away unannounced in the middle of the night. —Khaled Hosseini, *The Kite Runner*, 2003

In the Bible it says they asked Jesus how many times you should forgive, and he said seventy times seven. Well, I want you all to know that I'm keeping a chart. —Hillary Rodham Clinton, speech, National Prayer Luncheon (Washington, D.C.), 1994

The weak can never forgive. Forgiveness is the attribute of the strong. —Mohandas Gandhi, *Mind of Mahatma Gandhi*, 3rd ed., S. R. Tikekar, ed., 1968

The truth is incontrovertible. Panic may resent it, ignorance may deride it, malice may distort it, but there it is. —Winston Churchill, speech, House of Commons (London), 1916

Truth is the pearl without price .... Those who have the truth would not be packaging it and selling it, so anyone who is selling it, really does not possess it. —Peace Pilgrim, *Her Life and Work*, 1982

> Truth is tough. It will not break, like a bubble, at a touch; nay, you may kick it about all day, like a football, and it will be round and full at evening.
>
> —Oliver Wendell Holmes, *The Professor at the Breakfast Table,* 1859

Thus conscience does make cowards of us all .... —William Shakespeare, *Hamlet*, 1600

The plaque at the front of the courtroom, high on the wall, was permanent and yet its words were new each time Jack read them, read them half against his will, his eyes moving restlessly forward and up to them while testimony droned on: *Conscience Speaks the Truth.* —Joyce Carol Oates, *Do With Me What You Will*, 1970

Yesterday we obeyed kings and bent our necks before emperors. But today we kneel only to truth, follow only beauty, and obey only love. —Kahlil Gibran, *The Vision—Reflections on the Way of the Soul*, 1994

Truth has rough flavors if we bite it through. —George Eliot, *Armgart*, 1871

There was truth and there was untruth, and if you clung to the truth even against the whole world, you were not mad. —George Orwell, *Nineteen Eighty-Four*, 1948

This above all:—to thine ownself be true, / And it must follow, as the night the day, / Thou canst not then be false to any man. —William Shakespeare, *Hamlet*, 1600

It takes two to speak the truth—one to speak, and another to hear. —Henry David Thoreau, "Wednesday," *A Week on the Concord and Marrimack Rivers*, 1849

One can lie, but truth is more interesting. —Enid Bagnold, *The Chalk Garden*, 1955

Tell the truth or trump—but get the trick. —Mark Twain, *Pudd'n'head Wilson*, 1894

Truth burns up error. —Sojourner Truth, comment, c. 1882

The artlessness of unadorned truth, however sure in theory of extorting admiration, rarely in practice fails inflicting pain and mortification. —Fanny Burney, *Camilla*, 1796

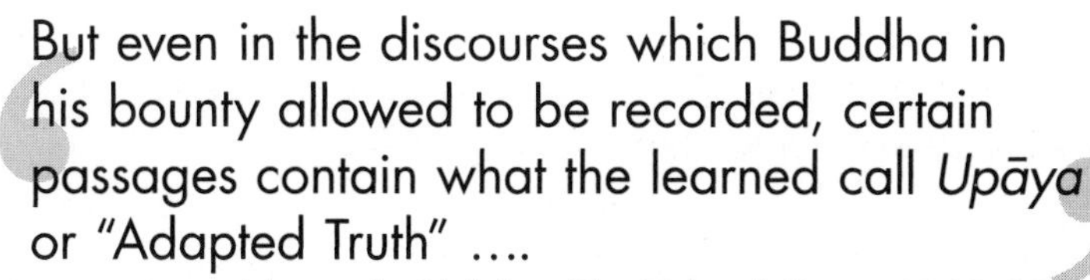

But even in the discourses which Buddha in his bounty allowed to be recorded, certain passages contain what the learned call *Upāya* or "Adapted Truth" ....
—Murasaki Shikibu, *The Tale of Genji,* 1001–1015

The truth is the most valuable thing we have. Let us economize it. —Mark Twain, *Following the Equator*, 1897

Truth ensures trust, but not victory, or even happiness. —Penelope Fitzgerald, *Human Voices*, 1980

Man is least himself when he talks in his own person. Give him a mask, and he will tell you the truth. —Oscar Wilde, *The Critic as Artist*, 1891

The truth is always something that is told, not something that is known. If there were no speaking or writing, there would be no truth about anything. There would only be what is. —Susan Sontag, *The Benefactor*, 1963

Circumstances should never alter principles. —Oscar Wilde, *An Ideal Husband*, 1895

Morality is a private and costly luxury. —Henry Adams, *The Education of Henry Adams*, 1907

I believe that the truth about any subject only comes when all sides of the story are put together, and all their different meanings make one new one. —Alice Walker, *In Search of Our Mothers' Gardens*, 1983

Never let your sense of morals prevent you from doing what is right.
—Isaac Asimov, "Foundation," *Astounding Science-Fiction*, 1944

Reformers who are always compromising, have not yet grasped the idea that truth is the only safe ground to stand upon. —Elizabeth Cady Stanton, *The Woman's Bible*, 1895

There's a world of difference between truth and facts. Facts can obscure the truth. —Maya Angelou, quoted by Brian Lanker, *I Dream a World*, 1989

Love all, trust a few, do wrong to none. —William Shakespeare, *All's Well That Ends Well*, 1602

The truth is balance, but the opposite of truth, which is unbalance, may not be a lie. —Susan Sontag, *Against Interpretation*, 1966

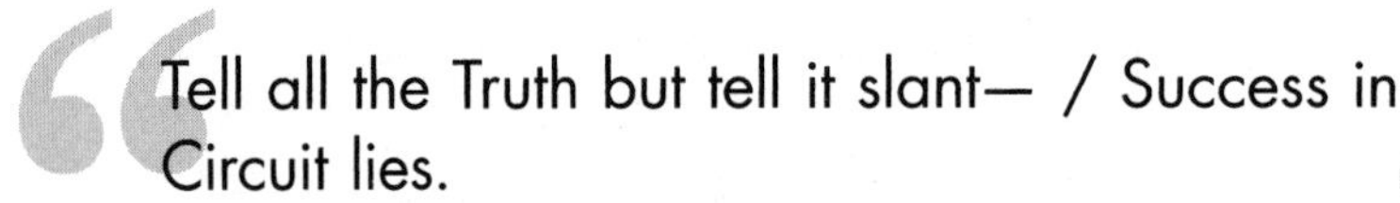

Tell all the Truth but tell it slant— / Success in Circuit lies.

—Emily Dickinson, No. 1129, *Poems*, Johnson

His morality is not in purple patches, ostentatiously obtrusive, but woven in through the very texture of the stuff. —Maria Edgeworth, *Helen*, 1834

Honesty is for the most part less profitable than dishonesty. —Plato, attributed

Yet it is in our idleness, in our dreams, that the submerged truth sometimes comes to the top. —Virginia Woolf, *A Room of One's Own*, 1929

Rich honesty dwells like a miser, sir, in a poor house; as your pearl in a foul oyster. —William Shakespeare, *As You Like It*, 1596

... like all virtuous people he imagines he must speak the truth ....
—Joyce Carol Oates, *Do with Me What You Will*, 1970

21 Love Makes the World Go 'Round

There are all kinds of love—romantic love, marital love, familial love, platonic love, love of a pet, love of God, and so on. You may not want to write a note to your dog or your God, but you very well may occasion to do so to a friend, a relative, or a mate. Tucking an appropriate quote into your note will spice it up quite nicely.

• • •

A woman can look both moral and exciting—if she also looks as if it was quite a struggle. —Edna Ferber, quoted in *Reader's Digest* (Pleasantville, New York), 1954

> “When women go wrong, men go right after them.”
>
> —Mae West, *Wit and Wisdom*

He kissed me and now I am someone else. —Gabriela Mistral, “He Kissed Me,” *Desolacion*, 1922

To be happy with a man you must understand him a lot and love him a little. To be happy with a woman you must love her a lot and not try to understand her at all. —Helen Rowland, *A Guide to Men*, 1922

I turn away reluctant from your light, / And stand irresolute, a mind undone, / A silly, dazzled thing deprived of sight / From having looked too long upon the sun. —Edna St. Vincent Millay, "When I too long have looked upon your face," *Second April*, 1921

Men want the same thing from their underwear that they want from women: a little bit of support, and a little bit of freedom. —Jerry Seinfeld, stand-up routine

He loved what he wanted me to be. —M. F. K. Fisher, *Stay Me, Oh Comfort Me*, 1993

The bravest thing that men do is love women. —Mort Sahl, stand-up routine

> "Oh, life is a glorious cycle of song, / A medley of extemporanea; / And love is a thing that can never go wrong; / And I am Marie of Roumania."
>
> —Dorothy Parker, "Comment," *Enough Rope*, 1927

Sex alleviates tension. Love causes it. —Woody Allen, *A Midsummer Night's Sex Comedy*, 1982

Your body was a temple to Delight …. —Edna St. Vincent Millay, "As to some lovely temple tenantless," *Second April*, 1921

Why does a man take it for granted that a girl who flirts with him wants him to kiss her—when, nine times out of ten, she only wants him to *want* to kiss her? —Helen Rowland, *A Guide to Men*, 1922

Familiarity breeds attempt. —Goodman Ace, *Easy Aces* radio show, 1930s–1940s

The only sin passion can commit is to be joyless. —Dorothy L. Sayers, *Busman's Honeymoon*, 1947

The difference between love and lust is that lust never costs over two hundred dollars. —Johnny Carson, *The Johnny Carson Show*

You mustn't force sex to do the work of love or love to do the work of sex. —Mary McCarthy, *The Group*, 1954

My boyfriend Ernie asked me, "Soph, how come you never tell me when you're having an orgasm?" // "Well, Ernie, you're never around." —Bette Midler, *Funny Women*, Unterbrink

France is the thriftiest of all nations; to a Frenchman sex provides the most economical way to have fun. The French are a logical race. —Anita Loos, *Kiss Hollywood Good-by*, 1974

I've always had a weakness for foreign affairs. —Mae West, quoted in *Time* (New York), 1959

Sonja: Sex without love is an empty experience! // Boris: Yes, but as empty experiences go, it's one of the best! —Woody Allen, *Love and Death*, 1975

And I try to teach my heart not to want nothing it can't have. —Alice Walker, *The Color Purple*, 1982

My love life is terrible. The last time I was inside a woman was when I visited the Statue of Liberty. —Woody Allen, *Crimes and Misdemeanors*, 1989

I know I am but summer to your heart, / And not the full four seasons of the year .... —Edna St. Vincent Millay, *The Harp-Weaver and Other Poems*, 1923

By the time you swear you're his, / Shivering and sighing, / And he vows his passion is / Infinite, undying— / Lady, make a note of this: / One of you is lying. —Dorothy Parker, "Unfortunate Coincidence," *Enough Rope*, 1927

The lovesick, the betrayed, and the jealous all smell alike. —Colette, "The South of France," *Break of Day*, 1928

Love without hope grows in its own atmosphere, and should encourage the imagination .... —Penelope Fitzgerald, *Human Voices*, 1980

> Love is an act of endless forgiveness, a tender look which becomes a habit.
>
> —Peter Ustinov, *Christian Science Monitor* (Boston), 9 December 1958

The Secret of Joy is … Resistance. —Alice Walker, *Possessing the Secret of Joy*, 1992

Where love is absent there can be no woman. —George Sand, *Lelia*, 1833

But the eyes are blind. One must look with the heart .... —Antoine de Saint-Exupéry, *The Little Prince*

People who make some other person their job are dangerous. —Dorothy L. Sayers, *Gaudy Nights*, 1936

> I am beginning to lose patience / With my personal relations. / They are not deep / And they are not cheap.
>
> —W. H. Auden, *The English Auden*, Edward Mendelson, ed., 1930

It is through action, based on a deep understanding of our interconnectedness and shared fragility, that love manifests, heals and builds the new relationships of trust and compassion in our social fabric. —Deepak Chopra, newsletter, The Alliance For a New Humanity For Global Transformation, 2007

Happiness is having a large, loving, caring, close-knit family in another city. —George Burns, attributed

What is family, after all, except memories?—haphazard and precious as the contents of a catchall drawer in the kitchen. —Joyce Carol Oates, *We Were the Mulvaneys*, 1996

All happy families resemble one another, each unhappy family is unhappy in its own way. —Leo Tolstoy, *Anna Karénina*, 1875–1877

One never knows how much a family may grow; and when a hive is too full, and it is necessary to form a new swarm, each one thinks of carrying away his own honey. —George Sand, *The Haunted Pool*, 1851

Many of us are living out the unlived lives of our mothers, because they were not able to become the unique people they were born to be. —Gloria Steinem, quoted by Joyce Tenneson, *Wise Women: A Celebration of Their Insights, Courage, and Beauty*, 2002

But the love of offspring … tender and beautiful as it is, can not as a sentiment rank with conjugal love. —Elizabeth Cady Stanton, *History of Woman Suffrage*, Anthony

My grief and my smile begin in your face, my son. —Gabriela Mistral, "Eternal Grief," *Desolacion*, 1922

He was not all a father's heart could wish; / but oh, he was my son!—my only son. —Joanna Baillie, *Orra*, 1812

We need to add to the pantheon of a holy family a divine daughter. For only then will we have a model for families in which all members are equally valued and respected. —Riane Eisler, *Sacred Pleasure*, 1996

Her parents had searched through the past, consulted psychiatrists, took every moment to bits. In no way should she be explained. —Muriel Spark, *Reality and Dreams*, 1997

To think that all in me of which my father would have felt a proper pride had I been a man, is deeply mortifying to him because I am a woman. —Elizabeth Cady Stanton, *Stanton*

I'm not a lady, I'm your daughter. —Dorothy Fields, remark to Lew Fields, Cotton Club (Harlem, New York), 1927

How sister gazed at sister / reaching through mirrored pupils / back to the mother. —Adrienne Rich, "Sibling Mysteries," *The Dream of a Common Language*, 1978

Let me not forget that I am the daughter of a woman who bent her head, trembling, over a cactus, her wrinkled face full of ecstasy over the promise of a flower, a woman who herself never ceased to flower, untiringly, during three quarters of a century. —Colette, *Break of Day*, 1928

Over the river and through the wood / To grandfather's house we'll go. —Lydia Maria Child, "A Boy's Thanksgiving Day," *Flowers for Children*, 1844

> ... I wish I'd a knowed more people. I would of loved 'em all. If I'd a knowed more, I would a loved more.
>
> —Toni Morrison, *Song of Solomon*, 1977

She hasn't had her full ration of kisses-on-the-lips today. She had the quarter-to-twelve one in the Bois, she had the two o'clock one after coffee, she had the half-past-six one in the garden, but she's missed tonight's. —Colette, *The Cat*, 1933

Oh cat; I'd say, or pray: be-*oooo*tiful cat! Delicious cat! Exquisite cat! Satiny cat! Cat like a soft owl, cat with paws like moths, jeweled cat, miraculous cat! Cat, cat, cat, cat. —Doris Lessing, *Particularly Cats*, 1967

> There are some people who begin the Zoo at the beginning, called WAYIN, and walk as quickly as they can past every cage until they get to the one called WAYOUT, but the nicest people go straight to the animal they love the most, and stay there.
>
> —A. A. Milne, *Winnie the Pooh,* 1926

He shut his eyes while Sasha [the cat] kept vigil, watching all the invisible signs that hover over sleeping human beings when the light is put out. —Colette, *The Cat*, 1933

To a pet nothing can be useless. —Samuel Johnson, *The History of Rasselas, Prince of Abissinia*, 1759

A dog needs God. It lives by your glances, your wishes. It even shares your humour. This happens about the fifth year. If it doesn't happen, you are only keeping an animal. —Enid Bagnold, *Autobiography*, 1969

"What makes the lamb love Mary so?" / The eager children cry. / "Oh, Mary loves the lamb, you know," / The teacher did reply. —Sarah Josepha Hale, "Mary's Little Lamb," *Poems for Our Children*, 1830

If a man aspires towards a righteous life, his first act of abstinence is from injury to animals. —Leo Tolstoy, *The First Step*, 1892

Is not general incivility the very essence of love? —Jane Austen, *Pride and Prejudice*, 1813

And a continued atmosphere of hectic passion is very trying if you haven't got any of your own. —Dorothy L. Sayers, *The Unpleasantness at the Bellona Club*, 1928

... of all devils let loose in the world there is no devil like devoted love .... —Dorothy L. Sayers, *Gaudy Nights*, 1936

Love does not consist in gazing at each other but in looking together in the same direction. —Antoine de Saint-Exupéry, *Wind, Sand, and Stars*, 1939

Joy's smile is much closer to tears than laughter. —Victor Hugo, *Hernani*, 1830

> Love is a full-length mirror.
> —Stephen Colbert, *The Colbert Report*

Love is not enough. It must be the foundation, the cornerstone—but not the complete structure. It is much too pliable, too yielding. —Bette Davis, *The Lonely Life*, 1962

Variety is the spice of love. —Helen Rowland, *Reflections of a Bachelor Girl*, 1903

… love's a nervous, awkward, overmastering brute; if you can't rein him in it's best to have no truck with him. —Dorothy L. Sayers, *Gaudy Nights*, 1936

Between lovers a little confession is a dangerous thing. —Helen Rowland, *Reflections of a Bachelor Girl*, 1903

Nobody dies from lack of sex. It's lack of love we die from. —Margaret Atwood, *The Handmaid's Tale*, 1986

"That love at length should find me out …." —Edna St. Vincent Millay, *The Harp-Weaver and Other Poems*, 1923

Four be the things I'd be better without: / Love, curiosity, freckles, and doubt. —Dorothy Parker, "Inventory," *Enough Rope*, 1927

Man will do many things to get himself loved, he will do all things to get himself envied. —Mark Twain, *Following the Equator*, 1897

You Can Do It! 22

Human nature, with all its foibles, embraces some pretty fine stuff. It's good to be reminded of our finer aspects on occasion—especially when the world seems to have gone amok. Of course, sometimes our memory seems to have gone amok as well. Here are some plums to rouse the spirit—and give us a good laugh at ourselves.

• • •

What a strange thing is memory, and hope; one looks backward, the other looks forward. The one is of today, the other is the Tomorrow. Memory is history recorded in our brain, memory is a painter, it paints pictures of the past and of the day. —Grandma Moses, *Grandma Moses, My Life's History*, Aotto Kallir, ed., 1947

> "I want to visit Memory Lane, I don't want to live there."
>
> —Letty Cottin Pogregin, *Deborah, Golda, and Me*

I said to my soul, be still, and wait without hope / for hope would be hope for the wrong thing; wait without love / For love would be love of the wrong thing; there is yet faith / But the faith and the love and the hope are all in the waiting. —T. S. Eliot, *Four Quartets*, 1935–1942

If failure, then another long beginning. / Why hope, / Why think that Spring must bring relenting. —Amy Lowell, "A Legend of Porcelain," *Legends*, 1921

Hope is the feeling you have that the feeling you have isn't permanent. —Jean Kerr, *Finishing Touches*, 1973

Uncertainty is the refuge of hope. —Henri-Frédéric Amiel, *Journal Intime*

When hope is taken away from the people moral degeneration follows swiftly after. —Pearl S. Buck, letter to the editor, *The New York Times* (New York), 1941

A great hope fell / You heard no noise / The Ruin was within. —Emily Dickinson, No. 1123, *Poems*, Johnson

If you lose hope, somehow you lose the vitality that keeps life moving, you lose that courage to be, that quality that helps you go on in spite of it all. And so today I still have a dream. —Martin Luther King Jr., *The Trumpet of Conscience*, 1968

If there is faith that can move mountains, it is faith in your own power. —Maria von Ebner Eschenbach, *Aphorisms*, 1905

Those who are animated by hope can perform what would seem impossibilities to those who are under the depressing influence of fear. —Maria Edgeworth, *The Grateful Negro*, 1802

Where there is hope there is life, where there is life there is possibility, and where there is possibility change can occur. —Jesse Jackson, attributed

Hope, like faith, is nothing if it is not courageous; it is nothing if it is not ridiculous. —Thornton Wilder, *The Eighth Day*, 1967

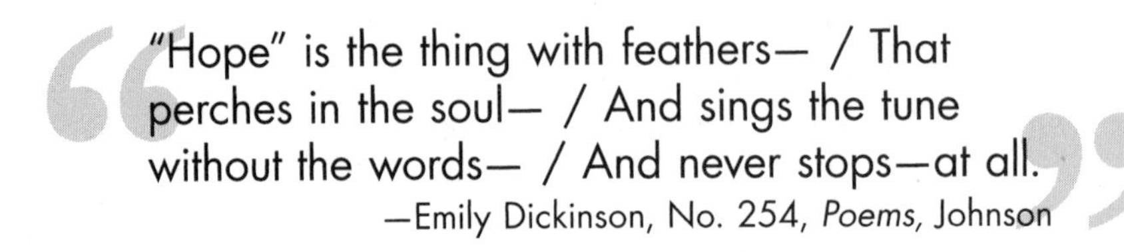
"Hope" is the thing with feathers— / That perches in the soul— / And sings the tune without the words— / And never stops—at all.
—Emily Dickinson, No. 254, *Poems*, Johnson

We live at a time when man believes himself fabulously capable of creation, but he does not know what to create. —José Ortega y Gasset, *The Revolt of the Masses*, 1930

The people will live on. / The learning and blundering people will live on. / They will be tricked and sold and again sold. / And go back to the nourishing earth for rootholds. —Carl Sandburg, *The People, Yes*, 1936

It is our choices, Harry, that show what we truly are, far more than our abilities. —J. K. Rowling, *Harry Potter and the Chamber of Secrets*, 1999

No act of kindness, no matter how small, is ever wasted. —Aesop, "The Lion and the Mouse," *Fables*

If I can stop one Heart from breaking / I shall not live in vain // If I can ease one Life the Aching / Or cool one Pain // Or help one fainting Robin / Unto his Nest again / I shall not live in Vain. —Emily Dickinson, No. 919, *Poems*, Johnson

Conquer, but don't triumph. —Maria von Ebner Eschenbach, *Aphorisms*, 1905

You have a good many little gifts and virtues, but there is no need of parading them, for conceit spoils the finest genius. There is not much danger that real talent or goodness will be overlooked long, and the great charm of all power is modesty. —Louisa May Alcott, *Little Women*, 1868

I think that everything he did, feeding the poor, giving money to friends in need, it was all a way of redeeming himself. And that, I believe, is what true redemption is, Amir jan, when guilt leads to good. —Khaled Hosseini, *The Kite Runner*, 2003

> "It is our time to rise again, to secure our future."
> —Al Gore, *An Inconvenient Truth*, 2006

What a joy it is to do a good deed! And this joy is strongest if no one knows that you have done it. —Leo Tolstoy, March 3, *A Calendar of Wisdom* (1908), Peter Sekirin, tr., 1997

An unrectified case of injustice has a terrible way of lingering restlessly, in the social atmosphere like an unfinished question. —Mary McCarthy, "My Confession," *On the Contrary*, 1961

When you take the high moral road it is difficult for anyone to object without sounding like a complete fool. —Anita Roddick, *Body and Soul*, 1991

There are men who can't be bought. —Carl Sandburg, *The People, Yes*, 1936

If you want to know what a man's like, take a good look at how he treats his inferiors, not his equals. —J. K. Rowling, *Harry Potter and the Goblet of Fire*, 2000

We praise a man who feels angry on the right grounds and against the right persons and also in the right manner at the right moment and for the right length of time. —Aristotle, *Nicomachean Ethics*, c. 325 B.C.E.

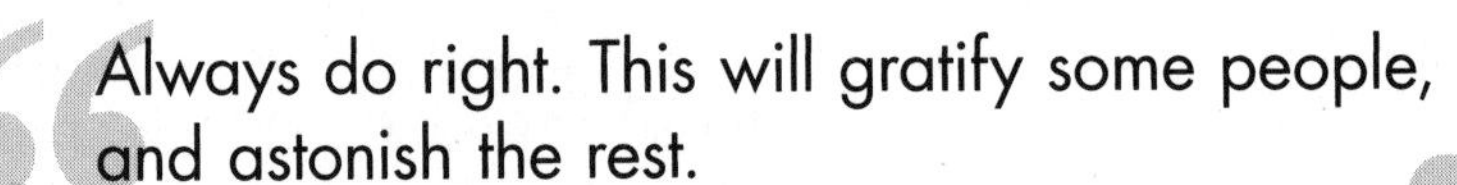

Always do right. This will gratify some people, and astonish the rest.

—Mark Twain, speech to the Young People's Society, Greenpoint Presbyterian Church (Brooklyn), 16 February 1901

Grief and tragedy and hatred are only for a time. Goodness, remembrance and love have no end. —George W. Bush, quoted in *Reader's Digest* (Pleasantville, New York), November 2001

Between grief and nothing I will take grief. —William Faulkner, *The Wild Palms*, 1939

Be as a bird that— / Pausing in its flight— / Alights upon a branch too slight / And feeling that it bends beneath it / Sings—knowing it has wings. —Victor Hugo, "Knowing It Has Wings"

Rosiness is not a worse windowpane than gloomy gray when viewing the world. —Grace Paley, *Enormous Changes at the Last Minute*, 1960

I have a dream that my four little children will one day live in a nation where they will not be judged by the color of their skin but by the content of their character. —Martin Luther King Jr., speech, "I Have A Dream," Lincoln Memorial (Washington, D.C.), 1963

> Let us never negotiate out of fear, but let us never fear to negotiate.
>
> "If a free society cannot help the many who are poor, it cannot save the few who are rich."
>
> Ask not what your country can do for you—ask what you can do for your country.
>
> —John F. Kennedy, *Inaugural Address* (Washington, D.C.), 1961

The only thing we have to fear is fear itself—nameless, unreasoning, unjustified terror which paralyzes needed efforts to convert retreat into advance. —Franklin D. Roosevelt, *First Inaugural Address* (Washington, D.C.), 1933

Great crises produce great men, and great deeds of courage. —John F. Kennedy, *Profiles in Courage*, 1956

Any coward can fight a battle when he's sure of winning; but give me the man who has pluck to fight when he's sure of losing. That's my way, sir; and there are many victories worse than a defeat. —George Eliot, *Scenes of Clerical Life*, 1857

I believe there is no devil but fear. —Elbert Hubbard, personal credo

It isn't for the moment you are struck that you need courage, but for the long uphill climb back to sanity and faith and security. —Anne Morrow Lindbergh, *Hours of Gold, Hours of Lead*, 1973

I make bean-stalks, I'm / A builder, like yourself. —Edna St. Vincent Millay, "The Bean-Stalk," *Second April*, 1921

The single most important quality you need in order to change the course of your life is courage. —Suze Orman, *The Courage to Be Rich*, 1999

Life is a do-it-yourself kit, so do it yourself. Work. Practice.

—Phyllis Diller, *Funny Women*, Unterbrink

We must overcome our fear of each other by seeking out the humanity within each of us. The human heart contains every possibility of race, creed, language, religion and politics. We are one in our commonalities. —Dennis J. Kucinich, speech, House of Representatives (Washington, D.C.), March 2002

A man does what he must—in spite of personal consequences, in spite of obstacles and dangers, and pressures—and that is the basis of all human morality. —John F. Kennedy, *Profiles in Courage*, 1956

… my heart is set / On living—I have heroes to beget / Before I die …. —Edna St. Vincent Millay, "Thou famished grave, I will not fill thee yet," *Huntsman, What Quarry?*, 1939

Fear of something is at the root of hate for others, and hate within will eventually destroy the hater. —George Washington Carver, newspaper column, "Professor Carver's Advice," 1920s

Vanity working on a weak head produces every sort of mischief. —Jane Austen, *Emma*, 1815

We boil at different degrees. —Ralph Waldo Emerson, "Eloquence," *Society and Solitude*, 1870

If everyone was sincere who says he's sincere there wouldn't be half so many insincere ones in the world and there would be lots, lots, lots more really sincere ones! —Tennessee Williams, *Camino Real*, 1953

How quick come the reasons for approving what we like! —Jane Austen, *Persuasion*, 1818

> "Differences of habit and language are nothing at all if our aims are identical and our hearts are open."
>
> —J. K. Rowling, *Harry Potter and the Goblet of Fire*, 2000

The reasonable man adapts himself to the world: the unreasonable one persists in trying to adapt the world to himself. Therefore all progress depends on the unreasonable man. —George Bernard Shaw, "Maxims for Revolutionists," *Man and Superman*, 1903

Gratitude is the sign of noble souls. —Aesop, "Androcoles," *Fables*

Fame is a fickle food / Upon a shifting plate. —Emily Dickinson, No. 1659, *Poems*, Johnson

Compassion is the antitoxin of the soul. —Eric Hoffer, *The True Believer*, 1951

There is nothing so catching as refinement .... —Emily Eden, *The Semi-Attached Couple*, 1830

As far as your self-control goes, as far goes your freedom. —Maria von Ebner Eschenbach, *Aphorisms*, 1905

Excess of joy is harder to bear than any amount of sorrow. —Honoré de Balzac, "Letters of Two Brides," *La Press*, 1841–1842

When the wayfarer whistles in the dark, he may be disavowing his timidity, but he does not see any more clearly for doing so. —Sigmund Freud, *The Problem of Anxiety*, 1925

There is no need to waste pity on young girls who are having their moments of disillusionment, for in another moment they will recover their illusion. —Colette, "Wedding Day," *Earthly Paradise*, Robert Phelps, ed., 1966

> "Laughter and tears are meant to turn the wheels of the same machinery of sensibility; one is wind-power, and the other water-power; that is all."
>
> —Oliver Wendell Holmes, *The Autocrat of the Breakfast Table,* 1858

Cheating may or may not be human nature, but it is certainly a prominent feature in just about every human endeavor. —Steven D. Levitt and Stephen J. Dubner, *Freakonomics*, 2005

The control of our being is not unlike the combination of a safe. One turn of the knob rarely unlocks the safe. Each advance and retreat is a step toward one's goal. —Eric Hoffer, *The Passionate State of Mind: And Other Aphorisms*, 1954

Pride is a sweetmeat, to be savoured in small pieces; it makes for a poor feast. —Laurie R. King, *The Game*, 2004

The happy ending is our national belief. —Mary McCarthy, "America the Beautiful," *Commentary* (New York), 1947

23 The Beast—and Best—Within

What is the nature of existence? What can I do to make my life more meaningful? Is memory a fiction? Am I as smart as I think I am? Such ruminations are second nature to we humans. When we look to great and sharp minds for their bead on such issues, it often helps us clarify our own.

• • •

Life in itself / Is nothing, / An empty cup, a flight of uncarpeted stairs. —Edna St. Vincent Millay, "Spring," *Second April*, 1921

Life is the farce which everyone has to perform. —Arthur Rimbaud, "Mauvais Sang," *Une Saison en Enfer*, 1874

I believe that I am in hell, therefore I am there. —Arthur Rimbaud, "Nuit de l'Enfer," *Une Saison en Enfer*, 1874

It is the mind that makes the body. —Sojourner Truth, interview (Battle Creek, Michigan), c. 1877

Is there no way out of the mind? —Sylvia Plath, "Apprehensions," 1971

Man is the only animal that blushes, or needs to. —Mark Twain, *Following the Equator*, 1897

The middlebrow is the man, or woman, of middlebred intelligence who ambles and saunters now on this side of the hedge, now on that, in pursuit of no single object, neither art itself nor life itself, but both mixed indistinguishably, and rather nastily, with money, fame, power, or prestige. —Virginia Woolf, "Middlebrow," *The Death of the Moth*, 1942

> It was a pity he couldna be hatched o'er again, an' hatched different.
>
> —George Eliot, *Adam Bede*, 1859

The thing that is really hard, and really amazing, is giving up on being perfect and beginning the work of becoming yourself. More difficult, because there is no zeitgeist to read, no template to follow, no masks to wear. —Anna Quindlen, commencement address, Mount Holyoke College (South Hadley, Massachusetts), 1999

The best way to find yourself is to lose yourself in the service of others. —Mohandas Gandhi, *Writings*

I is another. —Arthur Rimbaud, letter (1871), *Collected Poems*, Oliver Bernard, ed., 1962

She ransacked her mind, but there was nothing in it. —Joyce Carol Oates, *Them*, 1969

I am no prophet—and here's no great matter; / I have seen the moment of my greatness flicker, / And I have seen the eternal Footman hold my coat, and snicker, / And in short, I was afraid. —T. S. Eliot, "The Love Song of J. Alfred Prufrock," 1917

> Inner space is the real frontier.
>
> —Gloria Steinem, quoted by Michael Larsen, *Literary Agents*, 1996

Your mind is made of crumbs …. —Edna St. Vincent Millay, *Aria Da Capo*, 1919

Thank God for the head. Inside the head is the only place you got to be young when the usual place gets used up. —Grace Paley, "Zagrowsky Tells," *Later the Same Day*, 1985

Often, the truly great and valuable lessons we learn in life are learned through pain. That's why they call it "growing pains." It's all about yin and yang. And that's not something you order off column A at your local Chinese restaurant. —Fran Drescher, *Cancer, Schmancer*, 2002

When you turn the corner / And you run into yourself / Then you know that you have turned / All the corners that are left. —Langston Hughes, "Final Curve," *Montage of a Dream Deferred*, 1951

Idle youth, enslaved to everything .... —Arthur Rimbaud, "Song of the Highest Tower," *Collected Poems*, Oliver Bernard, ed., 1962

Life, to be sure, is nothing much to lose; / But young men think it is, and we were young. —A. E. Housman, No. VI, *More Poems*, 1936

... the inner voice; the human compulsion when deeply distressed to seek healing counsel within ourselves, and the capacity within ourselves both to create this counsel and to receive it. —Alice Walker, "A Letter of the Times," *You Can't Keep a Good Woman Down*, 1981

Here is my secret. It is very simple: It is only with the heart that one can see rightly; what is essential is invisible to the eye. —Antoine de Saint-Exupéry, *The Little Prince*

I don't want to achieve immortality through my work ... I want to achieve it through not dying. —Woody Allen, quoted by Edward Lax, *Woody Allen and His Comedy*, 1975

Eternity. It is the sea mingled with the sun. —Arthur Rimbaud, "Délires II: Faim," *Une Saison en Enfer*, 1874

"Faith" is a fine invention / When Gentlemen can see— / But Microscopes are prudent / In an Emergency. —Emily Dickinson, No. 185, *Poems*, Johnson

One of the most striking differences between a cat and a lie is that a cat has only nine lives. —Mark Twain, *Pudd'n'head Wilson*, 1894

> Particular lies may speak a general truth.
> —George Eliot, *The Spanish Gypsy*, 1868

That which is hateful to you, do not do to your fellow. That is the whole Law; the rest is the explanation; go and learn. —Hillel, quoted in *Talmud*

With malice toward none; with charity for all; with firmness in the right, as God gives us to see the right—let us strive on to finish the work we are in. —Abraham Lincoln, *Second Inaugural Address* (Washington, D.C.), 1865

Integrity without knowledge is weak and useless, and knowledge without integrity is dangerous and dreadful. —Samuel Johnson, *The History of Rasselas, Prince of Abissinia*, 1759

The true manipulator never has a reputation for manipulating. —Martin Amis, *Claus von Bulow*, 1983

There are no new truths, but only truths that have not been recognized by those who have perceived them without noticing. A truth is something that everybody can be shown to know and to have known, as people say, all along. —Mary McCarthy, "The *Vita Activa*," *The New Yorker*, (New York), 1958

Real integrity is doing the right thing, knowing that nobody's going to know whether you did it or not. —Oprah Winfrey, attributed

> The great enemy of the truth is very often not the lie—deliberate, contrived and dishonest—but the myth—persistent, persuasive, and unrealistic.
>
> —John F. Kennedy, commencement address, Yale University (New Haven, Connecticut), 1962

A thing worth having is a thing worth cheating for. —W. C. Fields, *My Little Chickadee*, 1940

Virtue, my pet, is an abstract idea, varying in its manifestations with the surroundings. Virtue in Provence, in Constantinople, in London, and in Paris bears very different fruit, but is none the less virtue. —Honoré de Balzac, "Letters of Two Brides," *La Press*, 1841–1842

... virtue that transgresses is but patched with sin; and sin that amends is but patched with virtue. —William Shakespeare, *Twelfth Night*, 1601

As always happens—sooner or later—to those who shake hands with the devil, they find out too late that what they have given up in the bargain is their soul. —Al Gore, speech, New York University (New York), 2004

I will have nought to do with a man who can blow hot and cold with the same breath. —Aesop, "The Man and the Satyr," *Fables*

> Truth is stranger than fiction, but it is because fiction is obliged to stick to possibilities, truth isn't.
>
> —Mark Twain, *Following the Equator,* 1897

There is nothing either good or bad, but thinking makes it so. —William Shakespeare, *Hamlet*, 1600

The time is always right to do what is right. —Martin Luther King Jr., "Letter from Birmingham City Jail," 16 April 1963

The fact that man knows right from wrong proves his intellectual superiority to the other creatures; but the fact that he can do wrong proves his moral inferiority to any creature that cannot. —Mark Twain, *What Is Man?*, 1906

I am free of all prejudice. I hate everyone equally. —W. C. Fields, quoted in *A Treasury of Humorous Quotations*, Herbert V. Prochnow and Herbert V. Prochnow Jr., eds., 1969

There are several good protections against temptations, but the surest is cowardice. —Mark Twain, *Following the Equator*, 1897

Beware lest you lose the substance by grasping at the shadow. —Aesop, "The Dog and the Shadow," *Fables*

Blessed is the man who, having nothing to say, abstains from giving wordy evidence of the fact.
—George Eliot, *The Impressions of Theophrastus Such*, 1879

Being inoffensive, and being offended, are now the twin addictions of the culture. —Martin Amis, quoted in *The Sunday Times* (London), 1996

It is a rare privilege to watch the birth, growth, and first feeble struggles of a living mind .... —Annie Sullivan, letter (1887), quoted by Helen Keller, *The Story of My Life*, 1903

They sicken of the calm, who knew the storm. —Dorothy Parker, "Fair Weather," *Sunset Gun*, 1928

I've been on a calendar, but never on time. —Marilyn Monroe, quoted in *Look* (New York), 1962

It's a strange thing, but when you are dreading something, and would give anything to slow down time, it has a disobliging habit of speeding up. —J. K. Rowling, *Harry Potter and the Goblet of Fire*, 2000

We are dancing in darkness on the edge of tragedy. And quite literally scared to death. —Leonard Pitts, quoted in *The Miami Herald* (Miami), 2003

Security is essentially elusive, impossible. We all die. We all get sick. We all get old. People leave us. People surprise us. People change us. Nothing is secure. And this is the good news. But only if you are not seeking security as the point of your life. —Eve Ensler, introduction, *Insecure At Last: Losing It in Our Security-Obsessed World*, 2006

Where we have reasons for what we believe, we have no need of faith; where we have no reasons, we have lost both our connection to the world and to one another. —Sam Harris, *The End of Faith*, 2005

Modern man must descend the spiral of his own absurdity to the lowest point; only then can he look beyond it. It is obviously impossible to get around it, jump over it, or simply avoid it. —Václav Havel, *Disturbing the Peace*, 1986

Scientific progress makes moral progress a necessity; for if man's power is increased, the checks that restrain him from abusing it must be strengthened. —Germaine de Staël, *The Influence of Literature upon Society*, 1800

"... what frosty fate's in store / For the warm blood of man,—man, out of ooze / But lately crawled, and climbing up the shore?

—Edna St. Vincent Millay, "Epitaph for the Race of Man," *Wine from These Grapes*, 1939"

The price of peace is to abandon greed and replace it with giving, so that none will be spiritually injured by having more than they need while others in the world still have less than they need. —Peace Pilgrim, *Her Life and Work*

Our best destiny, as planetary cohabitants, is the development of what has been called "species consciousness"—something over and above nationalisms, blocs, religions, ethnicities. —Martin Amis, quoted in *The Guardian* (London), 2001

The salvation of this human world lies nowhere else than in the human heart, in the human power to reflect, in human meekness and human responsibility. —Václav Havel, quoted in *The International Herald Tribune* (Paris), 1990

We for a certainty are not the first / Have sat in taverns while the tempest hurled / Their hopeful plans to emptiness, and cursed / Whatever brute and blackguard made the world. —A. E. Housman, No. IX, *Last Poems*, 1922

Graciousness has been replaced by surliness in much of everyday life. —Margaret Thatcher, interview, *The Washington Post* (Washington, D.C.), 1989

Memory is a nutriment, and seeds stored for centuries can still germinate. —Adrienne Rich, lecture, Scripps College (Claremont, California, 1983), *Blood, Bread, and Poetry*

Bless the gift of memory / that breaks unbidden, released / from a flower or a cup of tea / so the dead move like rain through the room. —Marge Piercy, interpretation of the She'ma, *The Art of Blessing the Day*, 1999

… memory is more indelible than ink. —Anita Loos, *Kiss Hollywood Goodbye*, 1974

... imagination took the reins, and Reason, slow-paced, though sure-footed, was unequal to a race with so eccentric and flighty a companion. —Fanny Burney, *Evelina*, 1778

> My imagination makes me human and makes me a fool; it gives me all the world and exiles me from it.
>
> —Ursula K. Le Guin, *Harper's* (New York), 1990

... women like to live on their imagination. // It's all they can afford, most of them. —Penelope Fitzgerald, *The Gate of the Angels*, 1990

Imagination is more important than knowledge. For knowledge is limited, whereas imagination embraces the entire world, stimulating progress, giving birth to evolution. —Albert Einstein, *The Saturday Evening Post* (Philadelphia), 1929

Imagination, which is the eldorado of the poet and of the novel-writer, often proves the most pernicious gift to the individuals who compose the talkers instead of the writers in society. —Marguerite Blessington, *The Repealers*, 1833

Imagination is not an empirical or superadded power of consciousness, it is the whole of consciousness as it realizes its freedom. —Jean-Paul Sartre, *Imagination: A Psychological Critique*, 1936

Now, I doubt that the imagination can be suppressed. If you truly eradicated it in a child, he would grow up to be an eggplant. —Ursula K. Le Guin, *Language of the Night*

When a man knows that the abstraction ten exists—nothing on earth can stop him from looking for the fact of eleven. —Lorraine Hansberry, *Les Blancs*, 1972

Your memory is a monster; you forget—it doesn't. It simply files things away. It keeps things for you, or hides things from you—and summons them to your recall with a will of its own. You think you have a memory; but it has you! —John Irving, *A Prayer for Owen Meany*, 1989

A little Madness in the Spring / Is wholesome even for the King, / But God be with the Clown.

—Emily Dickinson, No. 1333, *Poems,* Johnson

I never forget a face, but in your case I'll be glad to make an exception. —Groucho Marx, quoted by Leo Rosten, *People I Have Loved, Known or Admired*, 1970

It sometimes occurs that memory has a personality of its own and volunteers or refuses its information at its will, not at mine. —Ralph Waldo Emerson, "Memory," *Natural History of Intellect*, 1893

Men more frequently require to be reminded than informed. —Samuel Johnson, No. 2, *The Rambler*, 1750–1752

Memory is the diary that we all carry about with us. —Oscar Wilde, *The Importance of Being Earnest*, 1895

The real sin against life is to abuse and destroy beauty, even one's own—even more, one's own, for that had been put in our care and we are responsible for its well-being .... —Katherine Anne Porter, *Ship of Fools*, 1962

Life is a compromise between fate and free will. —Elbert Hubbard, *A Thousand and One Epigrams*, 1911

It disturbs me no more to find men base, unjust, or selfish than to see apes mischievous, wolves savage, or the vulture ravenous for its prey. —Molière, *Le Misanthrope*, 1666

Selected Bibliography

A

Most titles appear complete in the quotations section. But some titles are so long, or appear so frequently, I decided to shorten them in order to give you more quotes and less clutter. When you see a title in the quotation section without a publication year following it (for example: Ursula K. Le Guin, *Language of the Night*), that will signal you to look up Le Guin in this bibliography for the complete title (if you've a mind to).

Adams, F. P. D., D. Taylor, and J. Bechdolt, eds., *The Book of Diversion*, 1925.

Adams, Henry, *The Education of Henry Adams*, 1907.

Amiel, Henri-Frédéric, *Journal Intime*, Mary Augusta Ward, tr., 1892.

Anthony, Susan B., Mathilda Gage, and Elizabeth Cady Stanton, *History of Woman Suffrage*, vols. I & II, 1881.

Auden, W. H., *The Table Talk of W. H. Auden/Alan Ansen*, Nicholas Jenkins, ed., 1990.

Bontemps, Arna, ed., *Golden Slippers: An Anthology of Negro Poetry for Young Readers*, 1941.

Child, Julia, with Simone Beck and Louisette Bertholle, *Mastering the Art of French Cooking*, 1961.

Cowley, Malcolm, ed., *Writers at Work (First Series)*, 1958.

de Pange, Jean, ed., *Madame de Staël et François de Pange: lettres et documents inédits*, 1925.

Dickinson, Emily, *The Complete Poems of Emily Dickinson*, Thomas H. Johnson, ed., 1955.

Dukas, Helen, and Banesh Hoffman, eds., *Albert Einstein, The Human Side: New Glimpses From His Archives*, 1981.

Ehrenreich, Barbara, *The Hearts of Men: American Dreams and the Flight from Commitment*, 1983.

Einstein, Albert, *The Collected Papers of Albert Einstein*, 1987.

Eisler, Riane, *The Chalice and the Blade: Our History, Our Future*, 1987.

———, *Sacred Pleasure: Sex, Myth, and the Politics of the Body*, 1995.

———, *Tomorrow's Children: A Blueprint for Partnership Education for the 21st Century*, 2000.

Epstein, Lawrence J., *The Haunted Smile, The Story of Jewish Comedians in America*, 2001.

Fields, Ronald J. (his son), ed., *W. C. Fields By Himself*, 1972.

———, *W. C. Fields: A Life on Film*, 1984.

Flores, Angel, ed., *An Anthology of Spanish Poetry, From Garcilaso to García Lorca*, 1979.

Getlen, Larry, ed., *The Complete Idiot's Guide to Jokes*, 2006.

Goldman, Robert N., *Einstein's God: Albert Einstein's Quest As a Scientist and As a Jew to Replace a Forsaken God*, 1997.

Haedrich, Marcel, *Coco Chanel: Her Life, Her Secrets*, 1971.

Hubbard, Elbert, *The Note Book of Elbert Hubbard: Mottoes, Epigrams, Short Essays, Passages, Orphic Sayings and Preachments*, Elbert Hubbard II, comp., 1927.

———, *The Elbert Hubbard Notebook*, Orlando R. Petrocelli, ed., 1980.

Klagsbrun, Francine, ed., *The First Ms. Reader*, 1972.

Le Guin, Ursula, *The Language of the Night: Essays on Fantasy and Science Fiction*, Susan Wood, ed., 1979.

Levitt, Steven D., and Stephen J. Dubner, *Freakonomics: A Rogue Economist Explores the Hidden Side of Everything*, 2005.

Martin, Linda, and Kerry Segrave, *Women in Comedy*, 1986.

McGinley, Phyllis, *Times Three: 1932–1960*, 1960.

Montagu, Mary Wortley, *Letters of the Right Honourable Lady Mary Wortley Montagu*, 1767.

———, *The Letters and Works of Lady Mary Wortley Montagu*, Lord Wharncliffe, ed., 1861.

Niederman, Sharon, ed., *Shaking Eve's Tree, Short Stories of Jewish Women*, 1990.

Pilgrim, Peace, *Peace Pilgrim: Her Life and Work in Her Own Words*, 1982.

Piozzi, Hester Lynch, *Anecdotes of the Late Samuel Johnson*, 1786.

Pogrebin, Letty Cottin, *Deborah, Golda, and Me; Being Female and Jewish in America*, 1991.

Rich, Adrienne, *Blood, Bread, and Poetry: Selected Prose 1979–1985*, 1986.

———, *The Dream of a Common Language, Poems (1974–1977)*, 1978.

Saint-Exupéry, Antoine de, *The Little Prince*, Katherine Woods, tr., 1943

Schopenhauer, Arthur, *Essays of Arthur Schopenhauer*, T. Bailey Saunders, tr., 1851.

Sainte-Beuve, C. A., *Memoirs of Madame Desbordes-Valmore*, Harriet W. Preston, tr., 1872.

Shikibu, Murasaki, *The Tale of Genji*, vols. I & II, 1001–1015, Arthur Waley, tr., 1970.

Stanton, Theodore, and Harriot Stanton Blatch, eds., *Elizabeth Cady Stanton*, vols. I & II, 1922.

Taylor, Robert Lewis, *W. C. Fields: His Follies and Fortunes*, 1949.

Toklas, Alice B., *Staying On Alone: Letters of Alice B. Toklas*, Ed Burns, ed., 1973.

Unterbrink, Mary, *Funny Women, American Comediennes, 1860–1985*, 1987.

Warhol, Andy, *The Philosophy of Andy Warhol: From A to B and Back Again*, 1975.

West, Mae; *The Wit and Wisdom of Mae West*, Joseph Weintraub, ed., 1967.

Wilde, Oscar, *The Critic as Artist: With Some Remarks Upon the Importance of Doing Nothing*, 1891.

List of Contributors

A

Ace, Goodman (1899–1982): American radio personality, humorist, radio and television writer; husband of comedian Jane Ace. *See pages* 2, 49, 57, 79, 88, 93, 101, 170, 178.

Adams, Henry (B.) (1838–1918): American historian, journalist, novelist. *See pages* 36, 37, 131, 133, 157, 165, 175.

Adams, John (1735–1826): American political leader; second U.S. President. *See page* 45.

Aesop (sixth century B.C.E.): Greek fabulist, emancipated slave. *See pages* 62, 71, 73, 93, 117, 155, 166, 187, 191, 197, 198.

Alcott, Louisa May (1832–1888): American editor, writer; pseudonym A. M. Barnard. *See pages* 13, 14, 25, 51, 148, 187.

Allen, Fred (1894–1957): American radio personality, humorist. *See pages* 64, 88.

Allen, Woody (1935–): American actor, film director, comedian, writer; three-time Oscar winner. *See pages* 38, 48, 61, 64, 72, 76, 86, 90, 109, 132, 150, 178, 179, 195.

Allende, Isabel (1942–): Chilean-American journalist, novelist. *See pages* 5, 8, 46, 164.

Amiel, Henri-Frédéric (1821–1881): Swiss philosopher, poet, critic. *See pages* 104, 138, 168, 169, 186.

B

Barry, Dave (1947–): American humorist, newspaper columnist, author; Pulitzer, 1988. *See pages* 28, 80, 116, 121.

Baum, L. Frank (1856–1919): American author. *See pages* 54, 120, 159.

Behn, Aphra (1640–1689): English playwright, novelist, spy. *See pages* 5, 36, 56, 61, 136, 138, 158.

Bell, Dr. Bernard Iddings (1886–1958): American clergyman, educator, writer. *See pages* 33, 40

Benny, Jack (1894–1974): American comedian, radio and television personality, violinist. *See pages* 4, 68.

Berners, Juliana, Dame (1460?–?): English prioress, poet. *See pages* 119, 121, 133.

Bernhard, Sandra (1955–): American comedian, actor. *See pages* 50, 127.

Berra, Lawrence "Yogi" (1925–): American baseball player and manager, New York Yankees (1946–1963). *See pages* 89, 108.

Bierce, Ambrose (1842–1913/14): American satirist, critic, writer. *See pages* 1, 41, 45, 46, 59, 118, 129, 157, 158, 160, 171.

Blessington, Marguerite, Lady (1789–1849): Irish novelist, salonist, poet. *See pages* 6, 43, 74, 136, 201.

Boosler, Elayne (1952–): American comedian. *See pages* 54, 19, 112.

Brecht, Bertolt (1898–1956): German dramatist, poet, stage director. *See page* 57.

Bruce, Lenny (1925–1966): American comedian, political satirist. *See pages* 39, 76.

Buck, Pearl S. (1892–1973): American novelist, human rights activist; Nobel Prize, 1938; Pulitzer, 1932. *See pages* 46, 57, 91, 152, 162, 167, 172, 186.

Buffett, Warren (1930–): American investor, philanthropist. *See pages* 56, 57, 62.

Burgess, Anthony (1917–1993): English novelist, critic, composer. *See page* 143.

Burney, Fanny (1752–1840): English novelist, playwright. *See pages* 106, 174, 201.

Burns, George (1896–1996): American comedian, actor; husband of comedian Gracie Allen; Oscar, 1975. *See pages* 2, 30, 32, 66, 68, 124, 181.

Burroughs, William S. (1914–1997): American novelist, social critic, painter. *See pages* 79, 107, 117.

Bush, George W. (1946–), American political leader; fourty-third U.S. President; Texas governor (1995–2000). *See pages* 44, 98, 150, 161, 188.

C

Carlin, George (1937–): American comedian, actor, author; four-time Grammy winner. *See pages* 23, 110, 125, 154.

Carson, Johnny (1925–2005): American television personality, comedian, writer; hosted *The Tonight Show* (1962–1992). *See pages* 3, 10, 162, 179.

Carver, George Washington (1864–1943): American botanist, educator, columnist; Spingarn Medal, 1923. *See pages* 99, 190.

Carville, James (1944–), American political consultant, media personality. *See pages* 56, 57, 100.

Cavendish, Margaret (1623?–1673?): English-French poet, writer, playwright; a.k.a. Duchess of Newcastle. *See pages* 4, 47, 93, 130.

Centlivre, Susanna (1667?–1723): Irish-English playwright, actor. *See pages* 17, 60.

Chanel, Coco (1883–1971): French fashion designer. *See pages* 29, 133.

Chayefsky, Paddy (1923–1981): American playwright, screenwriter; Oscar, 1953. *See page* 48.

Child, Julia (1912–2004): American chef, author, television personality; Emmy, 1966. *See pages* 28, 110, 111, 112, 114.

Child, Lydia Maria (1802–1880): American writer, editor, abolitionist. *See pages* 22, 53, 91 182.

Chopin, Kate (1851–1904): American writer. *See pages* 4, 36, 56.

Chopra, Deepak (1946–): Indian-American physician, spiritual leader, writer; co-founded The Chopra Center, 1996; founded Alliance for a New Humanity, 2007. *See pages* 138, 180.

Christie, Agatha, Dame (1891–1975): English novelist, playwright. *See pages* 60, 65, 94, 103, 140.

Churchill, Winston, Sir (1874–1965): British political leader, British Prime Minister, writer; Nobel Prize for Literature, 1953. *See pages* 34, 66, 99, 106, 163, 166, 173.

Cleese, John (1939–): British comedian, actor; founding member, Monty Python; Emmy, 1987; Golden Globe, 1989. *See pages* 111, 139.

Clinton, Bill (1946–): American political leader; Arkansas Governor, forty-second U.S. President. *See pages* 13, 31, 125, 171.

Clinton, Hillary Rodham (1947–): American lawyer, children's rights advocate, health-care activist; U.S. forty-second First Lady, 1993–2000; New York Senator, 2001–; wife of Bill Clinton. *See pages* 6, 17, 21, 35, 76, 157, 173.

Cohen, Leonard (1934–): Canadian lyricist, singer, poet, novelist; Canadian Songwriters Hall of Fame. *See pages* 45, 76, 78.

Colbert, Stephen (1964–): American actor, comedian; three-time Emmy winner. *See pages* 40, 99, 127, 163, 184.

Colette (1873–1954): French writer. *See pages* 7, 11, 23, 103, 113, 116, 130, 138, 172, 180, 182, 183, 192.

Cosby, Bill (1937–): American actor, comedian, television personality and producer, activist; multiple Emmy and Grammy Awards. *See pages* 17, 19, 30.

Cottin Pogrebin, Letty (1939–): American journalist, author, activist; co-founder, *Ms.* Magazine. *See page* 10.

Cruz, Juana Inés de la, Sor (1651–1695): Mexican poet, scholar, nun. *See pages* 60, 92, 114.

cummings, e. e. (1894–1962): American poet, painter. *See pages* 70, 83, 96, 97.

D

Davis, Bette (1908–1989): American actor; two-time Oscar winner; two-time Emmy winner. *See pages* 18, 68, 95, 118, 184.

Desbordes-Valmore, Marceline (1786–1859): French poet, actor. *See pages* 51, 129, 150.

Diamond, Selma (1920–1985): Canadian-American comedian. *See pages* 45, 131, 134.

Dickinson, Emily (1830–1886): American poet. *See pages* 46, 48, 87, 90, 100, 105, 106, 170, 171, 176, 186, 187, 191, 196, 202.

Didion, Joan (1935–): American writer, screenwriter, journalist; wife of writer John Gregory Dunne; National Book Award, 2007. *See pages* 57, 94, 103.

Dillard, Annie (1945–): American writer, poet, magazine editor; Pulitzer, 1975. *See page* 47.

Diller, Phyllis (1917–): American writer, comedian, pianist. *See pages* 1, 7, 29, 50, 51, 69, 76, 78, 190.

Drescher, Fran (1957–): American actor, comedian; founder, Cancer Schmancer Movement, 2007. *See pages* 92, 103, 132, 135, 141, 195.

du Maurier, Daphne, Dame (1907–1989): English playwright, writer. *See pages* 27, 88.

Dubner, Stephen J. (1963–): American journalist, author. *See pages* 18, 23, 192.

Duncan, Isadora (1878–1927): American dancer. *See pages* 3, 12, 96, 98.

E

Eden, Emily (1797–1869): English-Indian novelist; a.k.a. Lady Auckland. *See pages* 2, 15, 191.

Edgeworth, Maria (1767–1849): Irish essayist, novelist. *See pages* 18, 24, 27, 65, 74, 89, 94, 123, 127, 176, 186.

Ehrenreich, Barbara (1941–): American columnist, author. *See pages* 10, 97, 121.

Einstein, Albert (1879–1955): German-American physicist; famed for his Theory of Relativity; Nobel Prize–winner. *See pages* 34, 35, 47, 58, 70, 72, 114, 115, 154, 201.

Eisler, Riane (1931–): Austrian-American author, macro-historian; founded Center for Partnership Studies; International Partnership Network. *See pages* 13, 14, 22, 47, 145, 153, 154, 181.

Eliot, George (1819–1880): English writer. *See pages* 2, 10, 16, 33, 70, 71, 72, 73, 90, 91, 97, 119, 122, 124, 130, 131, 132, 136, 168, 169, 170, 172, 172, 174, 189, 194, 196, 198.

Eliot, T. S. (1888–1965), American-British poet, literary critic, playwright; Nobel Prize for Literature, 1948. *See pages* 106, 185, 194.

Emerson, Ralph Waldo (1803–1882): American essayist, philosopher, poet. *See pages* 10, 15, 23, 32, 42, 52, 54, 69, 105, 107, 108, 113, 129, 130, 135, 136, 143, 152, 158, 165, 191, 202.

Ensler, Eve (1953–): American playwright, actor; founder and artistic director of V-Day; Obie, 1996. *See pages* 36, 78, 79, 126, 160, 199.

Ephron, Nora (1941–): American writer, screenwriter. *See pages* 24, 81, 132.

Eschenbach, Maria von Ebner (1830–1916): Austrian novelist. *See pages* 104, 134, 135, 172, 186, 187, 192.

F

Faulkner, William (1897–1962): American novelist, poet; Nobel Prize for Literature, 1949. *See pages* 29, 66, 84, 153, 188.

Ferber, Edna (1887–1968): American playwright, novelist, scenarist; Pulitzer, 1925. *See pages* 2, 8, 39, 51, 69, 115, 128, 155, 177.

Fields, W. C. (1880–1946): American actor, comedian, juggler. *See pages* 2, 16, 24, 25, 77, 79, 82, 115, 119, 123, 124, 125, 133, 197, 198.

Fisher, M. F. K. (1908–1992): American food writer. *See pages* 26, 86, 110, 114, 115, 116, 178.

Fitzgerald, Penelope (1916–2000): English novelist; Booker Prize, 1979. *See pages* 175, 180, 201.

Fonda, Jane (1937–): American actor, political activist, fitness expert; two-time Oscar winner. *See pages* 20, 81.

Freud, Sigmund (1856–1939): Austrian neurologist; known as "the father of psychoanalysis." *See pages* 22, 43, 80, 81, 161, 182.

Friedan, Betty (1921–2006): American feminist, writer; founded National Organization for Women (NOW), 1966. *See pages* 51, 52, 111.

Frost, Robert (1874–1963): American poet; four-time Pulitzer Prize winner. *See pages* 8, 66.

Fry, Stephen (1957–): British writer, comedian, director. *See pages* 25, 31, 95.

Fulton, Alice (1952–): American educator, poet, writer. *See pages* 9, 15.

G

Gabor, Zsa Zsa (1919–): Hungarian-American actor, business executive; Miss Hungary, 1936. *See pages* 4, 5, 7, 50.

Gandhi, Mohandas (1868–1948): Indian Political leader; recognized as the father of modern India; leading proponent of nonviolence. *See pages* 42, 45, 79, 113, 155, 173, 194.

García Márquez, Gabriel (1927–): Colombian novelist, journalist, political activist; Nobel Prize, 1982. *See pages*

Gates, Bill (1955–): American entrepreneur, philanthropist; co-founder and chairman of Microsoft; co-founded The Bill and Melinda Gates Foundation. *See page* 142.

Glaspell, Susan (1876?–1948): American writer, playwright; co-founded Provincetown Players; Pulitzer, 1931. *See page* 80.

Gordon, Ruth (1896–1985): American actor, screenwriter, playwright; wife of writer Garson Kanin; Oscar, 1968; Emmy, 1979. *See pages* 97, 101.

Gore, Al (1948–): American political leader, environmentalist, businessman; forty-fifth U.S. Vice President, 1993–2000; Oscar, 2006. *See pages* 163, 187, 197.

Greer, Germaine (1939–): Australian feminist, writer. *See pages* 2, 12, 93, 94, 129, 134.

H

Hale, Sarah Josepha (1788–1879): American writer, editor, poet; established Thanksgiving as a national holiday; established Mount Vernon as a national shrine. *See pages* 40, 53, 50, 116, 123, 183.

Hansberry, Lorraine (1930–1965): American playwright, author; New York Drama Critics Award, 1959. *See pages* 53, 154, 201.

Harris, Sam (1967–): American writer. *See pages* 46, 47, 48, 199.

Havel, Václav (1936–): Czech poet, political leader, activist; Czech President (1989–2003); Nobel Peace Prize, 1989. *See pages* 141, 148, 151, 158, 199, 200.

Hellman, Lillian (1905–1984): American playwright, writer, political activist. *See pages* 123, 138, 159.

Hemingway, Ernest (1899–1961): American writer; Nobel Prize for Literature, 1954. *See pages* 68, 84, 88, 103, 108.

Herold, Don (1889–1966): American cartoonist, writer. *See page* 9.

Hillel, Rabbi (fl. 50 B.C.E.–30 C.E.): Jerusalemite rabbi, scholar, woodcutter; fostered a liberal interpretation of the Hebrew Scriptures. *See pages* 35, 77, 90, 196.

Hoffer, Eric (1902–1983): American social writer, longshoreman; Presidential Medal of Freedom, 1983. *See pages* 27, 104, 105, 191, 192.

Holmes, Oliver Wendell (1809–1894): American physician, writer, poet. *See pages* 31, 55, 102, 159, 165, 173, 192.

Hope, Bob (1903–2003): English-American comedian, actor; two Honorary Oscars and Jean Hersholt Humanitarian Award; Congressional Gold Medal, 1962; Presidential Medal of Freedom, 1969. *See pages* 5, 31, 120, 123, 125.

Hosseini, Khaled (1965–): Afghan-American novelist, physician. *See pages* 23, 89, 173, 187.

Housman, A. E. (1859–1936): British poet, classical scholar. *See pages* 98, 117, 118, 195, 200.

Hubbard, Elbert (1856–1915): American writer, editor, philosopher. *See pages* 23, 34, 67, 73, 95, 103, 130, 171, 190, 202.

Hughes, Langston (1902–1967): American poet, playwright, author; Spingarn Medal, 1960. *See pages* 94, 99, 195.

Hugo, Victor (1802–1885): French novelist, poet, dramatist. *See pages* 67, 99, 105, 116, 137, 140, 184, 189.

Huxley, Aldous (1894–1963): English writer, novelist. *See page* 47.

I

Irving, John (1942–): American novelist, screenwriter; Oscar, 2000. *See pages* 37, 39, 43, 44, 102, 107, 142, 202.

Ivins, Molly (1944–2007): American newspaper columnist, writer, political commentator. *See pages* 35, 58, 109.

J

Jackson, Jesse (1941–): American civil rights leader, minister; founded Rainbow Coalition, 1984. *See pages* 70, 100, 186.

Jefferson, Thomas (1743–1826): American political leader, philosopher; one of America's Founders; third U.S. President; principal author of the Declaration of Independence. *See pages* 117, 149, 150, 162, 168.

Johnson, Dr. Samuel, (1709–1784): English poet, essayist, lexicographer, literary critic. *See pages* 2, 28, 59, 62, 70, 102, 110, 117, 118, 121, 122, 133, 144, 152, 183, 196, 202.

Jong, Erica (1942–): American writer, poet. *See pages* 4, 50, 80, 134, 136.

Jordan, June (1939–): American poet, civil rights activist. *See pages* 14, 15, 52.

Jung, Carl (1875–1961): Swiss psychiatrist; founder of analytical psychology. *See pages* 23, 38, 79, 81, 96, 143, 155, 160, 167.

K

Keillor, Garrison (1942–): American radio personality, humorist, author. *See pages* 11, 25, 94, 97, 132.

Kennedy, Florynce (1916–2000): American civil rights activist, lawyer, feminist. *See pages* 20, 63, 102, 105.

Kennedy, John F. (1917–1963): American political leader; thirty-fifth U.S. President. *See pages* 41, 61, 171, 189, 190, 197.

Kerr, Jean (1923–2003): American author, playwright; wife of Walter Kerr. *See pages* 61, 98, 118, 137, 186.

Key, Ellen (1849–1926): Swedish writer, feminist. *See pages* 6, 19, 24, 35, 38, 53.

Khayyám, Omar (1048–1131): Persian poet, astronomer, mathematician, philosopher. *See pages* 118, 122, 128.

Kiley, Brian (1967?–): American comedian, writer. *See pages* 35, 38.

King, Alan (1927–2004): American comedian, author, philanthropist. *See pages* 2, 57, 109.

King, Billie Jean (1943–): American tennis player; pioneer in raising recognition and pay for professional women athletes. *See page* 120.

King, Laurie R. (1952–): American novelist. *See pages* 126, 134, 141, 192.

King, Martin Luther Jr. (1929–1968): American civil rights leader, minister, orator; Nobel Peace Prize, 1968; Presidential Medal of Freedom, 1977; Martin Luther King Day, established as a national holiday, 1986; Congressional Gold Medal, 2004. *See pages* 153, 186, 189, 198.

Kipling, Rudyard (1865–1936): Indian-British poet, writer; Nobel Prize for Literature, 1907. *See pages* 25, 72, 100.

Koestler, Arthur (1905–1983): Hungarian-British novelist, philosopher, political activist. *See pages* 125, 163.

Kübler-Ross, Elizabeth (1926–2004): Swiss-American author, thanatologist, psychiatrist. *See pages* 85, 87, 89, 104, 168.

Kucinich, Dennis J. (1946–): American political leader, Cleveland Mayor, 1977-79; Ohio Congressmember, 1997–. *See pages* 148, 154, 190.

Kuhn, Maggie (1905–1995): American author, civil rights activist; founded Gray Panthers, 1970. *See pages* 68, 165.

L

Lamb, Mary Ann (1764–1847): English dressmaker, letter writer, poet. *See pages* 11, 12, 13, 103.

Landers, Ann (1918–2002): American newspaper columnist; twin sister of Abigail Van Buren (Dear Abbey). *See pages* 6, 8, 24, 96.

Le Guin, Ursula K. (1929–): American writer; multiple Nebula and Hugo Awards; Library of Congress Living Legends Award, 2000. *See pages* 38, 46, 96, 102, 150, 153, 165, 201.

Le Shan, Eda J. (1922–2002): American family counselor, educator, writer. *See pages* 6, 16, 24, 34, 80.

Lebowitz, Fran (1951–): American humorist, writer, journalist. *See pages* 12, 49, 115, 127, 134, 138.

Lennon, John (1940–1980): English singer, songwriter, peace activist; member of The Beatles; Grammy winner. *See pages* 67, 100, 146, 159.

Leno, Jay (1950–): American comedian, television personality; hosts *The Tonight Show*, 1992–. *See page* 26.

Lessing, Doris (1919–): English novelist, playwright. *See pages* 29, 149, 166, 182.

Levertov, Denise (1923–1997): English-American poet, translator, educator, poetry editor. *See pages* 6, 54.

Levitt, Steven D. (1967–): American economist, author, educator. *See pages* 18, 23, 192.

Liebman, Wendy (1961–): American comedian. *See pages* 1, 7, 26, 76.

Lincoln, Abraham (1809–1865): American political leader, lawyer; sixteenth U.S. President. *See pages* 40, 73, 94, 118, 144, 147, 148, 151, 163, 196.

Long, Earl K. (1895–1960): American political leader; Louisiana Governor, 1939–1940, 1948–1952, and 1956–1960. *See page* 138.

Longfellow, Henry Wadsworth (1807–1882): American poet. *See pages* 10, 11, 67, 144, 169.

Loos, Anita (1888–1981): American screenwriter, novelist, playwright, humorist. *See pages* 3, 6, 20, 37, 40, 122, 123, 179, 200.

Lowell, Amy (1874–1925): American poet, literary critic; Pulitzer, 1926. *See pages* 97, 185.

Lowell, James Russell (1819–1891): American poet, editor, abolitionist, diplomat. *See pages* 67, 105, 141.

Luce, Clare Boothe (1903–1987): American writer, political leader, playwright; Connecticut Congressmember, 1943–1947; U.S. Ambassador to Italy, 1953–1957; Presidential Medal of Freedom, 1983. *See pages* 7, 61, 156.

M

Maguire, Gregory (1954–): American novelist. *See pages* 18, 91, 124, 139, 146, 164.

Maher, Bill (1956–): American comedian, television writer and producer, free speech activist. *See pages* 59, 85.

Malcolm X (1925–1965): American civil rights leader, minister; national spokesman for the Nation of Islam; founded Muslim Mosque, Inc., and the Organization of Afro-American Unity. *See pages* 35, 45, 160, 164.

Marx, Groucho (1890–1977), American comedian; one of the Marx Brothers. *See pages* 5, 124, 150, 158, 202.

Maurois, André (1885–1967): French author. *See page* 142.

McCarthy, Mary (1912–1989): American writer, editor, drama and social critic. *See pages* 50, 67, 75, 104, 127, 158, 179, 188, 192, 196.

McGinley, Phyllis (1905–1978): American writer, poet, humorist; Pulitzer, 1961. *See pages* 11, 18, 22, 59, 74, 140.

McLuhan, Marshall (1911–1980): Canadian communications theorist. *See pages* 15, 80, 142.

Mead, Margaret (1901–1977): American anthropologist, museum curator, writer; Presidential Medal of Freedom, 1979. *See pages* 27, 68, 146.

Meir, Golda (1898–1978): Russian-American-Israeli political leader; Israel's first minister of labor, 1949–1956; foreign minister, 1956–1966; Prime Minister, 1969–1974. *See pages* 14, 31, 152, 158.

Midler, Bette (1945–): American actor, singer, writer; Grammy Awards, 1973, 1980; Tony, 1973; Emmy, 1978. *See pages* 7, 134, 179.

Millay, Edna St. Vincent (1892–1950): American poet, playwright, writer; Pulitzer, 1923. *See pages* 19, 30, 47, 83, 86, 88, 89, 92, 102, 108, 121, 122, 150, 168, 170, 178, 179, 184, 190, 193, 194, 199.

Miller, Arthur (1915–2005), American playwright, essayist; Pulitzer, 1949; Tony, 1947. *See pages* 13, 54, 65, 166, 169.

Milne, A. A. (1882–1956): English author, poet, playwright. *See pages* 2, 27, 75, 113, 183.

Mistral, Gabriela (1889–1957): Chilean poet, diplomat, educational activist; Chilean consul in Naples, Madrid, and Lisbon; first Latina to win Nobel Prize, 1945. *See pages* 9, 39, 46, 87, 177, 181.

Mitchell, Margaret (1900–1949): American writer; Pulitzer, 1937. *See pages* 14, 60, 62.

Molière (1622–1673): French playwright, director, actor; one of the masters of comic satire. *See pages* 3, 81, 96, 117, 122, 124, 139, 164, 168, 202.

Monroe, Marilyn (1926–1962): American actor, singer, pop icon; Golden Globe, 1960. *See pages* 3, 51, 64, 66, 81, 198.

Montagu, Mary Wortley, Lady (1689–1762): English poet, essayist, letter writer. *See pages* 18, 39, 75, 109.

Montessori, Maria (1870–1952): Italian physician, educator, writer; originated the Montessori Method of education. *See pages* 12, 38, 127.

Morrison, Toni (1931–): American novelist, book editor; first black woman to win Nobel Prize, 1993; Pulitzer, 1988. *See pages* 18, 51, 182.

Moskowitz, Faye (1930–): American writer. *See pages* 26, 88.

Moyers, Bill (1934–): American journalist, public commentator, author. *See pages* 42, 148, 159.

N

Nash, Ogden (1902–1971): American humorist, poet. *See pages* 3, 18, 19, 27, 67, 95, 116, 118, 122, 126, 128, 156.

Naylor, Gloria (1950–): American writer; National Book Award, 1988. *See pages* 34, 37, 112, 131.

Neruda, Pablo (1904–1973): Chilean poet, political leader; Nobel Prize for Literature, 1971. *See pages* 78, 86, 144.

Nhat Hanh, Thich (1926–): Vietnamese Zen Buddhist monk, educator, peace activist. *See page* 44.

Nichols, Mike (1931–): German-American director, producer, comedian, writer; Oscar, 1967; Golden Globe, 1968; four-time Emmy winner; eight-time Tony winner. *See page* 70.

Nightingale, Florence (1820–1910): English nurse, writer; pioneer of modern nursing; first woman to receive British Order of Merit, 1907. *See pages* 82, 102.

O

O'Brien, Conan (1963–): American comedian, television writer and producer; Emmy, 1989. *See pages* 95, 117.

O'Rourke, P. J. (1947–): American journalist, political satirst. *See pages* 44, 121, 124, 126, 161, 162.

Oates, Joyce Carol (1938–): American writer, educator; National Book Award, 1970. *See pages* 85, 89, 103, 104, 174, 176, 181, 194.

Obama, Barack (1961–): American political leader, author; Illinois Senator 2005–. *See pages* 33, 56, 140, 148.

Olsen, Tillie (1912–2007): American writer; O. Henry Prize, 1961. *See pages* 9, 12, 42.

Ono, Yoko (1933–): Japanese-American poet, painter, songwriter; widow of John Lennon. *See page* 146.

Orman, Suze (1952–): American financial writer. *See pages* 55, 60, 190.

Ortega y Gasset, José (1883–1955): Spanish philosopher, essayist, educator; founded *Revista de Occidente* magazine, 1923–1936. *See pages* 120, 140, 173, 187.

Orwell, George (1903–1950): Indian-British writer, journalist, cultural critic. *See pages* 149, 161, 166, 174.

P

Paley, Grace (1922–2007): American writer, poet, political activist. *See pages* 13, 88, 161, 189, 195.

Parker, Dorothy (1893–1967): American award-winning writer, poet, humorist; O. Henry Award, 1929. *See pages* 24, 62, 63, 125, 128, 131, 132, 169, 170, 178, 179, 184, 198.

Partnow, Al (1914–2002): American businessman; father of this book's author.

Peace Pilgrim (1908–1981): American pacifist, walker, philosopher. *See pages* 14, 45, 66, 119, 173, 200.

Pelosi, Nancy (1940–): American political leader; California Congressmember, 1987–; first woman Speaker of the House, 2007–. *See pages* 49, 95, 160.

Philips, Emo (1956–): American comedian. *See pages* 38, 45, 58.

Piercy, Marge (1936–): American award-winning writer, poet, magazine editor, feminist; founded the Movement for a Democratic Society (MDS). *See pages* 47, 114, 151, 155, 200.

Pitts, Leonard (1957–): American newspaper columnist; Pulitzer, 2004. *See pages* 62, 199.

Plath, Sylvia (1932–1963): American writer, poet; pseudonym Victoria Lucas; wife of poet Ted Hughes. *See pages* 50, 81, 89, 193.

Plato (427?–347 B.C.E.): Greek philosopher; pupil and friend of Socrates; founded the Academy, the ancient world's most influential school. *See pages* 16, 35, 36, 81, 154, 162, 176.

Pollan, Michael (1955–): American writer, journalist, educator. *See pages* 109, 110, 116.

Porter, Katherine Anne (1890–1980): American writer; Pulitzer, 1966. *See pages* 36, 77, 91, 123, 202.

Porter, Sylvia (1913–1991): American economist, writer, columnist. *See page* 58.

Q–R

Quindlen, Anna (1953–): American columnist; Pulitzer, 1992. *See pages* 37, 43, 120, 194, 120.

Radner, Gilda (1946–1989): American actor, comedian; wife of actor Gene Wilder; Emmy, 1978. *See pages* 77, 87, 104, 132.

Rand, Ayn (1905–1982): Russian-born American novelist, philosopher, screenwriter; originated the philosophy of "objectivism." *See pages* 59, 64, 150, 156.

Reagan, Ronald (1911–2004): American political leader, actor; fourtieth U.S. President. *See pages* 59, 73, 156, 162.

Repplier, Agnes (1858–1950): American writer, social critic. *See pages* 30, 138.

Resnik, Muriel (193–?–1995): American playwright. *See pages* 14, 58.

Rice, Condoleezza (1954–): American public servant; first woman to serve as U.S. Secretary of State, first African-American woman to serve in U.S. Cabinet. *See pages* 67, 70, 73.

Rich, Adrienne (1929–): American award-winning poet, educator, feminist; National Book Award, 1974. *See pages* 135, 143, 182, 200.

Rimbaud, Arthur (1854–1891): French poet. *See pages* 22, 43, 46, 193, 194, 195.

Rivers, Joan (1933–): American comedian, television personality, businesswoman; Emmy, 1990. *See pages* 4, 8, 51, 77, 112, 137.

Roddick, Anita (1942–): English business executive, entrepreneur; established The Body Shop retail chain. *See pages* 64, 188.

Roosevelt, Eleanor (1884–1962): American lecturer, humanitarian, government official, writer; thirty-second First Lady; wife of Franklin D. Roosevelt, niece of Theodore Roosevelt. *See pages* 48, 61, 71, 138, 140.

Roosevelt, Franklin D. (1881–1945): American political leader; thirty-second U.S. President; the only president to have served more than two terms. *See pages* 71, 189.

Roosevelt, Theodore "Teddy" (1858–1919): American political leader, conservationist; twenty-sixth U.S. president. *See pages* 71, 146, 152, 167.

Roth, Philip (1933–): American novelist; three-time Pulitzer Prize winner. *See pages* 31, 40, 65, 91, 107, 171.

Rowland, Helen (1876–1950): American journalist, humorist, writer. *See pages* 3, 4, 5, 20, 28 30, 34, 40, 49, 50, 55, 177, 178, 184.

Rudner, Rita (1956–): American comedian. *See pages* 1, 12, 14, 15, 16, 23, 28, 29, 62, 78, 111, 124.

S

Sahl, Mort (1927–): Canadian-American comedian, political satirist. *See pages* 3, 86, 156, 157, 178.

Saint-Exupéry, Antoine de (1900–1944): French aviator, author. *See pages* 11, 21, 52, 78, 96, 126, 131, 137, 138, 180, 184, 195.

Sand, George (1804–1876): French writer. *See pages* 100, 159, 180, 181.

Sandburg, Carl (1878–1967): American poet, novelist, folklorist; two-time Pulitzer Prize winner; Emmy, 1959. *See pages* 11, 89, 187, 188.

Sartre, Jean-Paul (1905–1980): French playwright, novelist, philosopher; leading existentialist. *See pages* 27, 43, 83, 101, 146, 201.

Sayers, Dorothy L. (1893–1957): English writer, translator. *See pages* 5, 8, 29, 32, 40, 44, 63, 83, 86, 88, 121, 142, 178, 180, 183, 184.

Schopenhauer, Arthur (1788–1860): German philosopher. *See pages* 3, 11, 92, 105.

Schreiner, Olive (1855–1920): French social critic, writer, feminist; pseudonym Ralph Iron. *See pages* 36, 46, 73, 88, 160, 164, 165.

Seinfeld, Jerry (1954–): American comedian, actor, writer; Emmy, 1993; Golden Globe, 1994. *See pages* 27, 30, 56, 121, 132, 178.

Seuss, Dr. (1904–1991): American writer, cartoonist. *See pages* 26, 110.

Shakespeare, William (1564–1616): English playwright, poet. *See pages* 22, 24, 42, 44, 48, 57, 68, 71, 89, 95, 100, 113, 117, 131, 139, 143, 144, 146, 164, 169, 171, 173, 174, 176, 197.

Shaw, George Bernard (1856–1950): Irish-English playwright, social critic. *See pages* 8, 79, 108, 112, 114, 120, 128, 139, 191.

Shikibu, Murasaki (974–1031?): Japanese poet, diarist, lady-in-waiting, novelist; reputed to have written the world's first novel. *See pages* 90, 92, 96, 110, 130, 171, 175.

Sontag, Susan (1933–2004): American cultural critic, novelist, dramatist; National Book Award, 2000. *See pages* 90, 161, 175, 176.

Spark, Muriel (1918–2006): Scottish poet, writer. *See pages* 1, 31, 36, 42, 54, 91, 181.

Staël, Germaine de (1766–1817): French-Swiss feminist, novelist, literary critic. *See pages* 102, 149, 154, 155, 165, 199.

Stanton, Elizabeth Cady (1815–1902): American abolitionist, suffragist, historian; co-organized first Women's Rights Convention in Seneca Falls, New York in 1848; co-founded three major women's rights organizations. *See pages* 19, 48, 50, 51, 60, 82, 147, 149, 150, 151, 176, 181, 182.

Stein, Gertrude (1874–1946): American-French writer, playwright, art collector, librettist; Obie, 1964. *See pages* 10, 21, 22, 56, 58, 74, 139.

Steinem, Gloria (1934–): American feminist, editor, writer; co-founded *Ms.* Magazine, 1972. *See pages* 8, 22, 60, 62, 65, 91, 149, 156, 165, 181, 194.

Stevenson, Adlai (1900–1965): American political leader; Illinois Governor, 1948–1951; U.S. Ambassador to the United Nations, 1961–1965. *See pages* 30, 34, 35, 37, 40, 110, 141, 155, 157, 163, 166.

Stewart, Jon (1962–): American comedian, political satirist, activist, author, producer; hosts Comedy Central's *The Daily Show*; nine-time Emmy winner. *See pages* 39, 44, 123, 142, 155.

Stoppard, Tom, Sir (1937–): Czech-British dramatist; Oscar, 1998; four-time Tony winner. *See pages* 94, 104, 143, 163.

Sullivan, Annie (1866–1936): American educator; tutored Helen Keller; invented manual alphabet. *See pages* 100, 198.

Swift, Jonathan (1667–1745), Irish-English writer, satirist. *See pages* 31, 43, 79, 112, 115, 117, 139, 153, 166.

T

Taylor, A. J. P. (1906–1990): British historian. *See pages* 31, 71, 166.

Thatcher, Margaret (1925–): English political leader, chemist, tax attorney; British Prime Minister, 1979–1990; first woman to head a major government in modern Europe; took up lifetime seat in House of Lords, 1992. *See pages* 58, 155, 157, 158, 161, 200.

Thoreau, Henry David (1817–1862): American philosopher, writer. *See pages* 30, 41, 52, 53, 54, 68, 76, 84, 112, 113, 116, 120, 128, 135, 144, 147, 160, 172, 174.

Thurber, James (1894–1961): American humorist, writer, illustrator. *See pages* 96, 122.

Toklas, Alice B. (1877–1967): American-French writer, art and literary figure; life partner of and secretary to Gertrude Stein. *See pages* 42, 77, 83, 111, 112, 115.

Tolstoy, Leo (1828–1920): Russian novelist, philosopher. *See pages* 114, 169, 181, 183, 188.

Trump, Donald (1946–): American real estate investor, television personality and producer. *See pages* 55, 70.

Truth, Sojourner (1797?–1883): American lecturer, abolitionist, mystic, former slave; first black woman to speak publicly against slavery. *See pages* 41, 145, 146, 151, 160, 174, 193.

Turner, Ted (1938–): American television executive, philanthropist; founded CNN. *See page* 62.

Twain, Mark (1835–1910): American humorist, novelist, lecturer. *See pages* 13, 15, 16, 17, 21, 32, 33, 37, 39, 42, 44, 45, 53, 55, 57, 68, 71, 72, 73, 82, 90, 91, 92, 98, 106, 107, 108, 115, 117, 126, 127, 133, 134, 136, 143, 148, 149, 152, 164, 165, 174, 175, 184, 188, 193, 196, 197, 198.

U–V

Ustinov, Peter (1921–): British actor, writer, director. *See pages* 12, 70, 93, 94, 130, 180.

Van Buren, Abigail (1918–2003): American advice columnist, lecturer; twin sister of Ann Landers. *See pages* 42, 80.

Viorst, Judith (1931–): American journalist, writer, poet; Emmy, 1970. *See pages* 10, 15, 28, 92.

Vonnegut, Kurt (1922–2007): American novelist. *See pages* 29, 73, 147, 153.

W

Walker, Alice (1944–): American writer, poet, civil rights activist; founded Wild Trees Press, 1984; Pulitzer, 1983 (first African-American woman to win); National Book Award, 1983; O. Henry, 1986. *See pages* 18, 43, 48, 66, 95, 97, 101, 125, 128, 175, 179, 180, 195.

Walters, Barbara (1929–): American television personality, journalist, producer, writer; Emmy. *See pages* 19, 74, 139, 140, 157.

Warhol, Andy (1928–1987): American pop artist, filmmaker, writer; founded *Interview* magazine. *See pages* 32, 65.

Washington, Booker T. (1856–1915): American educator, civil rights leader, author. *See pages* 72, 135.

West, Mae (1893–1980): American dramatist, nightclub entertainer, actor, stage producer. *See pages* 32, 52, 58, 59, 74, 95, 97, 98, 99, 105, 177, 179.

Wilde, Oscar (1856–1900): Irish playwright, novelist, poet. *See pages* 24, 28, 30, 105, 115, 139, 142, 143, 145, 168, 175, 202.

Wilder, Thornton (1897–1975): American novelist, dramatist; Pulitzer, 1938. *See pages* 2, 3, 60, 106, 186.

Williams, Robin (1952–): American comedian, actor; Oscar, 1997; five-time Golden Globe winner; four-time Grammy winner. *See pages* 126, 158.

Williams, Tennessee (1911–1983): American playwright; two-time Pulitzer Prize winner; Tony, 1952. *See pages* 62, 191.

Winfrey, Oprah (1953–): American television personality, actor, film and television producer, philanthropist; first Bob Hope Humanitarian Award, 2002; established the Oprah Winfrey Leadership Academy for Girls near Johannesburg in South Africa, 2007. *See pages* 80, 98, 100, 119, 134, 196.

Witkovsky, Burton (1914–2002): American businessman, novelist, poet. *See page* 89.

Woolf, Virginia (1882–1941): English writer, literary critic; she and her husband Leonard Woolf founded and operated Hogarth Press, 1917. *See pages* 21, 32, 53, 74, 86, 106, 116, 147, 176, 194.

Index

Numbers

A

B

C

D

E

F

G

H

I

J

K

L

M

N

O

P

Q

R

S

T

U

V

W

X-Y-Z